Mary Kassian speaks with rare insight, clarity, directness, and grace as she challenges the prevailing winds of our culture. She paints portraits of two contrasting kinds of women and sets forth a vision that calls women out of their dysfunction, pain, and deception, to walk in the light of God's redeeming truth and grace.

This book is extremely important, timely, and needed—I cannot think of any category of women (or men, for that matter) who could not benefit greatly from reading it and grappling with these critical issues. A "must-read" for women who desire to honor God with their lives and to influence others to do the same.

—Nancy Leigh DeMoss, author, host of Revive Our Hearts radio

This is a wonderful book with amazing insight into the hearts of women (and men!) who feel pressured by today's "wild" culture—and also deep, spiritual insight into the Bible's wisdom regarding the beauty of true womanhood as God created it to be.

—Wayne Grudem, Ph.D.
Research Professor of Theology and Biblical Studies
Phoenix Seminary, Phoenix, Arizona

Mary Kassian has done it again. With aplomb, grace, and wisdom, she sets the right course through some of the most treacherous and dangerous issues of our day. With just the right balance of truth and understanding, Mary calls girls and young women to a bold, strong, and biblical model of true womanhood—an understanding that honors God and shows the world a counter-revolutionary model of genuine womanhood. When Mary Kassian writes a book, women can count on sound advice and biblical wisdom from a gracious friend.

—R. Albert Mohler Jr., President
The Southern Baptist Theological Seminary

So much of life is broken because our standards come from the world rather than from the precepts of God's Word. Our young people are living in the rubble of destruction and need rescuing from the earthquake of the consequences of not building their lives on truth.

Mary's book *Girls Gone Wise . . . in a World Gone Wild* is a needed book for our times. May it grab our attention and drive us to His Word where Mary will take us.

—Kay Arthur, CEO and cofounder Precept Ministries International
Author of *The Truth about Sex: What the World Won't Tell You and What God Wants You To Know,* and *Return to the Garden: Embracing God's Design for Sexuality*

Girls today are growing up in a culture where "bad" has become the new "good." The glamorization of bad behavior among young women has become the new norm and left in its wake a tremendous amount of fallout and misery. Mary has penned a handbook for reversing the tide of the girls-gone-wild trend and replacing it with a new rank of girls-gone-wise. I can't wait to recommend this book!
—Vicki Courtney, bestselling author of *Your Girl* and *5 Conversations You Must Have With Your Daughter*

Many women today are eager for mentors. While a book is never a substitute for a real, live mentor, this one does connect women everywhere to the wise counsel of Mary Kassian. And we should heed her winsome, culturally relevant, and biblically sound words in *Girls Gone Wise*. This book provides an accurate gauge of the current feminine perspective in Western culture and contrasts it with the eternal wisdom found in Scripture. Easy-to-read, humble, humorous, and thoroughly sound, *Girls Gone Wise* is a book both long-time believers and new converts will benefit from reading. Highly recommended!
—Carolyn McCulley, author, *Radical Womanhood: Feminine Faith in a Feminist World*

This book sounds a clear and much-needed message regarding the ethics of biblical womanhood. Mary Kassian's energy and passion make it a readable book. Her eye-opening contrast between the wise and the wild make it a convicting book. Her faithfulness to Scripture makes it a compelling book.
—Susan Hunt, author, consultant for women's ministries for the Presbyterian Church in America

Girl's Gone Wise is a crucial message for such a time as this. In a culture where true femininity is in danger of extinction, young women desperately to catch a vision for God's pattern. Mary Kassian's relevant, practical, and biblically based insights give today's young women a clear, inspiring blueprint for the only version of womanhood that truly fulfills—God's version.
—Eric and Leslie Ludy, bestselling authors of *When God Writes Your Love Story*

Mary Kassian will help you navigate the overexposure we experience every day to messages that call us to be anything but what God created us to be as women. Her message will make you wise to that, and hungry to be what God intended. I think this would be a great book for moms to read with their teen girls. Though Mary navigates critical worldview issues and strong theology, she does it with a conversational and contemporary note in her writing voice. You'll never realize how hard you're thinking. It'll be too much fun!
—Dannah Gresh, coauthor, *Lies Young Women Believe*, founder, Pure Freedom

GIRLS GONE WISE

in a world gone wild

MARY A. KASSIAN

MOODY PUBLISHERS
CHICAGO

All Scripture quotations, unless otherwise indicated, are taken from *The Holy Bible, English Standard Version*. Copyright © 2000, 2001 by Crossway Bibles, a division of Good News Publishers. Used by permission. All rights reserved.

Scripture quotations marked NIV are taken from the *Holy Bible, New International Version*®. NIV®. Copyright © 1973, 1978, 1984 by Biblica, Inc.™ Used by permission of Zondervan. All rights reserved.

Scripture quotations marked NKJV are taken from the *New King James Version*. Copyright © 1982 by Thomas Nelson, Inc. Used by permission. All rights reserved.

Scripture quotations marked KJV are taken from the King James Version.

Scripture quotations marked HCSB are taken from the *Holman Christian Standard Bible*, Copyright © 1999, 2000, 2002, 2003 by Holman Bible Publishers. Used by permission. Holman Christian Standard Bible®, Holman CSB®, and HCSB® are federally registered trademarks of Holman Bible Publishers.

Scripture quotations marked NET are taken from the *NET Bible*®. Copyright © 2005 by Bible Studies Press, L.L.C. www.netbible.com. Used by permission. All rights reserved.

Names and details of stories have been changed to protect the privacy of the individuals involved.

The author uses feminine pronouns in some Scriptures for clarity and readability.

All websites and phone numbers listed herein are accurate at the time of publication, but may change in the future or cease to exist. The listing of website references and resources does not imply publisher endorsement of the site's entire contents. Groups and organizations are listed for informational purposes, and listing does not imply publisher endorsement of their activities.

Editor: Cheryl Dunlop
Interior Design: Ragont Design
Cover Design: Faceout Studio—formerly The DesignWorks Group, Inc.
Cover Image: RF Shutterstock and Fotolia
Cover Photo: JDS Portraits

Library of Congress Cataloging-in-Publication Data

Kassian, Mary A.
    Girls gone wise in a world gone wild / by Mary A. Kassian.
       p. cm.
    Includes bibliographical references.
    ISBN 978-0-8024-5154-5
    1. Christian women—Religious life. I. Title.
    BV4527.K37 2010
    248.8'43--dc22

                                        2009049616

We hope you enjoy this book from Moody Publishers. Our goal is to provide high-quality, thought-provoking books and products that connect truth to your real needs and challenges. For more information on other books and products written and produced from a biblical perspective, go to www.moodypublishers.com or write to:

Moody Publishers
820 N. LaSalle Boulevard
Chicago, IL 60610

7 9 10 8

Printed in the United States of America

for my k-pod,
the favorite tunes of my life

Brent
Clark & Jacqueline
Matthew
Jonathan

CONTENTS

WILD THING

"Wild thing . . . you make my heart sing.
You make everything groovy."
—The Troggs, 1966[1]

"Look carefully then how you walk,
not as unwise [wild] but as wise."
—Ephesians 5:15

From women exposing themselves for a camera crew on a beach in Florida, to cardio striptease classes in Los Angeles, to the infamous Manhattan Cake Parties, girls have gone wild! Many things that were once reviled as shameful—*Playboy*, strippers, wet T-shirt contests, and a porn aesthetic—are now embraced by young women as symbols of personal empowerment and sexual liberation. Videographer Joe Francis has built a multimillion-dollar empire on the backs (or I should say breasts) of college-age women who are willing to go wild on camera for the sake of a dare and a T-shirt. His multimedia *Girls Gone Wild* venture has become a household name and a distinguishing phenomenon of popular culture.

But as shocking as their behavior is, the phenomenon of girls going wild isn't really new. A generation ago, a British rock band called the Troggs paid tribute to the groovy, peacenik, hippy-beaded, flower-powered, grass-smoking, love-making Girl-Gone-Wild of that era, with what *Rolling Stone* magazine ranked as one of the five hundred greatest songs of all time: "Wild Thing." The fortuitous invention of the birth control pill ensured that she could be a Wild Thing and hook up in the back of a Volkswagen van without worrying about the usual risks of pregnancy.

The Girl-Gone-Wild of the 1920s was the flapper. She smoked, drank, danced, and had a giddy, risqué attitude. She bobbed her hair short, wore makeup, and went to petting parties. In an earlier era, the Girl-Gone Wild was the "bad girl" who crossed boundaries of propriety and wore clothing that was unencumbered by bustles, layers, or corsets. Her loose clothing and hair signified a "loosened-up" sexual standard. And let's not forget the Girl-Gone-Wild of the first century, who spent days getting her hair woven into intricate beaded creations that would rival the outrageous 'dos seen on models on the runway in Paris.

So does that mean that every woman who adopts the latest fashion is a Girl-Gone-Wild? And if we could set up a time-travel machine and transport a Girl-Gone-Wild from the past into our era, would she cease to be a Wild Thing because she isn't baring her breasts on video? Is a woman's "wildness" simply determined by the extent to which she is a fashion diva? Or the extent to which she pushes the boundaries of what's considered culturally acceptable? Although external appearance and sexual behavior certainly play a part in determining if a particular woman has or hasn't gone wild, the Bible teaches that there's a whole lot more involved than that. What's more, it teaches that Girl-Gone-Wild behavior isn't restricted to young single women. A woman can be a Girl-Gone-Wild at any stage of life.

It's easy for those of us who are older to distance ourselves from the bawdy college-age women who are sexting, or exposing themselves for cameras, or mud wrestling in a bar like pigs in a pen, or necking with other girls to turn on the guys, or adopting a *Sex and the City* multipartner lifestyle. It's easy to shake our heads, look down our noses, and self-righteously condemn them as Wild Things. It's easy to convince ourselves that if we don't happen to be young or single, and if we're not risqué, and if we stay a couple steps behind the cutting edge of fashion and propriety, that the Girl-Gone-Wild label couldn't possibly apply to us. But the truth of the matter is that it's not just over-the-edge, single, college-age girls who qualify as Wild Things.

According to Scripture, there is a measure of Girl-Gone-Wildness in all of us. I'll never forget the seventy-year-old woman who came up to me after a workshop with tears streaming down her face: "I came to your workshop to get some ideas about how to help my granddaughter," she said, "but I see now that it's *me* who is a Girl-Gone-Wild."

CONTRASTING WILD AND WISE

In this book, I want to contrast the attitudes and behaviors of a Girl-Gone-Wild with those of a Girl-Gone-Wise. I want to do this for two reasons. First, I hope that you'll grow in spiritual discernment, so you can spot the difference between wild and wise when it comes to the right biblical attitudes, thought patterns, and behavior for women. Second, I pray that this awareness will help you say yes to God's ideas about womanhood and no to the tremendous pressure to conform to the world's pattern and to the sinful tendencies in your own heart. My goal, in the final analysis, is that you might become more biblically savvy and godly in the way you think and conduct yourself in your relationships with men. As the title clearly indicates, I want you to become a Girl-Gone-Wise in a world gone wild.

Characteristics of both the wild and the wise woman are mentioned numerous times throughout Scripture, but perhaps nowhere more clearly than in the book of Proverbs. In this collection of writings, a Sage Father, Solomon, repeatedly warns his son to stay away from wild women. He talks about that kind of woman in some sixty-five verses, more than any other figure, even Lady Wisdom. In Proverbs 31, King Lemuel's mother chips in with some advice on how to spot and marry a woman who is wise. Don't worry. This isn't going to be another rehash of the Proverbs 31 woman. We've all heard our share of those. My approach is quite different. I intend to instruct by means of contrast.

Let me explain. When my middle son, Matt, played football, he had a pair of white practice pants. (White. Go figure.) Since Matt has always been an active, "let me at 'em" kind of a guy, he used to come home with all sorts of mud and grass and bloodstains ground into them. (White practice pants! White!!) Anyhow, it was my job to use Oxi-clean and Spray 'n Wash and bleach and to soak and scrub the stains out so that the practice pants would be clean for the next practice. (White! I never did find out which rocket scientist made that call.)

With some work, a substantial amount of elbow grease, and a lot of muttering under my breath, I managed to keep Matt's practice pants white. Ta da! Are you impressed? I was. I even thought about volunteering my services for a Tide commercial. But there's white, and then there's *white*. Halfway through the season, when Matt irreparably ripped his practice pants and I laid a newly purchased pair alongside, I saw that, in comparison, his old pants were not white at all. Lying beside the new white ones, the old ones looked grey. Comparison magnified the difference.

This book revolves around the story of the typical Girl-Gone-Wild as recorded for us in the Bible. The bulk of her story is recorded in Proverbs 7. Jesus' favorite and most powerful teaching tactic was the parable. We see this same method used by the Sage Father when he instructed his son to stay away from wild women. What I'm going to do is unpack the Proverbs 7 tale about the typical wild woman and contrast her characteristics with those of the typical wise woman. Over the course of this book, we'll look at twenty points of contrast. Like looking at my son's old football pants lying beside his new ones, it's the contrast between wild and wise that will magnify the difference.

The cautionary tale recorded in Proverbs 7 paints a picture of a typical Girl-Gone-Wild. For the purpose of the narrative, the author depicts her as a young, married woman—an ordinary, average, "typical" Jane Doe you could meet at the church down the street. But she could be any woman: young, old, single, married, divorced, widowed, childless; a mother, a teenager, a grandma . . . whatever. The point of the story isn't her age or marital status. It's about the "wild" characteristics she displays. As you'll soon see, these characteristics could show up in a woman of any age, of any marital status, at any stage of life.

Before we get into the text, I want to capture your imagination so you can picture the story happening in your surroundings—perhaps in the life of someone you know or even in your own life. If the Proverbs 7 cautionary tale about the Girl-Gone-Wild were told from today's vantage point, it might go something like this . . .

A TALE OF A MODERN GIRL-GONE-WILD

She stretched the satin sheet over the corner of the mattress. The sexual tension had been building for weeks. The looks. The banter. The innuendo.

It had started off innocently enough. They had both been volunteers for the big Easter musical. She was the backstage manager, and he was a stagehand. She discovered that his office was downtown, not far from where she worked. At her suggestion, they got together a half-dozen times for lunch and coffee—to discuss aspects of the production—just as friends, of course. They met at a cozy bistro tucked in an alley off Fifth and Main, a warm and homey place with checkered red drapes, booths aglow with candle-plugged wine bottles, rich operatic music, and delicious Italian fare.

The production ended, but their lunchtime get-togethers didn't. The thrill of the chase was too much to resist. Besides, he was such a good listener. He made her laugh. He understood. He empathized with her loveless existence. And the chemistry between them was electric.

Her heart quickened a beat. She plumped the pillows, arranged some cinnamon-scented tea lights, and scattered rose petals across the bed. After docking her iPod and sliding her wedding picture into a drawer, she went into the washroom to finish getting ready. A glance at her watch told her that her husband would soon be touching down in Seattle. The conference would keep him away for a week. The timing was perfect.

She carefully composed a text message: "I'm going to be lonely unless I happen upon a friend after Saturday night service. I hear it's Tuscany night at the bistro."

Her cheeks flushed with anticipation. Would he come? She felt certain he would. She had been reeling him in like a fish on a hook. And now it was time to make her big move. She touched up her hair and makeup, misted on some perfume, and stood back for a final appraisal.

Simple but sexy: tight designer jeans, stilettos, tank top. Oops. Too much skin and cleavage for church—better save that for later. She selected a little sweater from her closet. She'd whip it off on her way to the bistro. It would be too hot in there for a sweater. She smiled ever so slightly. Way too hot!

Later, her eyes scanned the church foyer. There he was. She moved close enough to entice him. She knew her craft. The toss of the hair. The ever-so-slight parting of the lips. The subtle display of her wares. The lingering sideways glance. The secret invitation was noticed by no one but the intended target. It gave her a rush to observe the effect it had on him. She waited until he selected his seat, and then positioned herself where he couldn't help but watch her. All through the service she kept sending little nonverbal cues to crank up the sexual tension. She caressed the back of her neck. Bent over to pick up a dropped pen. Licked her finger to turn the page. Every tiny move was calculated. Reel. Reel. Reel. She eased past him in the aisle on the way out, making certain he felt the brush of her skin. Another seductive look. Another toss of the hair. Reel. Reel. The fish was almost in the boat.

She waited for him in the corner of the bistro parking lot. After what seemed like an eternity, he appeared, walking from the direction of his office. Forget about Tuscany. This was the moment she'd been waiting for. She wouldn't be denied this chance at love. Grabbing hold of his shirt, she brazenly pulled him close and kissed him hard.

She could tell that he was tempted. She overcame his last bit of resistance with a barrage of smooth talk and flattery: "Thank God He sent you into my life. You're the answer to my prayers. You're the only one who understands me. You're the only one I can talk to. You are amazing! I feel so happy and safe when I'm with you. I finally found someone I can trust. Please come home with me. My husband's gone again. He's on the other side of the country and won't be back till the end of the month. I can't bear the thought of spending another night in that big house alone. I need you so much. I'm counting on you. I want to spend the whole night in your arms."

Her seductive words take hold. She kisses him again, fiercely. His breathing is thick. His hands begin to tremble. She takes a step back and holds out her car keys, locking her eyes with his—willing his fall. He only hesitates for the slightest second before grabbing them, helping her in, and driving off in the direction of her neighborhood.

He wasn't the first, and he wouldn't be the last. Though she's married now, she's had a history of revolving-door relationships with men. Consequences? She won't think about those. She's too caught up in the moment . . . and in the quest to fill the hole in her heart.

WALK NOT AS WILD BUT AS WISE

Did that modern-day take on Proverbs 7 sound at all familiar? Over the years, as I've ministered to women, I've heard hundreds of variations on the details, but it usually boils down to the same basic plot:

Rising Action: Girl sees guy. Girl thinks guy will meet her needs. Girl seduces guy. Girl gets guy.

The Climax: Girl has the whole thing blow up in her face.

Falling Action: Girl doesn't find what she was looking for. Girl is damaged by messy emotional, spiritual, and relational fallout.

Resolution: Girl buries her pain and starts looking for another guy.

I suspect most of you have also seen or heard of lives that have been damaged by this storyline. Maybe the damaged life is yours. The details may differ, but for untold numbers of women, the Proverbs 7 story isn't theoretical. It's real. The longing is real. The pull is real. The entanglement is real. The thrill is real. The sin is real. The inevitable breakdown is real. And the resulting devastation and heartache are real. Solomon points out that while this particular chick flick promises to be sweet as honey, those who buy tickets find themselves gagging on the bad taste it leaves in their mouths. They get a mouth full of "wormwood"—a strong, bitter-tasting plant that symbolizes bitterness and sorrow (Proverbs 5:4). So why do women sign up to be actors in this deceptive drama? The Bible says it happens because they are wild and not wise.

I doubt that anyone would disagree that wisdom is a valuable thing for women to have in their relationships with men. I think most women try to be wise and not stupid. But a quick glance at the current state of male-female relationships indicates that our own wisdom is woefully inadequate. We need a higher wisdom to guide our way.

All treasures of wisdom and knowledge are hidden in Christ Jesus (Colossians 2:3). So if we ever hope to be wise when it comes to male-female relationships, we need to align our thoughts and actions with His. We need to do what He says. The instruction of the Lord isn't just some good advice, in the same category as all the other "good" advice we get from friends, family, radio talk shows, reality TV, magazines, and pop psychology. The Bible says the Lord's instruction is *perfect*. It nourishes the soul. And it's *trustworthy*. It is what makes a woman wise (Psalm 19:7 NIV). A Girl-Gone-Wise is a woman who has committed herself to a relationship with Jesus Christ and who relies on Scripture to understand how she ought to conduct herself in her relationships with men.

What then, is a Girl-Gone-Wild? Wild is the polar opposite of wise. A wise woman's heart inclines her "to the right," but a wild woman's heart "to the left" (Ecclesiastes 10:2). Wild and wise go in two separate directions. This book equates "wild" with what Scripture calls foolish, wayward, evil, ignorant, or unwise.

In Proverbs 1:22, the Sage talks about three different types of unwise people—the simple, the fools, and the scoffers. The three Hebrew words all focus on moral rather than intellectual deficiencies. The first depicts the wild woman as lackadaisical or obstinate, unwilling to learn or do what is right. The second portrays her as being resistant to God's input and standards of morality. The third indicates that she is reckless, insolent, and rebellious. A Girl-Gone-Wise relies on God's Word to guide her conduct. A Girl-Gone-Wild doesn't.

Emily came up to me after a conference, wanting to know how to resolve her ongoing affair with her husband's brother. Her seven-year-old son hadn't been fathered by her husband, but by the man he called "Uncle." Emily had grown to despise her husband and wanted to start a new life with her lover, but they were hesitant because of the inevitable consequences. The son loved his "Daddy." And her husband, his parents, and the rest of his extended family had no idea of the long-hidden betrayal. Emily was convinced that she had married the wrong brother, and that it was God's will that she and her son and his real dad be together as a family.

I gotta admit, it was all I could do to keep from banging my fist against my forehead and exclaiming, "How could you be so *stupid*?!!!"

It's the thought that often crosses my mind when I listen to the impossible situations women get themselves entangled in. It's never, "How could you be so wise?", but always, "How could you be so stupid?" That's the thing. Sin makes us stupid. And I'm not exempt from this malady. Nor are you. None of us is beyond falling into the prideful assumption that we have enough smarts to make our own decisions about the way we live.

"Wild" is what we are whenever we disregard God and rely instead on the world's advice, or on what seems right in our own eyes. This was the mistake of Eve, the first Girl-Gone-Wild, who went with her own gut instinct instead of trusting and obeying the Lord. She fell for Satan's deceitful sales pitch (Genesis 3:1–5). The Evil One convinced her that:

1. God's ways are too restrictive ("Did God actually say?").
2. She wouldn't suffer any negative consequences by detouring from God's plan ("You will surely not die!").
3. She shouldn't let herself be denied ("When you eat, your eyes will be opened, and you will be like God!").

Eve fell into the trap of thinking that she had the right to judge the merits of the forbidden fruit for herself, rather than simply take God at His word. From her perspective, the fruit looked attractive ("a delight to the eyes"), harmless ("good for food"), and incredibly promising ("desired to make one wise"). So she took a bite. How many times has the Evil One used the same ploy? How many times have women fallen into the trap of viewing sin as attractive, harmless, and even promising? How many times have you?

Eve couldn't have begun to envision the ugly, painful, deadly consequences of her choice—in her own life, in her relationship with God, in her relationship with her husband, in her children, and grandchildren, and in every human being who would ever live. She bit because Satan convinced her that the fruit would be sweet. But tragically, from that day on, tragedy and bitterness dominated her life.

We are all Eve's daughters. All of us are born with Girl-Gone-Wild tendencies. Most of us have experienced bitterness, pain, and even death in our relationships. That's the bad news. The good news is that we have something infinitely more precious than Eve had. Because of the redeeming sacrifice of Jesus Christ on the cross, those who put their faith in Him get the gift of God's indwelling Holy Spirit and, therefore, a supernatural capacity to discern and follow the way of wisdom. God's grace is bigger than all of our sin. The power of Christ can transform even the most messed-up and broken Wild Thing into a Girl-Gone-Wise.

THE GIRL-GONE-WILD OF PROVERBS 7

Before we get into the twenty points of contrast between a Girl-Gone-Wise and a Girl-Gone-Wild, I'd like you to read the text in as it appears in Scripture. As always, God's inspired Word is rich with meaning and instruction that no paraphrase can mimic. We'll be coming back to this passage repeatedly throughout the rest of the book, so read it slowly and attentively. You might even want to read it a couple of times:

> Be attentive to my wisdom; incline your ear to my understanding. . . . [The wild woman's] feet go down to death; her steps follow the path to Sheol; she does not ponder the path of life; her ways wander, and she does not know it. . . .
>
> At the window of my house I have looked out through my lattice, and I have seen among the simple, I have perceived among the youths, a young man lacking sense, passing along the street near her corner, taking the road to her house in the twilight, in the evening, at the time of night and darkness. And behold, the woman meets him, dressed as a prostitute, wily of heart. She is loud and wayward; her feet do not stay at home; now in the street, now in the market, and at every corner she lies in wait.
>
> She seizes him and kisses him, and with bold face she says to him "I had to offer sacrifices, and today I have paid my vows; so now I have come out to meet you, to seek you eagerly, and I have found you.
>
> "I have spread my couch with coverings, colored linens from Egyptian linen; I have perfumed my bed with myrrh, aloes, and cinnamon. Come, let us take our fill of love till morning; let us delight ourselves with love. For my husband is not at home; he has gone on a long journey; he took a bag of money with him; at full moon he will come home."
>
> With much seductive speech she persuades him; with her smooth talk

she compels him. All at once he follows her, as an ox goes to the slaughter, or as a stag is caught fast till an arrow pierces its liver; as a bird rushes into a snare; he does not know that it will cost him his life.

And now, O sons, listen to me, and be attentive to the words of my mouth. Let not your heart turn aside to her ways; do not stray into her paths, for many a victim has she laid low, and all her slain are a mighty throng. Her house is the way to Sheol, going down to the chambers of death. (Proverbs 5:1, 5–6; 7:6–27)

In the next twenty chapters, we're going to unpack these verses phrase by phrase. They contain a wealth of instruction for women today. I wish I could get you to squeeze through the pages of the book and nestle down on a sofa in my den so we could talk about womanhood. I'd pour you a big steaming cup of my favorite African chai tea, and we'd share heart to heart. I have such a burden for you and for all the other daughters, sisters, and mothers of this generation. It's like we've lost our bearings and have no idea who we are or how we should live. So many of us are living with the brokenness, dysfunction, pain, and confusion that come from having gone wild.

As you read each chapter, make sure to visit the website Girls GoneWise.com, to download chapter questions for personal reflection. They'll help you apply the Word to your life. You can also download a leader's guide that will help you study the book with a girlfriend or with a group of girlfriends. Studying and discussing the book in a small group environment is the best way to learn. You'll also find additional Girls-Gone-Wise articles, resources, and a blog on the website. There, you can post your comments and interact with other women who are trying to figure out what it means to walk as wise and not wild.

The observer looking out from behind the lattice at the Wild Thing of Proverbs 7 could just as easily have been looking out at all the Wild Things of this generation. Update the fashion and technology, and not much has changed. The points of contrast between wild and wise are still the same. Lady Wisdom still calls. She cries aloud in the street; in the markets she raises her voice; at the head of the noisy streets she cries out; at the entrance of the city gates she speaks, beckoning women to listen. The Wild Thing of Proverbs 7 and all her foolish girlfriends ignore her. But Girls-Gone-Wise pay close attention. If you are wise, you will listen to Scripture's words of wisdom to figure out who you are and how you should live. You'll understand that "wisdom is better than jewels, and all that you may desire cannot compare with her" (Proverbs 8:11).

You'll find videos, a forum, and many other resources to help you learn how to walk wisely on the GirlsGoneWise.com website. And make sure to follow Gorls Gone Wise on Facebook (facebook.com/girlsgonewise) and Twitter (twitter.com/girlsgonewise) tool.

20 POINTS
OF CONTRAST

Point of Contrast #1

HEART
What Holds First Place
in Her Affections

Girl-Gone-Wild: **Christ Is Peripheral**	Girl-Gone-Wise: **Christ Is Central**
"Her feet go down to death; her steps follow the path to Sheol; she does not ponder the path of life; her ways wander, and she does not know it." (Proverbs 5:5–6)	"Her heart has not turned back, nor have her steps departed from your way." (Psalm 44:18)

He *swept her off her feet*. I'm sure you've heard the expression. People often use it when a girl gets emotionally overwhelmed by and infatuated with a guy. He gains her immediate and unquestioning support, approval, acceptance, and love. Like Wanda, the high school senior who was swept off her feet by the star of the football team. She loved him so much and was so certain they would have a future together, that she gave up her virginity and self-respect. Their relationship lasted a scant month. Or forty-four-year-old Tammy—who was swept off her feet by Omar, a new convert with a Muslim upbringing and twenty years her junior. He was an exotic foreigner, with a desire for a green card. She married him weeks after they met, convinced she had met the man of her dreams. Or Amanda, who was swept off her feet and into an affair with a married co-worker. Or Bridgette, who was swept off her feet and left her husband and teenage children for a guy she met on the Internet. Or Gretta, a lonely widow, who was swept off her feet into bankruptcy by a dashing elderly gentleman who was just a tad too fond of gambling.

The idiom "swept off her feet" indicates that there is a strong connection between a girl's heart and her feet. That connection is the first point of contrast between a Girl-Gone-Wild and a Girl-Gone-Wise. A wise woman gives the Lord Jesus Christ first place in her heart. Her feet follow the inclination of her heart, so she makes cautious, wise, godly decisions about her relationships with men. A wild woman, on the other hand, does not have Christ at the center of her affections. Other things—such as her desire to have a boyfriend or husband, to gain security or approval, or to have fun—take center stage. Her relationship to Christ is peripheral, shoved off to the side somewhere. The wild woman's feet also follow the inclination of her heart, but since Christ is not at the center of her affections, she makes missteps in her relationship with men. "Her ways wander, and she doesn't know it."

THE WAY SHE WALKS

The Sage Father tells his son that he'll be able to spot a Girl-Gone-Wild by the way she walks. He advises him to check out a woman's "feet," "steps," "path," and "ways." He's not being literal here. He's not telling his son to look to see whether the woman sports a crisp French pedicure or calluses rough as concrete, whether she wears designer heels or hiking boots, whether she prefers swaggering through a barn or strutting down urban pavement, whether she sways her hips or marches like a commando. It's obvious that the "walk" that he and his son are talking about is primarily figurative.

Biblical writers use the word *walk* metaphorically to describe the way human life is lived in relation to God. A girl's walk has to do with the overriding inclination of her heart. Her walk demonstrates where her loyalty lies. It reveals whether her heart is inclined toward the Lord or toward other things—whether she's moving toward Him or away from Him, whether she prefers the path of uprightness or the path of wickedness, God's way or the world's way—whether she favors being wise or wild. Her walk is her prevailing pattern of behavior. It's the key to determining which way she's headed. According to the Bible, you can tell the difference between a Wild Thing and a Wise Thing by the way she thinks, what she talks about, and all the small, daily decisions she makes. Her small, individual "steps" all add up to reveal the dominant direction of her heart.

If Christ is at the center—if He is the one who has forever swept her off her feet—she makes sure that her attitude and speech and conduct are pleasing to Him. She seeks to walk in His way. Her eyes are ever toward the Lord (Psalm 25:15). Her steps increasingly follow His path. She relies on Him to make each footstep secure (Psalm 40:2). If, on the other hand, Christ is not at the center, then she will walk in her own way, in a way that is "right in her own eyes" (Proverbs 12:15). She will follow her own desires, turn aside from the straight and narrow, go after things she has no right to, and mess around with sin (Job 31:7). Her way will be "a way that seems right to a man, but its end is the way to death" (Proverbs 14:12).

The wild woman makes poor decisions concerning her sexuality and relationships with men. If she doesn't have a guy, then she's probably obsessed with getting one. If she does have a guy, she's probably not content with him and is having trouble with the fairy-tale-ending part of the romance. If she's between guys, she may be licking her wounds and wrapping herself up in protective layers, telling herself that she'll be more careful next time. In any case, she schemes, dreams, manipulates, connives, controls, clamors, seduces, dominates, cowers, compromises, explodes, and/or implodes in this area of her life. All the while, her spirit dies a slow, withering death. When it comes to her love life, her "feet go down to death; her steps follow the path to Sheol; she does not ponder the path of life; her ways wander, and she does not know it."

It's important to remember that although her steps wander, the Wild Thing of Proverbs is a very religious woman who moves in religious circles. Nowadays, you might find her at a youth group, on the worship team, in a Bible study, on a mission trip, or teaching Sunday school. She could be the leader of the women's ministry in your church. Or the speaker at your next women's retreat. She could be me. She could be you.

On the surface, the Wild Thing does a lot of things right. She professes to worship God. She offers "fellowship offerings" at church and appears to fulfill her vows (Proverbs 7:14). But a closer examination reveals that her heart really isn't into it. Christ is not at the forefront of her affections. He has not captivated her heart. She loves herself and her own pleasure more. She only follows the Lord as long as it's convenient, and as long as it doesn't interfere with her quest to get what she wants (Zechariah 7:4–7; Isaiah 58:3–7). She lives a religious life, but does not love Jesus wholeheartedly. Though she calls Him "Lord, Lord," she does not know Him intimately, nor does she eagerly and obediently follow His ways (Matthew 7:21–22).

Several months ago, my young adult son, Matt, phoned and told me about a girl he had started seeing. My first question for him was, "Is Christ at the center of her heart?"

"Well," he tentatively replied, "she's super nice. She attended a Christian school. She goes to church. She went on a mission trip last year. Her family seems solid. We get along really well."

"That's not what I asked." I explained, "What I want to know is if she bubbles over with Jesus. Does He occupy her thoughts, purposes, dreams, and desires? Does she long to know Him better and obey Him more? Is she into His Word? Is He the sun around which all her planets revolve? Does she love Him with her whole heart?"

"Umm . . . I'm not really sure," he stammered. "We haven't really talked about it much." (By now, he's probably sweating, because it's dawned on him that his lack of an answer is an answer. If he's gone out with her several times, and they haven't talked about Jesus, chances are Jesus isn't at the center of her heart, at the center of his heart, or at the center of their relationship.)

"Son," I gently advised, "there is *nothing* more important than a girl's relationship to Jesus. Nothing. If her heart isn't sold out to Him, then she's not the woman for you. Plain and simple. A heart for God should be your number one criteria for a wife—number one—at the top of your list. Above all, make sure she loves Jesus and gives Him first place in her heart."

Thankfully, my sons have learned to politely tolerate and listen to what they refer to as my "mom-lecture moments." I pray that they take the wisdom of my words to heart. And I pray that you do too. It's one thing to be acquainted with Jesus. It's another thing to uphold Him as the Lord of your life—and to let your relationship with Him dictate how you conduct yourself in all other relationships. As my sports-chaplain husband often tells his pro athletes, "You can talk the talk. But it doesn't mean a thing unless you also walk the walk."

THE HEART-FOOT CONNECTION

When I was a kid at summer camp, we used to sit around the campfire late at night, belting out any song that came to mind. It was always an eclectic collection, ranging from old spirituals ("He's Got the Whole World in His Hands") to action songs ("Hokey Pokey"), from rounds of "Three Blind Mice" to repetitive counting songs like "Ninety-Nine Cans of Soup on the Wall" . . . (the counselors at the church camp made sure we substituted "cans of soup" for "bottles of beer"). We also sang an old traditional folk song, "Dem Dry Bones." It started with, "Ezekiel connected dem dry bones; I hear the word of the Lord," and then continued with a lesson in anatomy: "Your toe bone connected to your foot bone. Your foot bone connected to your ankle bone. Your ankle bone connected to your leg bone . . ." and so on, until you got to the final connection: "Your neck bone connected to your head bone—I hear the word of the Lord! Dem bones, dem bones gonna walk aroun'—I hear the word of the Lord!"

This song comes to mind because I believe that any girl who wants to *hear the Word of the Lord,* feel His Spirit breathe life into *dem dry bones,* and experience what it means to *walk aroun'* in His power needs to be very mindful of the connection between her heart and her feet. Anatomically, your foot bone is connected to your ankle bone. But spiritually and metaphorically, your foot and heart are directly connected to each other. Maybe the campfire song should add the line: "Your foot bone's connected to your heart bone!"

That's the way it's always been. Throughout the Old Testament, God repeatedly asked two things of His people: (1) follow Me with your feet, and (2) love Me with your heart (Deuteronomy 11:22; Joshua 22:5). Under the terms of the old covenant, the "feet" part came first. It was necessary for people to keep all the rules (the Law) in order to have any kind of a relationship with the Lord. But it may surprise you to know that the love relationship, and not obedience to the rules, was the main goal the Lord had in mind. His old covenant was a "covenant of love" (Deuteronomy 7:9 NIV). The rules were there because they made a love relationship possible. A holy, sinless God cannot enter into a relationship with a sinful creature. It is an utter impossibility. That's why the old covenant had a set of rules that defined God's standard of righteousness and a sacrificial system to atone for the penalty of falling short of that standard.

The sacrificial system of the old covenant had severe limitations. The sacrifices needed to be continual and were never quite "enough" to restore humanity to the sinless state that was required in order to approach and interact with a sinless, holy God. Because of the ongoing problem with sin, people's contact with Him, knowledge of Him, and relationship to Him were limited. Their feet and hearts continually strayed. They were unable to do what was necessary to remain in a committed love relationship. They couldn't hold up their end of the deal.

The Old Covenant didn't satisfactorily solve the problem of the sinful human condition. But God had the ultimate remedy in mind. Through the prophet Ezekiel, the Lord foretold:

> I will give you a new heart, and a new spirit I will put within you. And I will remove the heart of stone from your flesh and give you a heart of flesh. And I will put my Spirit within you, and cause you to walk in my statutes and be careful to obey my rules. (Ezekiel 36:26–28)

There it is again. The foot-heart connection. But this time, there's a different order—and an absolutely breathtaking promise. The prophecy pointed to a time when things would be radically different. The heart would come first. And the right heart wouldn't be the result of human effort. It would be the gift of God and a work of His Holy Spirit in the life of the individual. The feet would come second. The new heart would ensure that all who have it would walk in the way of the Lord. They would obey, not because they *had* to—contrary to the old covenant, there would be no obligation to fulfill—but because they *wanted* to. The new heart would contain the power, motivation, and guidance to walk the right way. Instead of being inclined toward sin, it would be inclined toward holiness.

Jeremiah prophesied that the new heart would have a far greater capacity to do the right thing, because God would engrave His ways directly on it (Jeremiah 31:33). Instead of relying on the external letter of the Law, the Spirit would provide internal guidance as to the intent of the command. (The Spirit might reveal, for instance, that imagining an affair is just as sinful as having one.) The capacity for holy living would be exponentially greater than under the old covenant, for God's Spirit would provide the impulse, guidance, and power to understand and follow God's Word.

God fulfilled the promise when He sent His Son to institute the new covenant in His blood. The sacrifice of Jesus Christ—the spotless Lamb of God—satisfied the requirements of God's justice and atoned for all sin. Through Jesus, we can receive the gift of God's Holy Spirit and enter into a close and intimate family relationship with our Father. We can be declared holy and enter into His presence boldly.

In the old covenant, the rules provided "the way." In the new covenant, Jesus is the Way (John 14:4–6). A relationship with Him sets us right with God. It results in a new heart and inspires and enables us to walk correctly, according to the directions in His Word. The heart-foot connection is still there, as it was in the old covenant, but God is the One who does everything. He gives us the heart, desire, and power to obey. It's a radically different approach.

So what does all this have to do with male-female relationships? We can draw several important conclusions. First, the way a woman relates to men has a lot to do with the state of her heart for God. Her behavior is a good indicator of the state of her heart.

Second, although behavior is a good indicator, it is not a *conclusive* indicator. A woman can have the "right" behavior, yet still miss the mark by failing to have the right heart. Conversely, a woman's heart may be right, but she could still be doing some things wrong. The Holy Spirit's conviction and instruction in her life might still be a "work in progress." Therefore, although it is our responsibility to evaluate behavior, discern right from wrong, and make judgment calls in our relationships, we need a strong dose of humility when doing so. Unlike the Lord, we are unable to see what is in a person's heart.

Third, when it comes to sexuality and male-female relationships, the Bible gives an *illustrative* list of behaviors that are out of step with God's way, but it doesn't provide an *exhaustive* list. Just because a certain behavior isn't prohibited in the Bible doesn't mean that it's a behavior the Lord condones.

For example, the Bible doesn't explicitly prohibit a girl from having her boyfriend sleep over on the couch at her apartment. I've heard several college students rationalize that if the couple does not have sex, this behavior is totally acceptable, that it's not sin. I agree that it technically doesn't go against the "letter of the Law." But it may be an offense against the Lord nonetheless. It may cause the girl and guy to toy with temptation, compromise purity of thought, engage in sensuality and impurity, dishonor the institution of marriage, disobey their parents, fail to flee the appearance of evil, muddy the reputation of the gospel in the eyes of unbelievers, and/or place their desire for convenience and pleasure above their desire to glorify Jesus Christ. They may have avoided the sin of fornication, but in all likelihood, there are a bunch of other sins they did not avoid. Furthermore, compromise of one protective boundary usually leads to the compromise of more protective boundaries. Couples who start with the intent of abstaining will often find that the circumstances are too tempting and, bit by bit, will give in to sexual immorality.

When the Holy Spirit writes God's law on our hearts, He calls us to a higher standard of purity than the "letter of the Law" ever did. Jesus did not come to abolish the Law or the Prophets. He came to fulfill them by having them blossom in the fertile soil of redeemed, Spirit-filled hearts (Matthew 5:17). The presence of God's Spirit increases our capacity to obey the Word of God and therefore our capacity for holiness. Through His Spirit's work in our hearts, the Lord wants to rid us of sinful behavior. But He also wants to rid us of sinful attitudes, thoughts, inclinations, and compromises. A growing love for the Lord inspires and empowers us to turn away from anything that is not completely spotless. When our hearts are captivated by Christ's glory, we are "transformed into the same image from one degree of glory to another" (2 Corinthians 3:18). And that affects our relationships with the opposite sex. As we become more and more holy, we become less and less tolerant of any hint of evil in our thoughts, words, or actions toward men.

Fourth, under the terms of the new covenant, success in our relationships with God does not depend on our personal resources or capabilities. God's Spirit provides us with all the power, love, wisdom, and self-discipline we need (2 Timothy 1:7). He equips us with *everything* we need to love Him and *everything* we need to be godly in our relationships. "His divine power has granted to us *all things* that pertain to life and godliness" (2 Peter 1:3, italics added). Therefore, proper conduct in our relationships with the opposite sex requires that we rely on Him. His divine wisdom, power, love, and self-discipline—and not our own—are what will enable us to do the right thing.

Fifth, though the order and the means have changed, the Lord still asks His children to do the same two things: (1) Love Me with your heart and (2) Follow Me with your feet. Our obedience is not a *requirement* for a relationship with God, but it is the expected *by-product* of it. Jesus said, "If you love Me, you will keep My commandments" (John 14:15).

GREAT AFFECTION

In the mid-1700s, New England and other colonies along the Eastern seaboard experienced a religious revival that historians call the Great Awakening. The people who became followers of Jesus at that time had a unique expression to describe their salvation experience. Instead of saying, "I've been born again," or "I gave my life to Jesus," or "I've become a Christian," they'd say, "I have been seized by the power of a great affection!" They'd say it with a loud voice and lots of enthusiasm. To get the inflection right, you have to put on a thick Philadelphian accent and divide the sentence into three separate phrases and emphasize it something like this:

> *"I have been SEIZED . . . by the POW'R*
> *. . . of a GREAT affection!"*

Try it. (Yes, out loud.) It sounds kinda cool. Being Canadian (and having no accent), I like to try to mimic the accents I hear in various parts of the continent. But more than that, I really like the idea that this declaration conveys. (Did you say it aloud? My dog came running and is staring at me, because I've hollered it out four or five times now.)

God fervently and unrelentingly pursues a love relationship with us. When the hearts of the New Englanders were "seized" by His affection, they responded with a fervent affection of their own. God's affection stirred their affection. They became passionate about Jesus. Jonathan Edwards, a well-known preacher at the time, made this observation:

> On whatever occasions persons met together, Christ was to be heard of, and seen in the midst of them. Our young people, when they met, were wont to spend the time in talking of the excellency and dying love of Jesus Christ, the glory of the way of salvation, the wonderful, free, and sovereign grace of God, His glorious work in the conversion of a soul, the truth and certainty of the great things of God's word, the sweetness of the views of His perfections, etc.[1]

For those who had been "seized," the great affection became the central focus of their lives. Edwards said, "The *engagedness of their hearts* in this great concern could not be hid, it appeared in their very countenances." They thought about Jesus. They talked about Jesus. They wanted to hear more about Jesus. They told others about Jesus. They read their Bibles. They sang worship songs on the streets. They stopped living the world's way and started living God's way. Bars emptied. Brothels went out of business. Broken relationships were restored. The poor, hungry, and needy received care.

Bottom line? The heart bone is connected to the foot bone. The more a woman's heart is seized with affection for Jesus, the more her life will be transformed to walk in His way. This is abundantly evident in the behavior of the people who were seized by the power of a great affection during the Great Awakening.

The first and most important characteristic of a Girl-Gone-Wise is that Jesus Christ occupies first place in her heart. He is the object of her greatest affection. A Girl-Gone-Wild loves the Lord little. A Girl-Gone-Wise loves Him much. The steps of her feet demonstrate the devotion of her heart.

THE HEART IS THE WELL

The inclination of a woman's heart is, by far, the most important factor in determining whether she will conduct herself in a godly way in her relationships with men. It's the most important point of contrast between a Wild Thing and a Wise Thing. As I constantly tell my eligible sons, "The first and most important thing to look for in a wife is a girl whose heart is overflowing with love for Jesus." A woman who attends to her heart will attend to her ways.

The remaining points of contrast in this book focus on the ways girls ought to "walk." But all these can be traced back to this first and central matter of the heart. The heart is the "well" from which all other behaviors spring. That's why the Sage Father instructed his son, "Keep your heart with all vigilance, for from it flow the springs of life" (Proverbs 4:23).

I hope you see the connection. I hope you understand that you will never get your behavior toward men or your relationships right until you first get your heart right before God. Girls-Gone-Wise cry out, as David did, "O Lord, teach me how you want me to live! Then I will obey your commands. Make me wholeheartedly committed to you!" (Psalm 86:1 1 NET).

Don't forget to watch the *Girls Gone Wise* DVD and do the first chapter in the *Girls Gone Wise Companion Guide*. They will help you examine the condition of your heart.

Point of Contrast #2

COUNSEL
Where She Gets
Her Instruction

| Girl-Gone-Wild: | Girl-Gone-Wise: |
| World Instructed | Word Instructed |

"Her feet go down to death; her steps follow the path to Sheol; she does not ponder the path of life; her ways wander, and she does not know it."

(Proverbs 5:5–6)

"She walks not in the counsel of the wicked, nor stands in the way of sinners, nor sits in the seat of scoffers; but her delight is in the law of the Lord, and on his law she meditates day and night."

(Psalm 1:1–2)

Imagine this. Let's say I wanted to do an experiment to determine the effects of popular culture on a girl's ideas about womanhood and male-female relationships. So I lock her in a lab and expose her to mass media every waking moment of every day. Her schedule looks something like this:

- Television: 8 hours
- Radio/iPod: 4 hours
- Video games/Internet: 2 hours

- Hollywood movie: 1.5 hours
- Women's magazines/romance novel: 1 hour
- Newspaper: 0.5 hour

After a full day of constant exposure, the girl goes to bed and sleeps for seven hours. As soon as she wakes up, the bombardment resumes. Every day—seventeen hours a day, seven days a week, for seven months—it continues. I make her watch, listen to, and read all the latest and most popular entertainment and news. That's all I allow her to do. She's exposed to nothing else.

What do you think would happen? How do you think it would affect her?

I asked my twenty-year-old son, Jonathan. He said, "She'd become what she was exposed to, because she wouldn't have any other influence."

I agree. She would become what she was exposed to.

Here's the shocker. This scenario isn't hypothetical. It's real. It's based on actual statistics and projections. According to research studies, the U.S. Census Bureau estimates that the average woman will expose herself to 3,596 hours of mass media this year.[1] That's seven full months of exposure! The only difference between the average woman and the girl in my scenario is that the average woman's exposure is spread out over twelve months instead of being crammed into seven. And she isn't locked into a room. She has other things going on in her life, like going to school, working at a job, or caring for a family. What's more, no one is forcing the mass media down her throat. She willingly indulges.

The ingestion of mass media starts at a very young age and continues year after year throughout a woman's life. If your daily intake of TV, Internet, radio, and women's magazines is about "average," by the time you are sixty-five, you will have spent forty solid years of all-day-every-day time sitting under the tutelage of worldly wisdom. Do you think you could possibly remain uninfluenced by its counsel?

The problem with popular media is that they constantly lie about the nature of truth, goodness, and beauty. They offer counterfeit versions of what womanhood, male-female relationships, romance, sexuality, marriage, and family are all about. They lie to a woman about who she is, what gives her significance, what she should do to be successful, and where she should spend her time and money. Mass media typically portray sin as natural and harmless. The things God calls the lust of the flesh, the lust of the eyes, and the pride of life are the very things they uphold as highly desired (1 John 2:16). They twist truth. They call evil good and good evil, put darkness for light and light for darkness, put bitter for sweet and sweet for bitter (Isaiah 5:20). They promote sin and mock godliness. I understand that not all media are bad. Some media are extremely good and do provide godly counsel. But few women exercise the necessary discernment and restraint to ensure that the media they expose themselves to are godly and not ungodly.

Where a woman gets "counsel" on how to live is the second point of contrast between a Girl-Gone-Wild and a Girl-Gone-Wise. A Wild Woman gets her instruction from the world. A Wise Woman gets it from the Word. A Girl-Gone-Wise does not walk in the counsel of the ungodly, stand in the path of sinners, or sit under the instruction of those who scoff at God. Instead, she delights in the Lord's instruction, and constantly meditates on His counsel. "Blessed is the man who walks not in the counsel of the wicked, nor stands in the way of sinners, nor sits in the seat of scoffers; but his delight is in the law of the Lord, and on his law he meditates day and night" (Psalm 1:1–2).

LIFE OR DEATH CONSEQUENCE

Proverbs tells us that the feet of a Girl-Gone-Wild follow the path to sheol. *Sheol* is a Hebrew word that means ravine, chasm, or underworld. In the Old Testament, sheol is the abode of the dead; a gloomy place of shadows and utter silence where existence is in suspense and life is no more. The psalmist describes it as the "land of forgetfulness" (Psalm 88:12 KJV). In the New Testament, *sheol* is translated as the Greek word *hades* and the English word *hell*. It's a place of separation from God, a place of torment where the wicked dead await judgment. In the end, God will judge sin and cast the wicked, death, and sheol (hades) into the lake of fire to suffer eternal punishment (Revelation 20:10–15).

Death. Sheol. Hades. Hell. Those are very strong words. The behavior of a Wild Thing isn't trivial or inconsequential. How she conducts herself in relation to men ends up having a horrific eternal consequence—one that she doesn't envision and certainly doesn't intend. So how does this church-going girl end up on the path to hell? Why do her feet wander? How does she end up unwittingly taking steps toward the land of forgetfulness? Our text tells us this happens because she does not *ponder* the path of life.

To ponder is to think over, to consider carefully, to weigh. The mistake of the Wild Thing is that she doesn't intentionally think about how to live a godly life. She forgets. She goes about her daily business and neglects to walk in the way of the Lord. It's not that she willfully scorns God's way. She just doesn't expend the necessary time or effort to figure out what it is or how to walk in it. Instead, the way of the world subtly sidetracks her. Like an intravenous drug dripping into the veins of an unconscious patient on a gurney, worldly thoughts get into her system and numb her sensibilities. Her constant exposure to the world poisons the way she thinks and behaves. Because she doesn't intentionally ponder and pursue the path of life, she unintentionally wanders onto the path of death.

The Hebrew word for "wander" literally means to stagger, topple, stumble, or haplessly fall. It conveys the idea of instability caused by aimlessness. The Bible teaches that if we walk aimlessly—if we aren't intentional about pondering and walking the way of life—we will wander onto the path of death. Life and death are the only two options. A woman who neglects God's way will begin to walk the world's way. It's bound to happen. She'll become what she is exposed to. And the consequence of this misstep isn't trivial. It is potentially deadly. No less than heaven and hell, eternal joy and eternal damnation rest in the balance.

I met Judy at a women's retreat. She told me the story of how she and her husband, John, had slowly wandered away from God. John and Judy both grew up in Christian homes. They met at Bible school. He got his degree in theology. She got hers in Christian education. Upon graduation, they both secured staff positions at a church in the Midwest. Their hearts were filled with love for God and a sense of hope and possibility for the future. But after a few years, they became disillusioned with the daily pressure and grind of church life and politics.

They decided they needed a break, so they resigned, found secular jobs, and moved to the East Coast. There, they just couldn't seem to find a church they liked. Eventually, they stopped going altogether. Their Bible reading and other spiritual disciplines also fell by the wayside. Although they still thought of themselves as Christians, they rarely talked about their faith, nor did they do anything to grow spiritually. No Christian friends lived nearby. Their circle of friends was unbelievers they knew from work and the community.

One Friday night, a new couple in the neighborhood invited John and Judy over to have some drinks and play cards. Judy wasn't entirely comfortable with the idea, but reasoned it could do no harm. The two couples hit it off and became close friends. Their Friday night card games became a regular highlight of the week. Judy couldn't remember exactly when, but at some point, hearts turned into poker, and poker turned into strip poker. And then, after they had grown accustomed to shedding all their clothes, the stakes got even higher. Sexual favors and sexual dares became the bets they placed on the table. By the time Judy sought me out to pray for her, their Friday night poker games had escalated into full-blown orgies with increasingly depraved sexual behavior. She had become a sexual addict, in severe bondage to pornography and sexual perversion. I prayed for her, but to this day, I do not know if she ever broke free.

If a friend in Bible college had asked Judy if she would ever participate in a sexual orgy, Judy would have scoffed at the question. It was preposterous! Of course she would never do that! She wouldn't compromise her morals. How could she? She was a Christian. She loved Jesus. Yet eight years later, Judy had all but forsaken Him and was walking in the land of forgetfulness. How did it happen? Very simply. *She stopped pondering the path of life.* A. W. Tozer warned, "The neglected heart will soon be a heart overrun with worldly thoughts; the neglected life will soon become a moral chaos."[2] With the decrease of godly influence and the increase of worldly influence, Judy slowly became what she was exposed to. Without her even realizing it, her way began to wander. She began to walk in the counsel of the ungodly, stand in the way of sinners, and sit in the assembly of scoffers. Each step was just a small compromise. But bit by bit, she became more and more entangled in sin.

THE COUNSEL OF THE UNGODLY

Bit by bit is the way it usually happens. A woman who faithfully follows Christ does not suddenly wake up one morning and decide to jump into bed with her neighbor. To get to that point, she will have made a series of small compromises along the way.

Compromise always begins by listening to the wrong counsel. That's exactly how the first woman, Eve, fell into sin. When the Serpent approached her, she listened to what he had to say. That was her first big mistake. After listening, she engaged in a conversation with him. Instead of rejecting his point of view, she mulled it over and let it percolate in her mind. She stared at the forbidden fruit and thought about all the benefits he said it had to offer. She entertained the idea that God was selfishly holding out and that He didn't really have her best interests at heart. Contemplating the Serpent's point of view was her second big mistake.

Eve's third big mistake was that she began to accept his ideas. She adjusted her beliefs to accommodate them. God's ways were definitely too restrictive. The consequences of disobedience were certainly overblown. She had a right to be happy and reach her full potential—she shouldn't let herself be denied. Her fourth big mistake was that she acted on her thoughts. She took the fruit and ate. The compromise in her mind led to a compromise in her behavior. And it all started by listening to the wrong counsel. Listening led to contemplating. Contemplating led to accepting. Accepting led to acting.[3]

What would have happened if Eve had declined to listen to ungodly counsel? What if she had refused to contemplate any point of view that differed from God's? What if she had repudiated instead of accepted the Serpent's faulty ideas? She would have nipped evil in the bud. She would not have compromised. She would not have sinned. She would not have wandered onto the path of death. Eve's biggest mistake of all was that she thought she was smart enough and strong enough to handle things without God's input and direction. She didn't think that something as simple as listening to the wrong counsel could get her into trouble or interfere with her relationship to the Lord.

Most of us recognize the danger of blatant evil, so we tend to set limits on the type and extent of sin to which we expose ourselves. When a TV show or movie presents us with occasional nudity, immorality, adultery, or profanity, we try to weigh the danger level. If it doesn't go beyond some arbitrary threshold of what we feel we are able to handle, we tolerate it, thinking it won't affect us. But evil is not benign. Author Josh Harris says we might as well ask how much of a poison pill we can swallow before it kills us.

> The greatest danger of the popular media is not a one-time exposure to a particular instance of sin (as serious as that can be). It's how long-term exposure to worldliness—little chunks of poison pill, day after day, week after week—can deaden our hearts to the ugliness of sin. . . . The eventual effect of all those bits of poison pill is to deaden the conscience by trivializing the very things that God's Word calls the enemies of our souls.
>
> Does anyone really believe that if I disapprove of the sin I'm watching, or roll my eyes and mutter about Hollywood's wickedness, or fast-forward through the really bad parts, my soul is not affected? Yeah, sure—and if you don't actually like chocolate cake, eating it won't add to your waistline.[4]

Pop culture is brim-full with the counsel of the ungodly. It's a poison-laced pill. As Harris says, it deadens our conscience by "trivializing the very things that God's Word calls the enemies of our souls." So should we throw away our DVRs and satellite dishes, ditch movies, disconnect from the Internet, cloister ourselves in a room, and refuse to go to the grocery store lest we expose ourselves to the images on the covers of the checkout counter magazines? No, of course not. But it is important that we do not shrug off the seriousness of exposing ourselves to evil, particularly when the exposure is constant. We must be cautious, wise, and vigilant, and ensure that listening to the counsel of the godly—and not the ungodly—remains our top priority and practice. "Whatever is true, whatever is honorable, whatever is just, whatever is pure, whatever is lovely, whatever is commendable, if there is any excellence, if there is anything worthy of praise, think about these things" (Philippians 4:8).

I have talked to thousands of women who have fallen into sin because they were unconcerned about their exposure to worldliness and complacent about pondering the way of the Lord. You are mistaken if you think that going to church for an hour a week will counteract the influence of thirty-three hours of TV. Do not think that you can constantly listen to ungodly counsel and remain uninfluenced by it—especially if you are not in the habit of pursuing godly input. Daily exposure to the world's way without a counteracting exposure to God's way will kill you just as surely as ingesting bits of poison without an antidote will.

TUNING IN TO GODLY COUNSEL

A Girl-Gone-Wise knows that God's ideas are radically different from the ideas of popular culture. Therefore, she tunes out what the world has to say and intentionally tunes in to what God has to say. She recognizes her need for ongoing godly input. She ponders the path of life. She disciplines herself and is not complacent.

A Wise Woman regularly feeds and nourishes her soul with the counsel of God's Word. Her *delight* is in the law of the Lord, and on His law she meditates *day and night*. She takes great delight in reading her Bible (Deuteronomy 17:19; Psalm 143:8). She studies it (Acts 17:11), memorizes it (Psalm 119:11), meditates on it (Psalm 119:97, 148), fixes her eyes on it (Psalm 119:14–16), and, above all, applies it (Psalm 119:1–3). She esteems the Word of God as a treasure and her safeguard against the way of evil:

> If you receive my words and treasure up my commandments with you . . . then you will understand . . . every good path; for wisdom will come into your heart, and knowledge will be pleasant to your soul; discretion will watch over you, understanding will guard you, delivering you from the way of evil. (Proverbs 2:1, 9–12)

The Counsel of the Godly

A Girl-Gone-Wise also counteracts ungodly influence by seeking out the counsel of the godly. Godly counsel comes from godly people. Ungodly people give ungodly counsel. "The thoughts of the righteous are just; the counsels of the wicked are deceitful" (Proverbs 12:5). That's why the wise woman makes sure she spends plenty of time in the company of those who are wholeheartedly following God.

Like the psalmist, she takes "sweet counsel" together with other believers (Psalm 55:14). She gathers with them regularly to worship, hear instruction, study the Bible, engage in fellowship, and encourage each other (Hebrews 10:25). She seeks out teachers who do not shrink from declaring the "whole counsel of God"—godly preachers, speakers, and authors who stand against the tide of popular culture and boldly teach sound doctrine (Acts 20:27). She listens to musicians whose lyrics faithfully extol Jesus Christ and His Word. She nurtures her closest friendships with those who are on fire for the Lord, and not with those whose hearts are lukewarm or cold toward Him (Psalm 141:4; 1 Corinthians 15:33). She seeks and listens to the instruction of older, godly female mentors (Titus 2:3–4).

The Bible teaches that older godly women, who love the Word and have figured out how to get life right, are a vital source of counsel for younger women. They have richer and more seasoned stores of advice than friends in the same stage of life. These older women can offer invaluable wisdom and training. They've been there, done that, gotten the T-shirt, the battle scars, and the know-how (and know-how-*not*). A Girl-Gone-Wise knows that when she walks in the counsel of God's Word and the counsel of the godly, her steps will be sure.

LEAVING THE LAND OF FORGETFULNESS

There's a scene in C. S. Lewis's Chronicles of Narnia, in the story of *The Silver Chair*, that reminds me of the effect that popular culture often has on us. The children and their friend the marshwiggle Puddleglum, go down to the Underworld to rescue a Narnian prince from the Witch-Queen's evil enchantment. They free him from the Silver Chair and are about to head back to the Overworld, when the Witch intervenes. She does not try to restrain them; instead, she throws a handful of green powder on the fire.

"It did not blaze much, but a very sweet and drowsy smell came from it. And all through the conversation which followed, that smell grew stronger, and filled the room, and made it harder to think." Next, the Witch began to strum on a mandolin-like instrument with her fingers—"a steady, monotonous thrumming that you didn't notice after a few minutes. But the less you noticed it, the more it got into your brain and your blood. This also made it hard to think."[5]

After the Witch has thrummed for a while, and the sweet smell is very strong, she begins to speak in a quiet, soothing voice, coaxing the Narnians to forget. As they breathe in the sweet, drowsy fragrance of the green powder and listen to the steady thrum, they do forget. Her subtle scheme lulls them into believing that there is no Narnia, no Overworld, no sky, no sun, no Aslan—that her Underworld is the only world that exists or matters—that they want to stay there with her. The enchantment is only broken when Puddleglum does a very brave thing. With his bare foot, he stamps on the fire, stops the overpowering smell from interfering with their ability to think, and loudly declares truth.

Do you see the lesson here? Satan tries to lull us with the sweet smell and steady thrum of worldliness. He wants us to forget God and become enchanted with evil. Stamping out his influence and listening to godly counsel is the only way to escape his subtle, yet powerful scheme. I want to challenge you to do a very brave thing. For the next thirty days, tune out the world so that you can tune in to the counsel of God. Reduce the amount of time you spend watching TV and movies, reading women's magazines, and surfing the net—cut it in half, or cut it out all together. Use that time, instead, to fill your mind with truth. Take the *Girls Gone Wise 30-Day Media Reduction Challenge*, and share your experience on www.GirlsGoneWise. com. Let me know what you did and how it went.

I think you'll be pleasantly surprised. The Bible says that tuning out the world and tuning in to God will increase your joy. It says "blessed" is she who walks not in the counsel of the ungodly, nor stands on the path of sinners, nor sits under the advice of those who scoff at God; but her delight is in the instruction of the Lord, and on His counsel, she meditates day and night (Psalm 1:1–2).

APPROACH
Who Directs
Her Love Story

Girl-Gone-Wild: Self-Manipulated	Girl-Gone-Wise: God-Orchestrated
"And behold, the woman meets him . . . *wily of heart*." (Proverbs 7:10)	"She trusts in the Lord with all her heart, and does not lean on her own understanding. In all her ways she acknowledges Him and He makes her paths straight." (Proverbs 3:5–6)

Wile E. Coyote is a cartoon character that stars in a Warner Brothers Looney Tunes cartoon series. His adventures all follow a typical pattern. The Coyote dreams up a new, elaborate plan to help him catch the Road Runner. Sometimes he obtains complex and ludicrous contraptions from the fictitious Acme mail-order corporation to help him: a rocket sled, jet-powered roller skates, or earthquake pills, for example. Invariably, his plot fails. And it always fails in an improbable and spectacular fashion. Instead of catching his prey, the Coyote ends up burnt to a crisp, squashed flat, or knocked senseless at the bottom of a canyon. Nevertheless, he egotistically calls himself "Super Genius" and compliments himself on his great ideas even as he watches them (or himself) go up in flames. Regardless of how often he blows himself up, falls from dizzying heights, and is flattened or mangled, Wile E. Coyote remains undaunted and tries again to catch his prey.

Creator Chuck Jones apparently based the character of Wile E. Coyote on Mark Twain's *Roughing It*, in which Twain describes the coyote as "a long, slim, sick, and sorry-looking skeleton" that is "a *living, breathing allegory of Want*."[1] When Wile E. Coyote made his debut in 1949, the audience assumed that he was just hungry, and had a good reason to chase the Road Runner. However, it soon became apparent that Wile E. Coyote wasn't just a silly coyote trying to get a meal. He had reasons for stalking the bird that were more nefarious. Desire and obsession had gripped him. He was "a living, breathing allegory of Want." Even if he were to catch the elusive Road Runner, Wile E. Coyote wouldn't be satisfied—or at least not for long. Just like an addict hooked on alcohol, drugs, or gambling, Wile E. Coyote was hopelessly addicted to the chase.

As you've probably figured out, the coyote's name is a play on phonics for the word *wily*. Wile E. Coyote is a wily coyote. *Wily* means crafty, cunning, sly, devious, or designing, characterized by subtle tricks and schemes. When Proverbs introduces the wayward woman, it identifies her as "wily of heart." A wily woman is calculating. She uses all sorts of tricks and schemes to insidiously entice, manipulate, and entrap. Desire and obsession have gripped her. She is a living, breathing example of Want.

A woman's *approach* to romance is the third point of contrast between a Wild Thing and a Wise Thing. A Girl-Gone-Wild is crafty. She plots and connives to manipulate her own love story. The Girl-Gone-Wise, on the other hand, trusts God to orchestrate the script.

A WILY WOMAN

The Sage Father tells his son that a Wild Thing is "wily of heart." The Hebrew word means guarded, blockaded, or secret. The phrase conveys the idea of a woman who has an underlying personal agenda, and secretly and skillfully manipulates men in order to get what she wants. The corresponding Greek term means "ready to do anything," usually in the bad sense of tricky and cunning behavior. The wily woman (1) has a personal agenda, (2) wants a man to satisfy it, and (3) does whatever is necessary to make that happen.

A famous biblical example of a wily woman is Delilah. Her story appears in Judges 16. Delilah was Samson's new girlfriend. After they started seeing each other, five Philistine rulers approached Delilah and offered her a considerable amount of money to seduce Samson into revealing the secret of his enormous strength. She had no qualms about using men, so she fast-forwarded their relationship and cranked up her feminine charm. "Please tell me where your great strength lies," she pleaded, "and how you might be bound, that one could subdue you." It's not hard to imagine her resting her head on Samson's chest, slowly tracing the outline of his bicep, and coyly teasing him until he gave her an answer.

Samson teased her back. "If they bind me with seven fresh bow-strings that have not been dried, then I shall become weak and be like any other man."

The next time Samson came, Delilah bound him with bowstrings. She had men hiding in an inner closet, ready to ambush him. But when she called out that the Philistines were on the doorstep, Samson jumped up and snapped his restraints like thread.

Seeing that her first attempt didn't produce the desired result, Delilah reverted to another tactic. She burst into tears. "Behold, you have mocked me and told me lies. Please tell me how you might be bound." She continued to sob and would not be comforted until Samson gave her the information she wanted. New ropes would do the trick. If she bound him with new ropes, he would be helpless as a kitten.

On his next visit, she had new ropes on hand. She seductively joked about taming her big kitten as she bound him hand and foot. Once again, when she called out to warn him of Philistines, Samson easily broke free. Seeing this, Delilah pouted and feigned offense at his continued lack of trust. When Samson tried to embrace her, she gave him the cold shoulder and pushed him away. Not until he told her that weaving his long hair into her loom would deprive him of strength did she cheer up, abandon her black mood, and allow him to embrace her.

Her loom went flying on a following visit, when Samson demonstrated for the third time that he had not been forthcoming with the information she wanted. Delilah was incensed. She lashed out in anger and began to accuse and badger him until he was "vexed to death" and finally gave in to her demand:

> And she said to him, "How can you say, 'I love you,' when your heart is not with me? You have mocked me these three times, and you have not told me where your great strength lies." And when she pressed him hard with her words day after day, and urged him, his soul was vexed to death. And he told her all his heart. (Judges 16:15–17)

You know the rest of the story. Delilah sent for the lords of the Philistines, made Samson fall asleep on her lap, and shaved off his hair—which represented his Nazirite vow and his special relationship to the Lord. "Then she began to torment him, and his strength left him." The Philistines seized Samson, gouged out his eyes, and threw him into prison. And Delilah got her bag of money.

PLANNING EVIL—DEVISING FOLLY

Delilah was exceptionally clever in the craft of manipulation. She obviously knew how to flirt, seduce, admire, compliment, pout, cry, reason, argue, lie, accuse, nag, and do whatever else was necessary to achieve her goal. Most women regard manipulating a man to get money as sordid and disgusting. So you may think that you and Delilah have very little in common. But is manipulating a man to get attention, love, or a ring on your finger that much different? Or is pouting, crying, or nagging to get him to comply with your demands? Or orchestrating circumstances to paint him into a corner? Or doling out physical affection as a reward? Or withholding it as punishment? If you have a noble end in mind, does that justify the means? Can scheming and conniving to manipulate someone for your own gain ever be justified? Is your craftiness any less wily or reprehensible than Delilah's?

The Bible teaches that crafty, cunning human wiles are "follies" (1 Corinthians 3:19). Folly is tragically foolish (thickheaded, dumb) conduct that goes against the ways of God. Folly is essentially a lack of wisdom. A "fool" in the Bible is a person who lives life as if God and God's way were of no consequence. It can mean a woman who, either by ignorance or by deliberate and calculated premeditation, relies on her own cunning to orchestrate what happens in her romantic relationship(s). Folly is more than just plain silliness. It actually demonstrates a disdain for God's truth and discipline. "Fools despise wisdom and instruction" (Proverbs 1:7).

In God's eyes, there is no difference between deliberately planning *evil* and devising a foolish, manipulative *scheme*. Delilah's plot to manipulate Samson to gain money and a contemporary woman's scheme to manipulate a man to get something from him, fall into the same category. Both are sin. Proverbs 24:8–9 says, "Whoever plans to do evil will be called a schemer. The devising of folly is sin, and the scoffer is an abomination to mankind."

Delilah was a schemer—a vixen. She planned to do evil. But according to this verse, "the devising of folly" is also sin. In God's eyes, wily behavior is sinful behavior. It is evil. So even if a woman has a noble goal in mind—love or marriage, for example—using underhanded cunning and craftiness to reach that goal is unwise. The end doesn't justify the means. The woman who uses her wiles to manipulate a man is just as guilty of sin as the vixen who plots evil. The verse concludes by pointing out that both are scoffers and an abomination to mankind.

Wow. That's pretty strong language! Wily, manipulative women are "scoffers" and an "abomination." What does that mean? To scoff is to scorn, to show contempt, to treat with disrespect or derision, to make fun of. According to Scripture, a wily woman scorns God. She demonstrates contempt for Him. When she decides to manipulate men and circumstances for her own gain, she treats God with derision and disrespect. When she relies on her own craftiness instead of relying on the Lord, it is just as though she mocks and makes fun of God's ways.

An "abomination" is something that greatly offends God's righteousness and evokes His extreme hatred and disgust. It is something that gives off a horrible, odious smell and is abhorrent and reprehensible to Him. The definition reminds me of the time I walked into an apartment defiled by numerous cats. The cat litter and feculence hadn't been cleaned for months and was everywhere. The sharp, caustic stench was more than I could bear. I ran from the room with my nose and eyes dripping, coughing, gagging, and gasping for clean air. An "abomination" is to God's senses what that room was to mine. It disgusts Him. Examples of abominations include defective sacrifices (Deuteronomy 17:1), magic and divination (Deuteronomy 18:12), idolatrous practices (2 Kings 16:3), homosexual conduct (Leviticus 18:22), and sexual immorality (Revelation 17:4–5).

Would you have expected scheming and devising folly to appear on the list of things that are an abomination to the Lord? Do you realize how offended He is by foolish, manipulative behavior? A "heart that devises wicked plans" is near the top of the list of things He absolutely hates (Proverbs 6:16–18).

SNARES, NETS, AND FETTERS

If you flip through the latest women's magazines, you're bound to find a generous amount of advice on what girls need to do in order to attract, snag, and keep a guy . . . how to bait the hook, cast the line, reel him in, or net the catch. Incidentally, did you know that the average woman reads twelve magazines a month? The demographic reading the highest average number of issues in a month is women aged eighteen to thirty-four. They read more than thirteen.[2] (That's more than 150 each year—which is a lot of worldly counsel!) The statistics aren't broken down into the types of magazines, but I think it's safe to assume that the majority of magazines read by women in that age group feature tons of advice on male-female relationships. They specifically instruct women how to be crafty so they can get what they want from men.

Popular magazines and media tell a girl to calculate every move in a romantic relationship. They teach her how to get noticed, how to signal interest, how to strike up a conversation, how to flirt, how to drop hints, how to stroke his ego, how to inflate his desire, how to please him sexually, how to maintain his interest, how to ward off the competition, how to get him to commit, and so on. They teach her to be a vixen, a fox—not only in the way she looks, but also in the way she thinks and behaves.

The problem is that this approach to male-female relationships trains a woman to develop the instincts of a hunter. Her foxy manipulations fill her heart with "snares" and "nets." The only way she knows how to get and keep the attention of a man is to entrap him in her "fetters." To the male writer of Ecclesiastes, this is a fate more bitter than death. "And I find something more bitter than death: the woman whose heart is snares and nets, and whose hands are fetters" (Ecclesiastes 7:26). He laments that although it may be rare to find a male who does not revert to manipulation, finding such a female is nearly impossible (v. 28). He had never met a woman without a hidden agenda.

I asked my son and three of his single, young-adult male friends to help me brainstorm and come up with a list of categories for the types of wily female manipulations they and I had either observed or encountered. We boiled it down to five general categories: sexual manipulation, verbal manipulation, emotional manipulation, spiritual manipulation, and circumstantial manipulation.

Sexual Manipulation

No surprise here. The number one scheme of women is to use their sexuality to control or manipulate a man's behavior. This includes, but is not limited to, immodest clothing, flirting, sexual banter and innuendo, the "come get me" look and other nonverbal turn-ons, all types of physical contact, and giving (or punitively withholding) physical affection and intimate sexual relations and acts. The world teaches us that sexuality is a woman's primary tool and/or weapon. She uses it to get the man she wants and then uses it to get what she wants from him.

Verbal Manipulation

A woman can use words to coax, reason, nag, explain, bombard, insinuate, lecture, harangue, cajole, accuse, wheedle, convince, and otherwise proselytize the guy so that he gives in to her way of thinking. The man leaves the conversation feeling like she has tap-danced on his head. He agrees to change his mind and do things her way, but he has no idea why, like Samson, who was "vexed to death" when Delilah urged him and "pressed him hard with her words day after day." The only way he was able to stop her incessant, confusing verbiage was to give in to her demands.

Emotional Manipulation

Any girl knows that one of the best ways to manipulate a guy is to turn on the waterworks. Many a woman has gotten her way by shedding tears. And then there are the tactics of pouting, sulking, acting hurt, lashing out, or emotionally withdrawing. Or how about securing his loyalty by manipulating him into feeling threatened and jealous? Or what about the "If you really loved me you would . . ." line?

A woman one of the young men in the room had dated tried to manipulate him by appealing to his protective nature. She made up stories about guys following her and insisted that she needed to come see him because she was so afraid. She also magnified symptoms of a physical ailment whenever she wanted more of his attention. Not only that, but when he tried to end their relationship, she threatened to do something to hurt herself. (Yup. This girl sounds like a real zinger!) The "I-need-you-so-much-you're-my-savior-my-life-would-fall-apart-without-you" scheme appeals to the protector-provider in almost every man.

I'm not saying that emotions are wrong. Nor am I saying that women shouldn't express them. The problem is not when a woman expresses her feelings, but when she does so with the subtle, underlying intent to control and manipulate the man.

Spiritual Manipulation

I didn't think of this one right off the bat. My son did. It's an "extra" form of manipulation that Christian girls will sometimes pull out of their purses. This is the "I-prayed-about-it-and-I-know-it's-God's-will-for-us-to-be-together (even-if-you-don't)" tactic. It, too, is a subtle form of manipulation.

Circumstantial Manipulation

It amazes me how much time and energy some women expend to plot and set up circumstances that give them an opportunity to get a man to do something he would not otherwise do. For instance, take the girl who just happens to be walking past the building when he leaves work. ("Fancy bumping into you!" she says, after waiting for him for an hour.) Or what about the girl who shows up at his apartment soaked to the skin from getting "caught" in the rain. ("Whoops—oh my goodness, it *would* have to happen on a day I wasn't wearing a bra!") Or the one who somehow locks herself out of her apartment at midnight and needs a place to stay? Or the one whose parents simply couldn't get two days off work to drive her out to college? Or the one who "falls" and sprains an ankle so he has to carry her to his car?

An example of circumstantial manipulation in the Bible is found in the story of Amnon and Tamar:

> Amnon had a friend, whose name was Jonadab, the son of Shimeah, David's brother. And Jonadab was a very crafty man. And he said to him, "O son of the king, why are you so haggard morning after morning? Will you not tell me?" Amnon said to him, "I love Tamar, my brother Absalom's sister." Jonadab said to him, "Lie down on your bed and pretend to be ill. And when your father comes to see you, say to him, 'Let my sister Tamar come and give me bread to eat, and prepare the food in my sight, that I may see it and eat it from her hand.'" (2 Samuel 13:3–5)

Amnon follows through with the manipulative scheme. He feigns illness, gets his dad to send Tamar to fix him a bowl of hot soup, gets Tamar into his bedroom alone, and declares his love for her. He tries to kiss her and win her over, but when she resists his advances, he forces her to have sex. The sex would have never happened had he not slyly manipulated circumstances to make the opportunity possible. In this instance, it was the manipulative behavior of a man, and not a woman, that set up the scenario for sin. But the story demonstrates the point nonetheless.

The most memorable instance of crafty behavior is, of course, the serpent's manipulation of the first woman, Eve. "Now the serpent was more crafty than any other beast of the field that the Lord God had made" (Genesis 3:1). His crafty, underhanded brilliance operated in stark contrast to the beautiful naked innocence of the first man and woman. The devil's craftiness deceived the woman and brought about the fall of humanity. At that time, women and men lost the beauty of innocence, and were infected with the evil tendency to be crafty and underhanded with one another. What's more, because of God's specific sentence on Eve, the tendency to manipulate men is a sin to which all women are particularly susceptible. Later we'll see how men are susceptible to their own particular type of sin.

The Lord "frustrates the devices of the crafty, so that their hands achieve no success. He catches the wise in their own craftiness, and the schemes of the wily are brought to a quick end. They meet with darkness in the daytime and grope at noonday as in the night" (Job 5:12–14). Have you ever noticed that a wily woman is rarely satisfied? Oh, she may get the guy, the ring on her finger, and her way, but she doesn't get what she needs to fill that gaping ache in her heart. Apart from abandoning her selfish, manipulative tendencies and trusting the Lord with her heart, she, like Wile E. Coyote, will experience a perpetual case of "Want."

A RADICALLY DIFFERENT APPROACH

Girls-Gone-Wise adopt a radically different approach to male-female relationships than the Wild Things of the world. A Girl-Gone-Wise renounces "disgraceful, underhanded ways" and refuses to "practice cunning" (2 Corinthians 4:2). She rejects the worldly belief that in order to get a guy, a woman must manipulatively toss out the bait and reel him in. She refuses to play that game. Instead, she seeks to be godly, above-board, unpretentious, and without guile in her relationships with men.

She trusts in the Lord with all her heart and does not lean on her own understanding. In *all* her ways she acknowledges Him, and He directs her paths. She does what my friend Leslie Ludy did. She gives up control, hands her pen to God, and lets Him write her love story. As Leslie says:

> The One who knows you better than you know yourself, and who loves you more than you can comprehend, wants to take you on a journey.
>
> This journey is for anyone who is searching for the beauty of true and lasting love, for romance in its purest form, and who is willing to do whatever it takes in order to find it. This journey is for anyone who has made mistakes, whether small or big, and said, "It's too late for me to discover *that* kind of love." It's a journey for anyone who is tired of the same old scene of physically intense relationships, devoid of meaning and purpose.
>
> This journey is for anyone who will dare to dream beyond the cheap and diluted romance our culture offers and hold out for an infinitely better way. This journey is even for the skeptic, who doubts that such a way exists.

No matter where you are or where you have been, this invitation is for you. The very One who is the Author of all true love and romance is standing before you, asking you gently, *Will you let Me write your love story?*[3]

The invitation is for the married as well as the single. It contains no guarantee of finding the perfect man, or of having your man transformed into one. But it does hold the promise of a spectacular story line—one that can satisfy the deep desires of a woman's heart to an infinitely greater extent than crafting her own love story ever could. Jesus wants to lavish you with love. He wants you to taste and see that *He* is good. And that good things happen when you stop being wily and trust Him with your love story.

(There are questions for personal reflection and a testimony of a woman who trusted God to write her love story, on GirlsGoneWise. com. Surf on over and check it out.)

Point of Contrast #4

ATTITUDE
Her Prevailing Disposition

Girl-Gone-Wild: **Clamorous & Defiant**	Girl-Gone-Wise: **Gentle, Calm, Amenable**
"She is loud and wayward . . ." (Proverbs 7:11)	Her heart reflects the imperishable beauty of a gentle and quiet spirit, which in God's sight is very precious. (I Peter 3:4)

I remember striding down the school hallway with a couple of girl-friends in the early seventies, belting out the words of Helen Reddy's chart-topping song, "I Am Woman." We sang about being strong and invincible. We were determined to show the world that we were in control. The words of the song summed up our resolve: We were women, and we would ROAR in numbers too big to ignore—no one would ever keep us down again! We were perched on the verge of womanhood. And we were confident that we would be the first generation to get the meaning of womanhood right.

Feminism taught the girls of my generation that men had terribly oppressed our mothers and grandmothers, and their mothers and grandmothers before them. Patriarchy had forced women to conform to an image of womanhood that men had conjured up to serve their own needs and egos. Men had seized all the positions of power. They had kept women in a subservient position by nefariously convincing them that there was no nobler female title or occupation than that of "wife" and "mother." (Gasp! What a travesty! How could they? Will someone please cue some heavy, ominous background music?)

Feminists informed us that marriage and motherhood catered to the selfish male agenda. Men got to do all the important stuff—like punch a time clock and earn money—while they forced women to stay home and do the trivial, demeaning work of homemaking and raising snotty-nosed kids. (At this point, the ominous music gets even more ominous!) The workplace provided men with prestige and power, and their wives provided them with sex and servitude. This arrangement totally favored the male. All he had to do was bring home the paycheck, fix the car, and cut the lawn.

When it came right down to it, men were nothing but lazy, power-hungry bums who married women for the men's own selfish ends. (And this is where the sound track screeches to its scariest, nail-biting crescendo . . .) I am being facetious, of course. But it's hard to believe how completely taken we were by those ideas. I know that you may be thinking that staying home and raising children while your husband financially supports the family sounds idyllic. Unbelievably, feminism claimed that this arrangement was inherently oppressive. And for the most part, the women of my generation swallowed the ruse.

According to feminism, not only did men seize power by occupying all the important roles in society, they also seized it by laying claim to all the important character traits. Patriarchy promoted the idea that the powerful attributes of strength, assertiveness, aggression, initiative, leadership, control, independence, self-reliance, and self-sufficiency were more characteristic of the male gender. All of the weak, insignificant traits belonged to women. Society upheld kindness, gentleness, purity, warm-heartedness, tenderness, and submissiveness as noble feminine virtues. The women of the past bought into the idea that these virtues were both womanly and noble. But this, too, was part of the male plot to keep women subservient to men.

Thanks to the brave efforts of the feminist movement, we women got wise to patriarchy's villainous scheme. We learned that what we needed to do, in order to remedy the age-old injustice, was to reclaim the *power* that men had stolen from us. Man (and not woman) had defined what womanhood was all about. It was time for women to fix that. It was time for Girl Power!

Feminism instructed us that the way to exert power was to reject all the traditional "male-defined" rules about marriage, motherhood, morality, and the meaning and nature of womanhood. So that's what we did. We embraced education, careers, prominence. We despised all relationships and responsibilities that might hold us back. We moved marriage, mothering, and homemaking from the top of our lists to the bottom—or crossed them off altogether. After all, we were so much more enlightened than our foremothers were. The world had revolved around men, but it was our turn now. We would make it bow to our demands.

We decided that the role of a housewife was passé. *Charlie's Angels* seemed so much more exciting. So we redefined boundaries. We changed the rules of male-female relationships. We boldly pushed back against traditional definitions of gender and sexuality. We claimed our freedoms and our rights. We bought into the feminist promise that woman would find happiness and fulfillment when she defined her own identity and decided for herself what life as a woman was all about.

Over the next few decades, culture's definition of womanhood did change. The ideal went from a home-based, nurturing wife and mom (think *Leave It to Beaver*) to a self-indulgent, promiscuous, narcissistic professional (think *Sex and the City*). The media stopped portraying women as sweet, nurturing wives and homemakers, and started portraying them as ripped, in-your-face, male-kicking, sassy heroines who were tough, dominating, hypersexual, and above all in control.

Nowadays we hold in high esteem the assertive, aggressive, tough, calculating, controlling, independent, self-reliant, self-sufficient, brazenly sexual women. Traits of kindness, gentleness, faithfulness, purity, warm-heartedness, tenderness, and submissiveness have all but fallen to the wayside. They are devalued and even scorned. The reason I took you on a trip down memory lane was to show you why. Due to the impact of the women's movement, today's women reject the very disposition that makes women uniquely "feminine"—the one that distinguishes them as God's perfect counterpart to men.

The traits that we value for women are not always the traits the Lord values. And the traits we scorn are often the very ones that are precious in His sight. The biblical stance on the appropriate demeanor for women is extremely countercultural. It goes directly against the grain of how pop culture has programmed us to think. According to the Bible, a Girl-Gone-Wise is not tough and aggressive. Nor is she clamorous and defiant. She forsakes this attitude for a soft, womanly disposition.

THAT GIRL'S GOT ATTITUDE!

"She is loud and wayward" is how the Sage Father pegs the Proverbs 7 woman. The phrase definitely describes her behavior, but more than that, it sums up her prevailing state of mind. She's a sassy, defiant, my-way-or-the-highway kind of a girl. Nowadays, the father might have described her by saying, "She's got attitude!"

The Hebrew word *loud* implies murmuring, growling, roaring, or being tumultuous or clamorous. The description applies to an untamable beast that refuses to bear the yoke. "Like a stubborn heifer" is how the prophet Hosea describes this mind-set among people who refused to obey God (4:16). I think it's ironic that Helen Reddy talks about women roaring in the lyrics of her song, because that's exactly what a Girl-Gone-Wild does. She roars. And it's not so much the volume of her voice, although it definitely can include that. It's her insolence. Synonyms for this clamorous type of attitude are *sassy, brassy, cheeky, cocky, flippant, mouthy, saucy, smart-alecky, barefaced, brash,* or *pushy*. It's an attitude that pop culture promotes and even admires. "Girl, you've got attitude!" is more compliment than insult.

The second adjective describing the Proverbs 7 woman is translated as *wayward*. The Hebrew word means "to be stubborn and rebellious." It reflects a defiant, self-willed, obstinate, "nobody-tells-me-what-to-do" frame of mind. According to the Bible, an attitude of stubbornness toward people often reflects an underlying attitude of stubbornness toward the Lord (Ezekiel 20:38). Ours is a "stubborn and rebellious generation," whose heart is not steadfast, whose spirit is not faithful to God (Psalm 78:8).

A Girl-Gone-Wild is stubborn. She gets irritated and sullen when someone tries to correct or rebuff her. She is not willing to give in or change. She turns a stubborn shoulder (Nehemiah 9:29), plugs her ears (Zechariah 7:11), turns aside and goes her own way (Jeremiah 5:23–26). A woman like this "sticks to her guns." She will not budge. Her way is right in her own eyes. She is not open to input (Proverbs 12:15). One theologian uses the word *unmanageable* to describe a woman with this type of attitude. Another suggests *ungovernable*. The bottom line is that this type of woman refuses to be led—especially by a man. No one has the right to tell her what to do.

Clamorousness (loudness) and defiance (waywardness) go hand in hand. Clamorousness loudly insists, "You better do it my way," and defiance reinforces the idea with, "I refuse to do it yours." They are like two sides of the same coin. Pop culture preaches that women *should* have a clamorous-defiant attitude. It extols it as a virtue. Oh, it often dresses it up nicely and calls it something that makes it sound a bit more respectable—like self-confidence, assertiveness, or personal empowerment—but it really boils down to the same thing: the brash, rebellious attitude of a Girl-Gone-Wild.

"Ms. Stupidity" is what the Bible calls a girl with this attitude. I'm not kidding. That's equivalent to what the Bible actually calls her! It says that Lady Folly is rowdy; "she is gullible and knows nothing" (Proverbs 9:13 HSCB). Folly is empty-headedness, craziness, absurdity, stupidity. Proverbs says that a brash, rebellious demeanor is foolish. It specifically warns women against adopting this mind-set. The Bible is very clear that embracing a defiant attitude isn't liberating and wonderful, as the world would have us believe. It's downright stupid. "Claiming to be wise, they became fools" (Romans 1:22). Janet's testimony shows the negative effect a rebellious attitude can have on a relationship:

> Not long ago, my husband of thirty plus years left me for another woman. Listening to you teach about biblical womanhood has opened my eyes to why this happened. I know that he is responsible for his infidelity and betrayal, and I won't justify his sin. But I know that my bad attitude over the years probably drove him to it.

If I were to pick a word to describe my manner toward my husband, it would be "resistant." I was forever resisting him. If he came up with an idea, I suggested a different or better one. If he wanted me to do something, I dug in my heels. If he tried to make a decision, I objected. If he asked me to reconsider, I would refuse. I continually corrected him and put him down. And I always had a sharp comeback ready on the tip of my tongue.

You have to understand that my husband was not a demanding man. He was very kind. But because I believed that compliance was a sign of weakness, and that women should *never* subject themselves to men, I constantly undermined him. I would not let him lead. Even in the smallest, most insignificant matters, I absolutely refused to follow.

Looking back, I can sadly see how my constant resistance chipped away at his manhood and at our relationship. I resisted and resisted until he gave up, and walked away and into the arms of a woman who welcomed his strength. I was very foolish. If I had the chance to do it all again, I would try to do things God's way. Sadly, it's too late for me, but it isn't too late for all the young women you teach. The world may not believe it, but a gentle, quiet, submissive spirit doesn't demean women. This attitude is precious to God. If it would have been precious to me, I probably would have celebrated my thirty-second anniversary last week. Instead, I was mocked by an empty house and a heavy heart full of regret.

The world thinks a sassy, defiant attitude is the epitome of empowered womanhood. It breaks my heart when I see Christian women fall for this lie. The Evil One has deceived us. A rebellious attitude does not strengthen a woman, nor does it strengthen her love relationship. Quite the opposite, in fact. As Janet and countless others have discovered, rebellion diminishes rather than enhances a woman's life.

STEEL MAGNOLIA

A brazen, defiant attitude stands in stark contrast to the soft receptiveness that the Lord intended for women. When I think of His original design, the Southern phrase "steel magnolia" comes to mind. I'm a Northern woman, so I don't know all the nuances of Southern talk. I wouldn't know when to drawl, "Well bless your heart!" if my life depended on it. I'm just not the pink, frilly, fluffy type. Nevertheless,

I do like the phrase "steel magnolia", because to me it speaks to the essence of womanhood. The image melds beauty with perseverance, softness with backbone, delicacy with durability, sweetness with stamina. It reminds me of what the first man exclaimed when he saw the first woman. When Adam laid his eyes on her, he broke into an exuberant, spontaneous poem:

> "This at last is bone of my bones and flesh of my flesh; she shall be called Woman (*Isha*), because she was taken out of Man (*Ish*)." (Genesis 2:23)

The first man called himself *"Ish"* and the woman *"Isha."* This appears to be an extremely clever and profound play on words. The sound of these two Hebrew words is nearly identical—*Isha* merely adds a feminine ending—but the two words have a complementary meaning. *Ish* comes from the root meaning "strength," while *Isha* comes from the root meaning "soft."

The implication becomes clearer when we observe the biblical meaning of a man's "strength." The Hebrew root is commonly associated with the wisdom, strength, and vitality of the successful warrior. It carries the idea of a champion valiantly serving his people by protectively fighting on their behalf. Strength can also refer to a man's manhood—his virility (Psalm 105:36; Proverbs 31:3; Genesis 49:3). Woman's corresponding trait is her fertility—her unique capability to nurture and bring forth life. He is "strong" directed by inner softness. She is "soft" directed by inner strength.

The bodies of male and female reflect the idea of this complementary distinction. A man's body is built to move toward the woman. A woman's body is built to receive the man. But the pattern goes beyond the mere physical difference between men and women to encompass the totality of their essence: The man was created to joyfully and actively initiate and give. The woman was created to joyfully and actively respond and receive. The woman is the beautiful "soft" one—the receiver, responder, and relater. The man is the "strong" one with greater capacity to initiate, protect, and provide. Each is a perfect counterpart to the other.

Although our culture portrays the ideal woman as aggressive and tough—both physically and sexually—this is a far cry from what woman was created to be. According to Scripture, it's woman's soft-ness, her ability to receive, respond, and relate, that is her greatest strength.

THE RIGHT STUFF

You don't have to be a girly-girl to cultivate a soft, beautiful wom-anly disposition. A woman who rides a Harley or spends her days in chaps wrangling steers, can be just as womanly as the daintiest south-ern belle. Womanliness has to do with a female's demeanor rather than her occupation, hobbies, or talents. It's more of an *internal* than an *external* characteristic. It involves *who she is* more than it involves *what she does*.

The primary passage that outlines the disposition of godly women is 1 Peter 3:4–6. Peter talks about "the imperishable beauty of a *gentle* and *quiet* spirit." He also talks about *deference*—a willingness to respond that expresses itself in a married woman's life as her submission to her husband. Scripture maintains that these three basic qualities are foun-dational to godly womanhood. A Girl-Gone-Wise is not clamorous and defiant. She is (1) gentle, (2) calm, and (3) amenable.

Gentle

Godly women are gentle. Gentleness (often translated as "meek-ness") is a mild, friendly, kind, considerate disposition. Here are some synonyms that my thesaurus lists for *gentle*:

affable, agreeable, amiable, biddable, compassionate, considerate, culti-vated, disciplined, genial, humane, kindly, lenient, manageable, meek, mer-ciful, moderate, pacific, peaceful, pleasant, pliable, soft, softhearted, sweet-tempered, sympathetic, tame, taught, temperate, tender, tractable, trained, warmhearted.

Gentleness isn't weakness. It's the strength of character that enables a person to respond in a kind, considerate way to others' weakness— to put up with their impositions and imperfections. In 1 Thessalo-nians 2:7, gentleness is portrayed as the type of disposition a nursing mother has as she cares for and caters to her fussy child. Gentleness is the reverse of being insistent on one's own rights, being rude or pushy, or demanding one's own way. It's the exact opposite of the loud, clamoring attitude of a Girl-Gone-Wild.

Gentleness is a disposition in which we see the Lord's dealings with us as good and therefore accept them without disputing or resisting. Gentleness means we wholly rely on God rather than our own strength to defend ourselves against inconvenience, hardship, or injustice. It stems from trust in God's goodness and control over the situation. Gentleness isn't self-abasement. It's the mark of the wise woman who remains calm even in the face of other people's shortcomings.

According to the Bible, there are numerous benefits to having this type of attitude. The gentle "delight themselves in abundant peace" (Psalm 37:11). They constantly obtain "fresh joy in the Lord" (Isaiah 29:19). Jesus said, "Blessed are the meek [gentle], for they shall inherit the earth" (Matthew 5:5).

Calm

Calmness is the second characteristic of a Girl-Gone-Wise. Most translations use the word *quiet* to describe this attitude of serenity and tranquility. Being calm means being settled, firm, immovable, steadfast, and peaceful in spirit. A calm disposition is like a still, peaceful pool of water, as opposed to a churning whirlpool that's agitated and stirred up. It's the opposite of the anxious, distressed, disorderly, and clamorous spirit of the Girl-Gone-Wild. "For the wicked are like the tossing sea; for it cannot be quiet, and its waters toss up mire and dirt" (Isaiah 57:20). When women lack a calm spirit, they toss up all kinds of "mire" and "dirt" in their relationships.

According to the Bible, a calm spirit goes hand in hand with trusting the Lord. "In quietness and in trust shall be your strength" (Isaiah 30:15). God's love quiets us and is the source of our calm (Zephaniah 3:17). What's more, calmness and trust are both a result of righteousness: "the result of righteousness [is] quietness and trust forever" (Isaiah 32:17). "Quietness" has more to do with the state of our hearts than the quantity and volume of our words (although the one definitely influences the other). Even women who are gregarious, extroverted, and sociable can achieve a calm, tranquil spirit.

Amenable

A third aspect of a beautiful womanly disposition is the inclination to bend, comply, or submit. Godly women are amenable. The word comes from the French *amener* (to lead). An amenable woman is "leadable" as opposed to "ungovernable." An amenable woman is inclined to say, "Amen!"—which means, "Yes!" She's responsive to input and likely to cooperate. I believe that the Lord created women (all women) with an amenable disposition. He created us with a soft, deferent spirit—a disposition or tendency that joyfully responds and yields to the will of others.

Amenability is really a more sophisticated way of saying "respect." Amenability is an attitude that respects others and esteems God's proper lines of authority. An amenable woman gladly foregoes personal desires and preferences to honor that authority. Other words for amenability are *deference, homage, submission, reverence,* and *consideration.* Antonyms (opposites) include *insolence, irreverence, disesteem, disfavor, discourtesy,* and *rudeness.* The amenable disposition of a Girl-Gone-Wise is the exact opposite of the wayward, rebellious attitude of the Girl-Gone-Wild.

Amenability is the disposition that made Eve beam with joy when Adam named her. It's the disposition that made Mary respond to the angel's startling news of her coming pregnancy with "Behold, I am the servant of the Lord; let it be to me according to your word" (Luke 1:38). And it's the beautiful disposition that the Lord desires each one of His daughters to cultivate.

FEAR FACTOR

The beautiful softness of womanhood was severely damaged when Eve sinned. The Lord informed Eve that sin's horrible consequence was that her "desire" would be for man, but that man would "rule" over her (Genesis 3:16). Theologians have spent a lot of time figuring out what this verse means, but what it boils down to is this: Sin twisted the positive desire of woman to respond amenably to man into a negative desire to resist and rebel against him. It twisted the positive drive of man to use his strength to lead, protect, and provide for woman, into a negative tendency to abuse or refuse that responsibility.

Read that statement again. It's important that you understand the far-reaching consequences of how your womanhood has been affected by sin. Sin damaged woman's inherent softness. Sin also damaged man's inherent strength. That's why maintaining the right disposition can be such struggle.

The world leads us to believe that we must fight for our rights. It teaches us that we need to look out for number one. It teaches women that an attitude of clamorousness and defiance is necessary to ensure we don't become doormats or punching bags. It suggests that those who exchange the Girl-Gone-Wild attitude for the Girl-Gone-Wise attitude will surely lose power and be diminished. I call this the "fear factor."

First Peter 3:6 says that we are Sarah's daughters if we seek a gentle, calm, amenable disposition and *don't give in to fear.* If truth be told, the reason women are clamorous and defiant is that they're scared not to act this way. They're scared of softness. They're scared of vulnerability. In essence, they're scared of womanhood (and of manhood). They're scared that if they become soft and vulnerable, that they will be taken advantage of, and will be reduced to weak, quivering, spineless blobs, devoid of will or personality. They're scared that adopting womanly traits will cause them to be "less" and not "more."

Is it true? If you adopt a gentle, calm, amenable spirit, will it diminish your personality? Will you get stomped on? Will it make you less than who you are? That was Cindy's fear:

> I cut my teeth on feminist philosophy. I was a strong, independent, capable woman who wasn't afraid to elbow her way to the top. If I had to steamroll over some men in the process, well, so be it. I was loud, brash, self-confident, self-promoting, and aggressive, the epitome of what feminism taught me womanhood was all about.
>
> It was with great dismay that I discovered, in a Bible study, that God had a very different perspective on womanhood than I did. When I read adjectives like "quiet," "gentle," "meek," and "submissive," I balked. Being those things went against every fiber of my being. I was literally terrified that pursuing these traits would diminish me into a quivering bowl of jelly. I would lose my personality and become less of a person . . . less of who I am.
>
> Conviction won out, and I begrudgingly told the Lord I was willing

to die to self and be what he wanted me to be, even if it meant losing "me." I would be obedient and to try to cultivate the type of womanhood taught in Scripture.

It wasn't easy. I had to work hard at it, and I can't say that the process is complete yet. Did I sacrifice and give up some things? Yes, definitely. But it dawned on me the other day that I have gained so much more, and that my fear was unfounded. I didn't lose myself. In fact, quite the opposite happened.

In trying to be the woman God wanted me to be I found out who I really am. It's as though Jesus removed the ugly, cracked paint so that the beautiful pattern of the wood could shine through. The joy and peace are incredible. I love being a woman according to His design. And paradoxically, my personhood did not diminish. I am more "Cindy" now than I ever was before.

When it comes to attitude, you have a choice to make. Will you accept the deceptive lie that God's way will diminish you? Or are you going to fight the fear factor? Will you hang on to sin's twisted distortion of what it means to be a woman? Or will you be transformed into whom the Lord created you to be? Will you choose the clamorousness and defiance of a Girl-Gone-Wild? Or the gentle, calm, amenable spirit of a Girl-Gone-Wise?

SWIMMING UPSTREAM

"Wait a minute," you may argue. "Godly attributes are not unique to gender. They're the same for both genders. Women ought to possess strength, initiative, resourcefulness, and enterprise just as men ought to possess gentleness, calmness, and amenability. The Bible doesn't say that the last three attributes belong exclusively to women. It's just as important for men to be gentle, calm, and amenable!" To this, I answer yes and no.

Yes, these attributes are characteristic of both genders. And yes, men should seek to be gentle, calm, and amenable. (Just as women should seek to possess strength, initiative, resourcefulness, and enterprise.) But no, these characteristics are not the same in men as they are in women. Gentleness, calmness, and amenability look different in a man than they do in a woman. The texture is markedly different. In a man, the traits have a uniquely masculine texture. In a woman, they have a uniquely feminine one. His gentleness is strong and initiatory. Hers is soft and responsive. His gentleness moves out and toward. Her gentleness accepts and welcomes in. Therefore the traits should not receive the same emphasis for both genders. Some traits are uniquely important to what it means to be a man, and some are uniquely important to what it means to be a woman. The Bible identifies the ones that deserve special sex-specific attention.

The idea that women should cultivate a soft-spirited attitude is very countercultural. Those who accept and try to live out this idea will find themselves swimming upstream against the current—even against ideas about womanhood that are prevalent in the church. Our cultural milieu makes biblical concepts seem very abrasive.

I'm aware of how foreign some of these ideas may seem to you—especially if you are hearing them for the first time. When I was a young woman and first encountered some ideas about biblical womanhood written by some fuddy-duddy lady, I pitched her book across the room in disgust. I find it amusing to think that I am now the fuddy-duddy one, and that some of you may pitch *my* book across the room in disgust. That's OK. I understand. You don't have to agree with everything I say. All I ask is that you consider these ideas and hold them up to the light of Scripture to see if they are true. I have no doubt that this will be a journey for you, as it was for me.

The Bible has a spectacular vision for what womanhood is all about! With the right heart, the right counsel, the right approach, and the right attitude, you will be well on your way to being a Girl-Gone-Wise.

To go deeper, watch the *Girls Gone Wise* DVD and do the next chapter in the *Girls Gone Wise Companion Guide*.

Point of Contrast #5

HABITS
Her Priorities and Routines

Girl-Gone-Wild: Self-Indulgent	Girl-Gone-Wise: Self-Disciplined
"Her feet do not stay at home; now in the street, now in the market, and at every corner." (Proverbs 7:11–12)	"She looks well to the ways of her household and does not eat the bread of idleness." (Proverbs 31:27)

Texans are familiar with the saying, "Red touches yellow, kill a fellow; red touches black, venom lack." This old reminder helps people distinguish between the deadly, venomous coral snake and the harmless milk snake. Both snakes have alternating bands of red, black, and yellow, but the order and pattern of the colors is different. Red-to-black-striped milk snakes are quite docile. Some people even keep them as exotic pets. But the red-to-yellow-striped coral snake's bite can be fatal. Its fangs inject a potent neurotoxin that paralyzes nerves and breathing muscles. Mechanical or artificial respiration, along with large doses of antivenom, is often required to save a victim's life.

Just as folks in Texas can tell a milk snake from a coral snake by looking at the order and pattern of the stripes, it's possible to differentiate a Wise Thing from a Wild Thing by observing the order and pattern of her conduct. Her priorities and routines are a dead giveaway. If the Sage Father were to dream up a ditty for his son about a woman's habits, he might come up with something like this: "Homeward-faced, wisdom-graced; out-to-the-max, wisdom lacks." A Girl-Gone-Wise is settled and self-disciplined. She puts first things first by giving precedence to intrinsic, home-based priorities. A Girl-Gone-Wild is restless and self-indulgent. She is undisciplined and gives precedence to the pursuit of extrinsic social pleasures and amusements.

OUT AND ABOUT

The Proverbs 7 woman is a prime example. "Her feet do not stay at home; now in the street, now in the market, and at every corner she lies in wait." The words *street, market,* and *corner* refer to the broad, public, open spaces in towns and cities where people in Bible times gathered. Markets were located at the city gate and were often ornamented with statues and colonnades. This is where merchants displayed their goods (2 Kings 7:18). Generally, the marketplaces of the ancient Near East were much like the open-air bazaars one can still see in many cities throughout Greece, Turkey, and Israel. Trade goods included ivory, ebony, emeralds, coral, rubies, wheat, honey, oil, balm, wine, wool, wrought iron, cassia wood, lambs, rams, goats, horses, gold, silver, bronze, iron, tin, lead, carpets of colored material, embroidery work, fine linen, purple cloth, clothes of blue, and choice garments (Ezekiel 27:12–25).

The point that the Sage Father was trying to convey is that the Wild Thing spent her time frequenting public places. She was always out and about. She wanted to be where the action was. She wanted to be amused and entertained, and to feed her appetite for attention and admiration. She was self-indulgent rather than self-disciplined. Shopping, hearing the latest gossip, having a good time, being noticed, and potentially hooking up with a good-looking guy took precedence over other, more important things. "Now at the mall, now at the club, now at the movie theater, now at the party, now at the game" is how the Sage Father could have described her habits, given our contemporary circumstances.

The problem was not so much that this woman went out, but that she went out at the expense of what she should have been doing. "Her feet do not stay at home." That means that her house was probably messy, her laundry undone, her mail unopened, her bills unpaid, her exam unstudied for, her pantry unfilled, and her supper unmade. What's more, she probably couldn't even remember the last time she read or studied her Bible, picked up a good, instructive Christian book, or listened to a sermon she downloaded from the Internet. When she was at home, her overriding purpose was to get herself ready to go out again. This girl could find plenty of time to paint her toenails, but couldn't possibly find time to paint the badly peeling fence. She was far too busy for that!

The Proverbs 7 woman was married. But undoubtedly, her habit of out-and-about behavior was established long before she had a husband. She had never learned the discipline of giving first priority to the things that deserved first priority. She had never learned to attend to her private life first.

Home is far more than a place of residence with a requisite set of domestic duties. One's home is her inner private sanctum. It's the "place"—physically and spiritually—where the most important stuff in life happens. Home is crucial. If a woman's surroundings are neglected, out of order, cluttered, and chaotic, chances are her inner, private life shares the same fate. And her habitual pattern of neglect affects far more than just her. It affects her husband, her marriage, her children, and, ultimately, her own capacity to live a godly, fruitful, productive life and to make a difference in this world.

EYE ON THE HOMEFRONT

The habits of the Proverbs 31 woman stand in marked contrast (vv. 10–31). The writer describes them in a poem he learned from his mother. The structure of the poem is a Hebrew acrostic. The starting consonant of each verse follows the order of the alphabet. The first verse starts with the Hebrew A, the second with B, and so on. It's like an A to Z guide of how to spot a great woman. The beautifully structured poem points out six key characteristics of the habits of a Girl-Gone-Wise:

1. Her habits are self-disciplined and not self-indulgent.

> "She looks well to the ways of her household and does not eat the bread of idleness." (v. 27)

2. She habitually attends to matters of personal faith and character.

> "She dresses herself with strength and makes her arms strong." (v. 17)

> "Strength and dignity are her clothing, and she laughs at the time to come." (v. 25)

> "She opens her mouth with wisdom, and the teaching of kindness is on her tongue." (v. 26)

> "Charm is deceitful, and beauty is vain, but a woman who fears the Lord is to be praised." (v. 30)

3. She habitually attends to the needs of her household.

> "An excellent wife who can find? She is far more precious than jewels." (v. 10)

> "She does him good, and not harm, all the days of her life." (v. 12)

> "She is like the ships of the merchant; she brings her food from afar. She rises while it is yet night and provides food for her household and portions for her maidens." (vv. 14–15)

> "She seeks wool and flax, and works with willing hands." (v. 13)

> "She puts her hands to the distaff, and her hands hold the spindle." (v. 19)

> "She is not afraid of snow for her household, for all her household are clothed in scarlet." (v. 21)

> "She makes bed coverings for herself; her clothing is fine linen and purple." (v. 22)

4. She habitually attends to kingdom mission and ministry.

> "She opens her hand to the poor and reaches out her hands to the needy." (v. 20)

5. She habitually attends to beneficial (and not idle) pursuits.

> "She perceives that her merchandise is profitable." (v. 18)

"She makes linen garments and sells them; she delivers sashes to the merchant." (v. 24)

"She considers a field and buys it; with the fruit of her hands she plants a vineyard." (v. 16)

6. She and her household reap the reward of her disciplined lifestyle.

"Her lamp does not go out at night." (v. 18)

"The heart of her husband trusts in her, and he will have no lack of gain." (v. 11)

"Her husband is known in the gates when he sits among the elders of the land." (v. 23)

"Her children rise up and call her blessed; her husband also, and he praises her: 'Many women have done excellently, but you surpass them all.'" (vv. 28–29)

"Give her of the fruit of her hands, and let her works praise her in the gates." (v. 31)

The habits of the Girl-Gone-Wise are very different from the Wild Thing. Both are busy, but they are busy with different things. The Wild Thing is busy indulging herself. She is constantly out and about, looking for a good time. And she neglects things on the home front. The Girl-Gone-Wise attends to her home life. Her habits are self-disciplined, self-sacrificing, and directed by the needs of her household. "Her feet stay at home."

FEET AT HOME

Having feet that "stay at home" has more to do with a woman's focus than her actual physical location. The Proverbs 31 woman obviously went to the marketplace on a regular basis. She managed her own wholesale business, trading linen garments and sashes. She was also involved in kingdom business, ministering to the poor and needy. But even though she physically went out of the home to do these things, she still maintained a homeward focus and did spend a significant amount of time in her home. It's important to note that a woman's physical location is not the only nor the main part of what it means to have "feet at home." Just because a woman stays at home physically does not necessarily mean that she is attending to her household. She could be procrastinating, self-indulging, and living an undisciplined life just as much as the woman who is always out and about.

The Bible teaches that God created woman with a uniquely feminine "bent" for the home. "Working at home" is on its top ten list of important things that older women need to teach the younger ones (Titus 2:5). It encourages young women to "manage their households" (1 Timothy 5:14). It praises her who "looks well to the ways of her household"—keeping her antennas up to the physical, emotional, relational, and spiritual well-being of everyone in her family, and making sure that everything and everyone is connected and doing well (Proverbs 31:27). The Bible casts women whose hearts are inclined away from the home in a negative light (Proverbs 7:11).

A woman's role in the home is a hot topic. Feminism has taught us to bristle at the idea that a woman's responsibility to the home is any different from a man's. The very suggestion conjures up the classic, oppressive notion of woman being perpetually "barefoot, pregnant, and chained to the kitchen sink." So I feel as though I'm treading on a field full of landmines here. One wrong word or phrase, and my mailbox will explode with angry e-mails. I risk being vilified, mocked, and misrepresented by bloggers in cyberspace forever. Nevertheless, I believe that it is crucial that women understand their special connection to the home. God "wired" women with a unique homeward bent. We can argue until we are blue in the face that it should not be so—that men ought to function in the home the same way as women. But Scripture and a simple observance of male-female behavior indicate that there is indeed a difference. Because of women's nurturing, responsive spirit, we are equipped to be attentive and attuned to the affairs of our households in a way that men are not.

The "ways of the household" involve the cleanliness and orderliness of its physical environment. But more important than that, they involve the cleanliness and orderliness of its relational and spiritual environment. Have you ever noticed that, generally speaking, women have a far greater sensitivity to disorder than men do? (Just think of the typical bachelor pad.) It has always amazed me that my husband and sons can step over something that is out of place (like a jacket or book on the floor in the hallway, for example) a hundred times without even noticing that it is there. It's not that they are intentionally negligent, or averse to picking it up. If asked, they are glad to do so and to contribute to keeping the house clean. But until I draw their attention to it, or until the disorder becomes a significant problem, they simply don't see it. They don't notice that the item is out of place. I do! And it's the same way with "seeing" things that are out of order with a family member's emotions, relationships, or spiritual life. The guys usually don't notice it as readily. Most of you who have been married for a time can attest to the fact that women generally notice a problem in the home long before the men do.

This bent of woman toward the home is an incredible responsibility and an incredible blessing. I can't count the number of times my watchfulness for "things out of place" has saved my family from emotional and spiritual injury. I notice the "disorder" and deal with it with prayer, counsel, and correction. Or I draw my husband's attention to it so we can set it straight and deal with it together. We address the thing that is "out of place" before it becomes a chaotic mess.

I am not the type of woman who loves housekeeping chores (who does?), but over the years I have learned that my vigilance for physically maintaining order in my home is a reflection of what I do for my family spiritually. The two are interconnected. And both are necessary. Attending to the physical condition of a household is of little value if one does not attend to its emotional and spiritual condition. Attending to a household's emotional and spiritual condition is not possible if one does not also attend to its physical condition. Given my personality and gifts, and distaste for all things "trivial," this has been a very tough lesson for me. But I have learned that in order to "look well to the affairs of my household" spiritually, I must physically and practically order my priorities and routines to put first things first. The inward must precede the outward. My feet need to be "home" before they are "out and about."

A single woman might say, "I have no household. I need to get out and about so I can find a husband and get a household!" It's true that a single woman may have more discretionary time for socializing, but it's not true that she does not have a household. Nor is it true that she can neglect it and suffer no ill consequence. Every woman has a household—even if she is the only one in it. A Girl-Gone-Wise cultivates habits, routines, and priorities to keep her home life in order. This happens long before she is ever married. Home is not all she does, but it is what she does first.

FIRST THINGS FIRST

Most of us have a sense for what's important. We know that we ought to develop habits that nurture our personal faith and character, attend to the needs of our households, and minister to others. We know we ought to expend our energy on beneficial and not idle pursuits. However, ordering our lives to put first things first takes discipline. The Wild Thing sadly lacks this character trait. "The woman Folly is . . . undisciplined" (Proverbs 9:13 NIV). Unlike her wise counterpart, the Wild Thing habitually eats "the bread of idleness" (Proverbs 31:27).

The apostle Paul admonished believers not to be idle (1 Thessalonians 5:14). He specifically identified unmarried women as being susceptible to this sin (1 Timothy 5:13). When we use the word *idle*, we usually think of inactivity. We assume that an idle woman has lots of time on her hands. But "inactive" is not exactly what idleness means. The Greek word refers to someone or something that is not in good order. It means "careless" and "out of line." The word was used to describe an undisciplined soldier who would not keep rank but insisted on marching his own way or someone who failed to remain at his post of duty. In the Bible, idleness doesn't mean "doing nothing"—it means "not doing what you should." An idle woman is often busy. Perhaps even excessively busy. Our Proverbs 7 woman was constantly on the go, doing all sorts of things. But she was idle nonetheless. Women are idle when they have the wrong priorities. They are idle when they fail to stay at their post of duty, and busy themselves with other things instead. An idle woman's life is undisciplined and out of order. She does not do what she ought to do.

An orderly, disciplined life is a hallmark of those who follow Jesus. According to the apostle Paul, the grace of God trains us "to renounce ungodliness and worldly passions, and to live self-controlled, upright, and godly lives in the present age . . . zealous for good works" (Titus 2:11–12, 14). Paul set an example by his own self-disciplined lifestyle. He explained, "Every athlete exercises self-control in all things. . . . So I do not run aimlessly; I do not box as one beating the air. But I discipline my body and keep it under control" (1 Corinthians 9:25–27). He expected that all believers would follow his example.

To Paul, self-discipline was a discipleship issue. He wanted the older women to teach younger women how to live "self-controlled" lives (Titus 2:4–5). He implied that self-control was the virtue that ensured that a woman ordered her priorities in the right way. Self-discipline was so important to Paul that he warned his friends to "keep away from any brother who is walking in idleness" (2 Thessalonians 3:6). He didn't want his friends hanging out with undisciplined people and being influenced to adopt a self-indulgent, undisciplined lifestyle.

Is your life orderly and disciplined? Are you putting first things first? A well-known American journalist once said, "Don't waste your breath proclaiming what's really important to you. How you spend your time says it all. . . . There's no sense talking about priorities. Priorities reveal themselves. We're all transparent against the face of the clock."[1] There's a lot of truth in those words. Priorities reveal themselves in habits. If asked, most of us could come up with quite a good-looking list of priorities. Unfortunately, for most people, this list would itemize the things we know should take precedence in our lives, but that really don't. It's not what we *say* but what we *do* that reveals our true priorities. That's why I titled this chapter, "Habits," and not "Priorities." Looking at what you routinely *do* reveals what your priorities really are. For instance, if you routinely sleep in instead of getting up to read your Bible, then sleep is a higher priority to you than Bible reading. There's no sense trying to pretend otherwise.

If you were to evaluate your priorities based on your habits, would "what you do" match up with "what you know you *should* do"? I don't know about you, but for me, taking a look at my habits shows me how very far I still have to go in the area of self-discipline. My life is not as ordered and balanced as it should be. It seems that I am always reevaluating habits and struggling to keep priorities in the right order. But if there's anything I've learned, it's that the battle for a godly, self-disciplined lifestyle is ongoing.

In order to determine whether I am putting first things first, I need to clarify what should come first in this particular season of my life. I need to evaluate my habits to see if what I am doing lines up with what I should be doing. A high priority of every woman is to attend to her spiritual growth through the Word and prayer, and to attend to her personal health and physical fitness. Other priorities will differ, depending on a woman's stage of life and circumstances. A single college student will have her studies as a priority. A new mom's priority is to attend to the needs of her baby. A widow might put ministry first. A wise woman constantly checks her habits to see if she is putting things in the right order and giving everything the right emphasis. She prayerfully evaluates her life, clarifies her God-given priorities, and adjusts her habits to match.

Clarifying what we should do is a whole lot easier than actually doing it. The natural, sinful inclination of our flesh is to be self-indulgent and not self-disciplined. I want to sleep more than I want to get up with the alarm. I want to relax more than I want to exercise. I want to eat chocolate and drink Coke more than I want string beans and milk. I want to be entertained more than I want to work. I want to receive more than I want to give. I want others to wait on me more than I want to wait on them. I want to have fun more than I want to sacrifice. I want things easy. I don't want to be inconvenienced or to exert too much effort. My sinful nature is the reason I need help. I do not have the necessary motivation or self-discipline to do what I ought to do. It's just too tough. And there's usually no one to blame but me. My own desires interfere and keep me from doing what I want to do: "For the desires of the flesh are against the Spirit, and the desires of the Spirit are against the flesh, for these are opposed to each other, to keep you from doing the things you want to do" (Galatians 5:17).

Given my own strength and willpower, my ability to live a self-disciplined life is extremely limited. That's why I need to depend on my "Helper." The Lord gives me His Spirit to help me in my weakness. The Holy Spirit is the Spirit of power, of love, and of self-discipline (2 Timothy 1:7 NIV). The truth of the matter is, I don't have enough *power* to overcome the sinful pull toward self-indulgence. I don't *love* God or others enough to sacrifice my own comfort and pleasure for the sake of theirs. I don't have the *self-discipline* to make myself do what I ought to do.

On my own, I do not have the capacity to put first things first. But thankfully (and this is the wonder of the Gospel), it doesn't matter. The Lord gives me all I need. He provides the power, love, and self-discipline that I so desperately lack. Therefore, doing the right thing doesn't depend on me drumming up enough willpower. Success is a matter of depending on the Holy Spirit and not on my own capacity.

The "rubber hits the road" at decision time. I know what I should do . . . and I know that God gives me the power and self-discipline to do what I should do . . . so all that remains is for me to surrender my will to His and actually do it. I need to live by the Spirit and not by my flesh. And that's the toughest part. Every day, I make dozens of "rubber hits the road" decisions about whether I'm going to gratify the desires of my flesh or walk by the Spirit of God. All these decisions add up to a self-indulgent or self-disciplined pattern of living.

The alarm rings. I know I should get up. I know that God's Spirit gives me the power to get up. I know that if I don't get up, I won't have time to read my Bible, pray, exercise, straighten the kitchen, throw in a load of laundry, and put on a pot of coffee for my husband. So it's decision time. Do I gratify the desires of my flesh, or do I surrender my will and walk in the power of the Spirit of God? I stumble downstairs and rub the sleep out of my eyes. On the way to the laundry room, I pass by my office. Should I check my e-mail? There might be an important or interesting message in my inbox. I want to read my e-mail more than I want to read my Bible and definitely more than I want to exercise! So it's decision time again. Do I gratify the desires of my flesh, or surrender my will and walk by the Spirit of God? When I get to the kitchen, I notice that someone left an open bag of potato chips on the counter. I know I shouldn't have any, especially that early in the morning, but they're my favorite brand. It's decision time. Do I gratify the desires of my flesh and dig in? All day I make tiny decisions that are either self-disciplined or self-indulgent.

Ten p.m. End of the day. My son just flicked on an entertaining movie in the family room. I should be taking the meat out of the freezer, running the dishwasher, hanging up some clothes, checking tomorrow's schedule, and getting ready for bed. I know that a lack of discipline at bedtime often sets me up for an unproductive day tomorrow. But all I want to do is plop down on our comfy sofa, curl up in a blanket, and watch the DVD. It's decision time again.

Each day we make dozens and dozens of small decisions. Each individual decision seems trivial and inconsequential. But together they add up to a habitual pattern that is either life-giving or life-quenching. Paul warns, "If you live according to the flesh you will die, but if by the Spirit you put to death the deeds of the body, you will live" (Romans 8:13). The problem of the Wild Thing is that she gave in to her own sinful inclination and lived according to her flesh. She habitually chose to go out and about, looking for a good time. In the end, the consequence of her behavior was deadly. Her relationship with the Lord stagnated and died.

You can tell if a girl is wise or wild by the order and pattern of her habits. "Homeward-faced, wisdom-graced; out-to-the-max, wisdom lacks." The Girl-Gone-Wise recognizes the importance of daily habits. She orders her ways and lives a self-disciplined, rather than self-indulgent life. She keeps an eye on the home front, and diligently works to make sure all is in order there.

Point of Contrast #6

FOCUS
What Commands
Her Attention

Girl-Gone-Wild: **Getting**	Girl-Gone-Wise: **Giving**

"She lies in wait." (Proverbs 7:12)	"She opens her hand to the poor and reaches out her hands to the needy." (Proverbs 31:20)

She looked so cute. But her appearance was at odds with her inclination. Our pretty cat, Truffles, had a killer instinct. It was obvious by the number of mice and birds she dragged into my kitchen and triumphantly dropped at my feet. You could also see it in her eyes. Especially when she got the evening crazies. Her eyes had an intense, focused look—highly alert for prey. The tiniest bit of movement from any small object, and she immediately crouched into a predatory stance—ears pricked forward, tip of her tail flicking, every muscle taut, ready to pounce. If she ever spotted a bird through the window, she'd fixate on it, chatter her teeth, and emit a guttural growl.

And she didn't restrict herself to small prey. Once, our adorable tabby trapped an electrical repairman in the basement storage room. She positioned herself in the doorway, then snarled, spit, and threatened to attack when he tried to escape. Being a skilled predator, Truffles obviously derived pleasure from stalking, pouncing, chasing, and playing with her victim. She was always on the lookout for another good hunt.

The Sage Father of Proverbs likened a Girl-Gone-Wild to a predator. He advised his son that this kind of woman "lies in wait." She has a hunting instinct. She's always alert and on the prowl. The Wild Thing focuses on what she can *get*. She particularly wants to get the guy. The Girl-Gone-Wise, on the other hand, focuses on what she can *give*. The Wise Thing extends her hands outward. "She opens her hand to the poor and reaches out her hands to the needy" (Proverbs 31:20). The Wild Thing closes her hands inward. Hers is a predatory *me-focus* and not the productive *kingdom-focus* of the Girl-Gone-Wise.

CAUGHT IN A TRAP

In the last chapter, we learned that the Girl-Gone-Wild is always out and about. The reason she is out and about is that she is on the prowl. Like my cat, she gets the evening crazies. "Her feet do not stay at home; now in the street, now in the market, and at every corner she lies in wait." Lying in wait is traditional hunting behavior. The Bible often uses a hunting metaphor for people who take advantage of unsuspecting victims. It compares their behavior to animals such as lions and bears, which lie in wait to ambush their prey (Lamentations 3:10). But the hunting metaphor it uses the most is that of the "fowler." The wicked "lurk like fowlers lying in wait. They set a trap; they catch men" (Jeremiah 5:26).

Fowlers were professional bird catchers. They supplied the marketplace with doves and other birds that people kept as caged pets. They also sold wild pigeons and doves for temple sacrifices, and small birds such as partridge and quail for food. The many biblical references to the fowler and his hunting devices are likely due to the fact that Palestine lies on one of the main flight routes of certain migratory birds (Exodus 16:13). A fowler catching and selling birds was a common sight and thus a concept with which the ancients were very familiar.

The Bible refers to the "snare of the fowler" as an alluring but dangerous trap. Fowlers generally caught birds in snares or traps. A passage in Job uses six Hebrew words for traps, more synonyms for these objects than in any other Old Testament passage (Job 18:8–10). Scripture's point is that the traps of foolish, ungodly people are many and varied and highly dangerous. They are "snares of death" (Proverbs 13:14). And this is particularly the case with a Girl-Gone-Wild, who dangles herself out as bait to catch a man. Here's how the Bible describes her predatory hunting behavior:

- She lurks and "lies in wait" (Proverbs 7:11–12; 23:28).
- Her "heart is snares and nets" (Ecclesiastes 7:26).
- Her "mouth is a deep pit" (Proverbs 22:14).
- She "hunts down a precious life" (Proverbs 6:26).
- She traps him like a stag in a trap or a bird in a snare (Proverbs 7:22–23).
- Her "hands are fetters" (Ecclesiastes 7:26).
- "He who pleases God escapes her, but the sinner is taken by her" (Ecclesiastes 7:26).
- Like a bird, the young man rushes into her snare. "It will cost him his life" (Proverbs 7:23).

The Lord warned the men of Israel that getting involved with this ungodly type of woman would be "a snare and a trap for you, a whip on your sides and thorns in your eyes" (Joshua 23:12–13). The Sage Father agreed. He warned his son that taking the bait would lead to spiritual death (Proverbs 7:27). He directed his son to steer clear of Wild Things. He didn't want him falling for the wiles of a predatory woman.

If the father had written his proverbs for a daughter, he would have warned her against *becoming* a Wild Thing, for he knew that the trap of a predatory woman doesn't just snag the man. It also entangles her. Scripture makes it clear that predators are trapped by their own devices. "For in vain is a net spread in the sight of any bird, but these [predators] lie in wait for their *own* blood; they set an ambush for their *own* lives" (Proverbs 1:17–18). The wicked are snared in the work of their own hands (Psalm 9:16).

I want to make sure that you carefully note this point: *predators will not avoid getting caught in their own traps!* This is incredibly important for women to understand. I cannot stress it enough. Being out and about, dangling your body as bait, and lying in wait to hook a man isn't just bad for the man who walks into your trap; it's also bad *for you!* It's a foolish strategy. Ultimately, it will backfire. You will hurt yourself. You won't find the long-term, loving relationship you yearn for. Your own schemes will throw you down. You will be ensnared and injured by your own devices (Job 18:5, 7–10).

I think of Meagan, the twenty-two-year-old who has given herself away to multiple guys and has had her heart broken numerous times, yet fails to see that her Girl-Gone-Wild behavior sets her up for failure, and therefore refuses to change. I think of Gloria, the fifty-six-year-old who is on marriage number four, sobbing on my shoulder, "If only I could find a man to love me!" Or Vicky, the dental hygienist who, disappointed by the husband she caught in a club, became infatuated with her married boss and then turned her charms on him. I think of the thousands of women I have met who think that "getting the guy" is what life is all about. I think of the thousands more who have been deeply disappointed and hurt by the guys they've caught, but who nevertheless continue to "lie in wait."

LYING IN WAIT

A Girl-Gone-Wild expends enormous amounts of time and energy lying in wait. She is like the fowler who bides his time to lure the birds onto his net and then bides it again to determine when he should pull the cord. Biding time is the major part of his job. He repeatedly watches and waits. Where are they? Are they coming? Do they see the bait? Do I need to put out more? Here they come . . . I hope they keep moving in this direction. Are they close enough? Have they taken the bait? Is the bird in the net? Should I spring the trap? Will I catch my prey?

Like the fowler, the Wild Thing perpetually waits. She constantly scopes things out and evaluates the situation. She preoccupies herself with "the hunt." Thinking about it takes up a great deal of mental energy. She dreams up possible scenarios and schemes for the hunt. She talks about it with her girlfriends. She makes sure she reads the latest *Cosmopolitan* to find the latest techniques for it and constantly evaluates how it is progressing. She watches sitcoms and Blu-rays about the hunt. She texts her girlfriends to find out how they are faring in the hunt. She cries when it is going poorly. She's happy when she has a new prospect on the horizon and the hunt is going well. She's elated when she finally catches her bird. But her satisfaction is short-lived. She may busy herself with getting the bird tethered down and taking him to market, but she will soon grow restless. She's a hunter, after all. It's not long before she will return to the lipstick jungle to once again lie in wait.

Lying-in-wait behavior isn't restricted to getting a guy and getting married. It extends to getting other things too. After she gets the guy, the Wild Thing may turn her attention to getting the house, getting the furniture, getting a car, getting new clothes, getting a job, getting some kids, getting a break, getting her husband to change, getting the money to retire . . . Many women spend their whole lives lying in wait. They perpetually wait and watch for their next big catch, and hope that it will bring them the fulfillment they so desperately desire.

Predators "lie in wait" because they rely on others to satisfy their desires. They are greedy at heart. Their primary focus is to satisfy their own appetites. They are ravenously intent on filling their own stomachs. They will disregard the needs of others and steal or destroy to get what they want. The devil is the greatest predator of all. He prowls around like a roaring lion, seeking someone to devour (1 Peter 5:8). His motivation is utterly selfish. He ensnares people so that they might be "captured by him to do his will" (2 Timothy 2:26). The Girl-Gone-Wild operates with a similar motivation. A man is "taken by" her just as a sinner is "captured by" the devil (Ecclesiastes 7:26). The language indicates that the Girl-Gone-Wild is the perpetrator. Yes, men can be just as guilty of predatory sins, but in this instance, the woman is the one doing the "grabbing" and "taking." She is the one who is intent on getting.

The Girl-Gone-Wild captures a guy with the expectation that he will do *her* will. She expects that he will give her what she wants—a good time, love, acceptance, security, marriage, kids, a home. Almost everything that she gives him is bait. It has "strings attached." It's motivated by her desire that he will meet her needs in return. A girl will *give* a guy a peek at her hardware . . . to *get* his admiration. She'll *give* him a boost to his ego . . . to *get* him to engage in conversation. She'll *give* him physical pleasure . . . to *get* another date. She'll *give* him sex . . . to *get* him to love her. She'll *give* him what he wants . . . if it will *get* her what she wants.

Her heart is "snares and nets," and her hands are "fetters" (Ecclesiastes 7:26). A fetter is a chain or shackle fastened to somebody's ankles or feet. It's a means of restraint. When the Girl-Gone-Wild extends her hand and gives something to a man, it's with the hope and expectation that she will bind him to her with obligation. Because of her need and greed, she is incapable of loving freely like Jesus—with a pure, no-strings-attached kind of love. In the end, her "me-focus" doesn't deliver. She ends up forsaking the right way, selling out to sin, and having a partner that she has to restrain like a dog on a leash in order to keep him from wandering. She entangles herself in a terrible mess.

FROM PREDATORY TO PRODUCTIVE

The predatory behavior of a Girl-Gone-Wild stands in marked contrast to the productive behavior of a Girl-Gone-Wise. A Girl-Gone-Wise doesn't waste time "lying in wait." She's too busy putting first things first. She has a *kingdom-focus* instead of a *me-focus*. She's far more concerned about what she can give than what she can get. Why is her life so different? Because she believes the old creed that says, "The chief end of man is to glorify God and enjoy Him forever." To "glorify" something is to extol it and "show it off" or "make it famous." The wise woman's life is all about enjoying God and making Him famous. That's what commands her attention.

People intuitively get the part about "enjoying" and "glorifying." Everyone has an innate drive to enjoy and glorify something. The Girl-Gone-Wild wants to enjoy and glorify herself. Her me-focus governs everything she does. She tries to make men, sexuality, marriage, family, money, career, her volunteer work—everything in life—cater to her personal enjoyment and affirm her personal sense of self-worth. For her, that's what life is about.

The difference between the Girl-Gone-Wise and the Girl-Gone-Wild is not that one "enjoys and glorifies" something and the other does not. The difference lies in *what* each enjoys and glorifies. The overriding purpose of the Girl-Gone-Wise is to enjoy and glorify Christ in all she does. She seeks to enjoy Christ and make Him famous in her relationships. She seeks to enjoy Christ and make Him famous in the way she interacts with men. She seeks to enjoy Christ and make Him famous in her marriage. She seeks to enjoy Christ and make Him famous in her sexuality, in her family, with her money, and with her career. In everything she does—from the way she dresses to the way she orders her day—she seeks to delight in Christ and put His beauty and excellence on display. Getting love, getting a guy, getting "stuff," or getting herself to the point where she feels "self-actualized" isn't her overriding goal. Enjoying and glorifying God is. She focuses on building His kingdom—not on building her own. And that makes a major difference in how she interacts with men.

A WOMAN ON A MISSION

The Girl-Gone-Wise doesn't lie in wait for a man, because she doesn't need a man to fulfill her life's purpose. Although marriage is a good and legitimate goal, her life is about so much more. She has a profound sense of mission. More than anything, she wants to know Christ and make Him known. She wants to display His greatness by doing the good works that He prepared in advance for her to do. "For we are his workmanship, created in Christ Jesus for good works, which God prepared beforehand, that we should walk in them" (Ephesians 2:10). The Girl-Gone-Wise understands that regardless of whether she is single or married, her overriding purpose is to display Christ and to be busy with the kingdom work that He has for her in that season of her life. As my twenty-two-year-old friend Vanessa told me, "I just had this overwhelming sense that the Lord had a purpose for me that was not all about me. . . . The reason I'm here is so much bigger than that!"

I invited Vanessa over for coffee to talk about her focus in life. I had met her eight years before when she and my son were both in eighth grade. She and the rest of the kids in their class had come over to our house for a birthday party. Vanessa and several others hung out in the kitchen while I readied some pizza buns for the oven. It didn't take long for me to notice that Vanessa had a different focus than the other girls. The others had that "truffles" look in their eyes. They were intent on watching the boys and trying to get the boys' attention. You could tell by the way they dressed and did their makeup, the way they positioned themselves around the room, what they talked about, and the way they giggled and tossed their heads.

Vanessa didn't play that game. She seemed rather uncomfortable with the whole scene. But when I asked her about how she was planning on spending the weekend, she came alive. Her beautiful dark eyes sparkled as she told me about the quilt she was making to send to the family of a firefighter killed in 9-11.

Vanessa's dad is a firefighter, and when she watched the events of 9-11 unfold, she wanted to do something to reach out and comfort the kids who had lost their dads. That night, the fourteen-year-old knelt by her bed and asked the Lord what she could do to help. He gave her the idea to sew and send handmade quilts to wrap the grieving children in Arms of Compassion. The quilt would be "like a big hug of comfort." The next day, Vanessa took out a big pair of shears, cut up her dad's old firefighting uniform, and started making quilts. Her goal was to make three hundred quilts to send to all the children affected by the tragedy.

She soon realized that she couldn't do it alone. So she called up all the churches and youth groups and schools in the area, asking for volunteers. She made templates and patterns. She canvassed businesses for supplies: old blue jeans, cloth, sewing machines, cutters, mats. Soon, box after box of supplies landed on her doorstep. If she needed cloth, she prayed for cloth. If she needed batting, she prayed for batting. Department stores donated vans full of display material. The Salvation Army gave large boxes of old blue jeans. Laundromats offered cleaning services. Thousands of volunteers donated their time. Businesses gave money. Vanessa witnessed miracle after miracle as she asked the Lord to supply her needs. One time, she needed thread. So she specifically prayed for thread. Soon afterward she got a call from the Levi Strauss Company. They were shutting down one of their factories. Could she possibly use some massive cylinders of thread?

Vanessa's Arms of Compassion soon reached beyond the children in New York to sick kids at the local children's hospital, to families who lost homes in fires, to needy children and orphans in Nicaragua, and to many other people who were suffering and in need. Quilting volunteers delivered the precious handmade "hugs" as symbols of the love and compassion of Christ. "The needs were overwhelming," Vanessa explained. "Everywhere I looked there was a need." While the other girls were flaunting tight-fitting, low-rise denim to lie in wait for guys, Vanessa was cutting up denim to make patchwork quilts to give to those who were suffering and in pain. During her high school years, her Arms of Compassion wrapped more than six hundred hurting kids and families in homemade quilts.

Vanessa was a young woman with a profound sense of mission. And it wasn't long before the world sat up and took notice. When she was fifteen, the Governor General awarded her with the Queen's Golden Jubilee Medal for outstanding citizenship; she was the youngest Canadian ever to receive this honor. Other accolades followed—a Premier's Citizenship award, a Centennial Medal, and a Stars of the Millennium award. When she was seventeen, Soroptimist International, a worldwide women's organization associated with the United Nations, recognized her with yet another award. At that ceremony, she stood in front of thousands of women from nations all around the world and spoke of the importance of purpose, compassion, and making a difference in the lives of the poor and needy.

Vanessa shrugs and looks somewhat embarrassed as she lists off the awards. She wasn't really looking for awards. She just wanted to reach out to kids who were hurting. She just wanted to be faithful to what the Lord wanted her to do. "I just want to make a difference every day—whether in a small capacity or large."

It shows. For the past few years, Vanessa has quietly ministered to the homeless in downtown Edmonton. Last year, at age twenty-one, this remarkable young woman dropped out of college to care full-time for her mother, who is recovering from a brain tumor, and her father, who was stricken with lung cancer from his many years firefighting. It has been very, very difficult. But Vanessa is undaunted. When I ask the reason for her resolve she says, "You have to realize that life is bigger than you. It's bigger than what we can see. We all have a purpose. God has a purpose for each and every person."

Would Vanessa like to meet and marry her Prince Charming? Of course she would! But she knows that the God who satisfied her need for thread can also satisfy her desire for a husband. Vanessa doesn't have to take matters into her own hands. She doesn't have to worry. She doesn't have to lie in wait. She can busy herself with doing the things that are proper for women who profess godliness to do—the good works of the kingdom of God (1 Timothy 2:10). She knows she needs to be about His business. Like my eighty-one-year-old mom often says to me, "I'm still here. There must be something God wants me to do today."

Vanessa learned the importance of a Godward focus as a teen. Some of you may not have. But it's never too late. Whether you are eight or eighty-eight, you can shift your attention from a predatory *me-focus* to a productive *kingdom-focus*. Don't squander your life. Don't waste your time lying in wait. Christ is too important. Time is too precious. The needs are too great. Too much is at stake. Be like the wise woman of Proverbs 31, who opens her hand to the poor and reaches out her hands to the needy (31:20). Focus on kingdom business. Enjoy God and glorify Him. A Girl-Gone-Wise does not lie in wait for men or worldly "stuff." Instead, she busies herself with her mission and trusts the Lord to take care of the rest.

Point of Contrast #7

APPEARANCE
How She Adorns Herself

Girl-Gone-Wild: Unbecoming, Indecent, Excessive	Girl-Gone-Wise: Becoming, Decent, Moderate
"And behold, the woman meets him, dressed as a prostitute." (Proverbs 7:10)	"[She] adorn[s] [herself] in respectable apparel, with modesty and self-control." (1 Timothy 2:9)

I was at a hockey game. But it was hard to focus on hockey. The low-rise skirts and jeans of the six young women sitting in front of me revealed everything from colorful thongs, to fleshy love handles, to the most intimate crevices of a woman's body. Their tops were equally immodest. I kept thinking very disturbing thoughts about where all the ice in my drink would land if I happened to spill it. At the end of the first period, I relocated to a different seat so I could enjoy the rest of the hockey game without the distraction of the skin show. It was that bad. And if I was having a hard time not staring, I can't imagine how difficult it was for the young men seated across the aisle to avoid gawking at the display and keep their minds on ice (the sheet of ice the players were skating on, that is).

The girls at the hockey rink looked more like hookers than hockey fans. In my city, hookers peddle their wares on a certain street downtown. It used to be easy to pick them out. They were the ones with the extreme high heels, micro-mini skirts or shorts, protruding cleavage, heavy makeup, and attention-getting hair. But if a prostitute from the street had seated herself next to those six girls, chances are I wouldn't have been able to tell her apart. She would have blended right in. Nowadays, there is little difference between the appearance of a prostitute and the appearance of what the world upholds as a sexy, attractive woman.

The hooker look has gone mainstream. You can see it paraded by women in malls, restaurants, schools, the workplace, and even in churches. Popular culture encourages very young girls to dress in a provocative manner. Toddlers play with dolls dressed in fishnets, miniskirts, and heavy eye makeup. Clothing stores sell tiny tank tops printed with Playboy bunnies and such expressions as "Hottie," "Porn Star," "Wet," "Princess," "Party Girl," and "No Angel." In 2002, retailer Abercrombie and Fitch produced a line of thong underwear with expressions such as "Eye Candy" and "Wink Wink." The thongs fit girls as young as seven.[1] From the adolescent Lolita to the middle-aged "cougar," looking "hot" is promoted by the media as a desirable, life-long pursuit.

The Sage Father tells his young son that one of the telltale marks of a Wild Thing is that she dresses "as a prostitute." It's important to note that the Proverbs 7 woman is *not* a prostitute. But *like* a prostitute, she relies on her "wares" to entice men. Looking "hot" is her aim. Though her desired remuneration is not as tawdry as money, she peddles her looks for payment of another kind . . . attention, self-esteem, acceptance, or affection, for example.

What does it mean to dress "as a prostitute"? It definitely involves how a woman puts herself together—the type of shoes, clothing, and makeup she chooses to wear. But far more than that, it has to do with her underlying attitude. A prostitute is excessively concerned about personal appearance. She believes that the payment she'll receive from men is dependent on her external packaging. Packaging equals payment. "Getting" depends on "looks." A Girl-Gone-Wild has this same sort of attitude. A Girl-Gone-Wild might try to look sexy or despair that she cannot. She might expend a tremendous amount of energy to make herself look like a "Pretty Woman" or be self-conscious that her body doesn't measure up. Her body type may prevent her from wearing the tight, highly revealing type of clothing that a prostitute commonly wears, but she would wear that type of clothing if she could. She believes that her level of "sexiness" and "hotness" will dictate whether men will buy into a relationship with her.

The prostitute-like mentality of a Girl-Gone-Wild will motivate her to dress in a way that is unbecoming, indecent, and/or excessive. Her counterpart, the Girl-Gone-Wise, has a very different mind-set. She neither obsesses over, nor neglects her appearance. Mindful of Christ, the Girl-Gone-Wise adorns herself in a way that is becoming, decent, and moderate. Her external appearance reflects the beauty of her inner self. Later, we'll take a look at what all that means, but first, I'd like to explore the biblical reason for covering our bodies. Why do we wear clothing anyway?

THE PURPOSE FOR CLOTHING

In the church, most discussions about clothing revolve around the need for modesty. Teachers place much emphasis on the fact that men are visually stimulated. Women are told that if they dress in a way that is overly sexual, they can tempt their Christian brothers to sin, and may end up in sexual sin themselves. The issue of clothing is thus often reduced to the question of the best way to help men avoid temptation: How low is too low? How short is too short? How tight is too tight? How sheer is too sheer? How much skin is too much skin? How stylish is too stylish? How do I reduce the chance that men will lust after me? How do I divert their attention away from my private parts?

Some try to come up with a checklist of what is and is not appropriate for Christian women to wear. Others propose that the best solution is to dress in clothes that are outdated or ugly: wear long, faded, baggy jean jumpers, along with white socks and sneakers, and pull your hair up in a bun. Some Christians believe that those who dress in colorful, stylish, attractive clothing, wear high heels, and get their hair styled are rather unspiritual, if not downright carnal. Frumpy and out-of-style equals holy. All this can leave a woman with the impression that curbing wrongful sexual desire and activity is the ultimate goal of the way she dresses. Taken to its logical end, this mentality supports the *burka*—the tentlike garment worn by women in some Islamic traditions that cloaks the entire body. If the ultimate point of clothing is to prevent wrongful sexual temptation and activity, then it makes sense that covering a woman's entire body would be the best way to accomplish that goal.

It's true that women must take care not to willfully tempt or mislead their Christian brothers. But curbing wrongful sexual activity is not the main reason behind the Bible's teaching on dress. Don't get me wrong. It is an important consideration. But it's not the main one. And those who focus on it can miss the point. How we ought to dress has something to do with curbing wrongful sexual activity, but it has a whole lot more to do with the Fall, when God originally covered the nakedness of human beings. It has to do with why we wear clothing in the first place.

NAKEDNESS AND SHAME

"What's the Problem with Nudity?" was the title of a recent program on BBC. The show pointed out, "All humans are sensitive to sexual modesty," even in cultures where nudity or partial nudity is normative. To find out if modesty could be "unlearned," the BBC took eight ordinary people—none of them nudists—and had them spend a few days together naked. The producers wanted to test some scientific theories that explain why naked bodies make us so uncomfortable. The big question was whether people could unlearn their naked shame.

The volunteers did unlearn their shame. By the final nude wine and cheese reception, they appeared to be entirely comfortable with each other's nakedness. As a parting challenge, the director asked them to walk out naked onto the street to waiting taxis. Emboldened by their experience, they suppressed any remaining shame and did so. In the end, the moderator concluded, "We're not born with sexual modesty," and added, "So long as everyone agrees, we can create new rules and avoid the risk of offense."[2]

Why does nakedness normally cause shame? The BBC suggests it's because of cultural conditioning. But the Bible has an entirely different answer. It reveals that there was once a day when there was nudity and no shame. "And the man and his wife were both naked and were not ashamed" (Genesis 2:25). Then sin entered the world. Adam and Eve suddenly became aware that they were naked. They felt shame, and tried to cover up.

> Then the eyes of both were opened, and they knew that they were naked. And they sewed fig leaves together and made themselves loincloths. And they heard the sound of the Lord God walking in the garden in the cool of the day, and the man and his wife hid themselves from the presence of the Lord God among the trees of the garden. But the Lord God called to the man and said to him, "Where are you?" And he said, "I heard the sound of you in the garden, and I was afraid, because I was naked, and I hid myself." . . . And the Lord God made for Adam and for his wife garments of skins and clothed them. (Genesis 3:7–10, 21)

Nakedness was natural and fitting for Adam and Eve when they were pure and innocent. But when that purity and innocence was lost, they became painfully embarrassed by their naked condition. Why? What's the connection between sin and nakedness? Why were they ashamed of nudity? Why did they feel the need to cover their private parts? What were they trying to hide? Who were they trying to hide from? Why were their fig leaves inadequate? Why did the Lord shed the blood of an animal to make them garments? How did He propose to solve the problem of their shame? As you'll soon see, these questions all relate to the matter of why we wear clothing and the appropriate attitude we ought to have toward adorning our bodies.

It all started when Eve decided that she wanted to be like God and call her own shots. The Serpent convinced her that she would receive all kinds of benefits if she did. He promised that a whole world of knowledge and experience would open up to her. ("Your eyes will be opened.") He assured her that she would be equal with God—that is, she could be her own god. ("You will be like God.") Finally, he promised that she would be able to decide for herself what was right and wrong. ("Knowing good and evil.")

The Serpent's promises came true, but in a horribly twisted way. Eve's eyes *were* opened to a new world of knowledge and experience—it was awful. She felt the horrible, oppressive force of evil wrap its ugly black tentacles around her heart. She *did* act "like God"—it was a farce. In trying to usurp His position, she enslaved herself to the Prince of Darkness, who was cast from heaven for the same rebellious sin. She *did* make her own decision about good and evil—it was a disaster. Apart from God, she was totally inept at discerning right from wrong. Eve's sin was self-exaltation. She arrogantly refused to acknowledge that God alone was God. When she took the fruit, she defied who He was and made herself out to be something that she was not.

After she sinned, Eve's eyes opened to the fact that she was not the goddess she had presumptuously made herself out to be. Nor was she the woman that God had created her to be. Not anymore. A massive chasm had opened up between what she once was and what she had become. For the first time ever, she experienced imperfection. She was flawed. Feelings of inadequacy swept over her like the rushing muddy waters of a Mississippi flood. She was not who she should have been. Her created beauty was marred. And this resulted in excruciating shame.

Shame is a negative emotion that combines feelings of dishonor, disgrace, unworthiness, and embarrassment. Eve's attempt to clothe herself was a pitiful effort to conceal her disgrace. The ugliness in her heart made her feel physically ugly. For the first time ever, she felt unattractive. Imperfect. Flawed. Self-conscious. Her nakedness felt too revealing and too vulnerable. So she tried to conceal the gap between what she was and what she should have been by covering her most intimate, vulnerable parts with leaves.

The leafy apron Eve stitched together may have helped a bit when it came to covering the shame she felt in Adam's presence. After all, Adam had also sinned and had donned a leafy loincloth to cover his shame. But neither she nor Adam could cover their inadequacy before the Lord. When God drew near, they realized that the leafy aprons didn't suffice. They still felt naked. Eve couldn't cover her sin. Adam couldn't cover his. Nothing could hide the dishonor, disgrace, and embarrassment of their rebellion against their Creator. They could not conceal the fact that they no longer measured up to who He created them to be. So they ran and hid from His presence.

Pre-Fall nakedness symbolized the purity and innocence of humans before God. Post-Fall nakedness symbolizes the inability of humans to make themselves presentable before Him. God did what Adam and Eve were unable to do. He covered them and made them presentable. He shed the blood of an animal—probably a lamb—and clothed them with its skin. By means of a bloody sacrifice, *He* covered their sin and shame. Do you see the symbolism here? Do you feel the surge of hope? God's merciful solution to Adam and Eve's sin, and their inadequate attempt to cover shame, was to clothe them with something infinitely more adequate. The skin of the sacrificed animal pointed to the time when God would sacrifice His Lamb—the Lord Jesus Christ—to atone for sin, alleviate shame, and clothe us in His righteousness. "And the Lord God made for Adam and for his wife garments of skins and clothed them" (Genesis 3:21).

The Lord did not pretend that nothing had happened. He did not tell Adam and Eve to strip off the silly leaves and go back to being naked. He knew that Adam and Eve could never go back to their sinless state. It was impossible for them to return to their naked and shame-free existence. In clothing them, the Lord confirmed that they needed something other than their own skin. Covering up was the appropriate response to the disgrace of sin. The shame of their fallen condition demanded a covering, not to *conceal* it, but to *confess* and *redeem* it. This is a very important point. Clothing bears witness to the fact that we have lost the glory and beauty of our original sin-free selves. It confesses that we need a covering—*His* covering—to atone for our sin and alleviate our shame. It testifies to the fact that God solved the problem of shame permanently and decisively with the blood of His own Son. It also directs our attention forward to the time when we will be "further clothed" with spotless, imperishable garments (2 Corinthians 5:3 NKJV, Revelation 3:5).

Clothing is an outward, visible symbol of an inward, spiritual reality. When you "put on Christ," He covers your shame and makes you what you should be. He offers you his garments "so that you may clothe yourself and the shame of your nakedness may not be seen" (Revelation 3:18). His covering makes us decent (Galatians 3:27). Without it, we are indecent. The physical clothing we wear is supposed to bear witness to that fact. It testifies that the Lord covers our sin and makes us presentable. That's why we need to cover our bodies in public. That's why public nakedness is inappropriate.

In private, within the covenant relationship of marriage, being naked is a very good thing! A husband and wife are presentable and shameless to each other within the context of their covenant. But when they are in public, they clothe themselves to bear witness to their covenant relationship with God. When we see Jesus face-to-face, He will transform our lowly bodies to be like His glorious one. But it's significant to note that even then, we won't go back to being naked. Immortal, imperishable clothes will replace our mortal, perishable ones (2 Corinthians 5:3, Revelation 3:5). Until that that time, we must wear clothes in public as a visible witness to our fall and redemption (Philippians 3:17). We must adequately cover up. As John Piper says:

> Our clothes are a witness both to our past and present failure and to our future glory. They testify to the chasm between what we are and what we should be. And they testify to God's merciful intention to bridge that chasm through Jesus Christ and his death for our sins.[3]

Piper also points out:

> Those who try to reverse this divine decision in search of the primal innocence of the Garden of Eden are putting the cart before the horse. Until all sin is gone from our souls and from the world, being clothed is God's will for a witness to our fall. Taking your clothes off does not put you back into pre-Fall paradise; it puts you into post-Fall shame. That's God's will. It's why modesty is a crucial post-Fall virtue.[4]

Let's relate this back to the BBC's question of "What's the Problem with Nudity?" and its conclusion that people can and ought to unlearn their naked shame. One practical implication of the divine decision to clothe the sinful human race is that public nudity is not a return to pre-Fall innocence, but a rebellion against God's remedy for sin. God ordains clothes to testify about the glory we have lost and to testify about His solution for this shame. Taking off our clothes in public or wearing revealing clothes, adds insult to injury. It is added rebellion. Doing this is like shaking my fist at God and saying, "I'm proud of my sin!" "I'm proud of my fallen condition!" "I don't need to cover up!" "I don't need You or Your clothes!" "I'm proud of my shame!"

Is this possible? Can people be proud of their shame? Can it be unlearned? Most definitely. The volunteers in the BBC study discovered that in an environment that encouraged nakedness, they could readily throw off personal inhibitions and be proud and unashamed of doing so. It comes as no surprise. The Bible informs us that sinners "glory in their shame" (Philippians 3:19). They take pride in defying God. They strip off clothing, morality, and God's directives, and unabashedly display their shame for the world to see. Instead of confessing their need for the clothing of Christ, they brashly proclaim that they feel "comfortable in their own skin." They glory in their naked shame.

The question is not whether shame can be unlearned. It can. The question is whether it *ought* to be. The passage in Philippians explains that those who glory in their shame walk as enemies of the Cross of Christ. When Jesus Christ died for us, He "despised the shame" of the cross and bore it in our stead. His death and resurrection removes our disgrace and the accompanying shame. Only when we cover ourselves with His garments can we truly be free of shame and disgrace. The appropriate response to this moral reality is not to throw off our clothing and inhibitions and thumb our noses at shame, but to be all the more careful about the way we dress.

CLOTHED WITH CHRIST

What then shall we wear? Paul tells us in Romans 13:14 to wear Christ. "*Put on the Lord Jesus Christ*, and make no provision for the flesh, to gratify its desires" (italics added). A Christian woman clothes herself with Christ. That's what she wears. That's how she covers herself. That's how she makes herself beautiful. The clothing of Christ is the most important item in her wardrobe. Her external appearance should display, and not deny or distract from, the righteous clothing of Christ that she wears. The visible should point to the invisible. The temporal should point to the eternal. The symbol should point to the reality. In the final analysis, your clothing is not meant to be about you—it's meant to display deep and profound spiritual truths about the gospel. That's why it's highly important that you wrestle with the practical question of what and what not to wear.

It's not an easy question. Pitfalls exist all around. Sin encourages us to throw off clothing and inhibition, and proudly display our nakedness. It tempts us to exalt external appearance and make clothing our god. It tempts us to deny the importance of appearance and walk around like slobs. It tempts us to become sirens. It tempts us to despise beauty and deny our femininity. It tempts us to slavishly follow contemporary fashion or haughtily spurn it by adopting the fashion of another era. It tempts us to think that clothing is overly important. It tempts us to think it is unimportant. It tempts us to be self-righteous about the way we dress and downright uncharitable toward the way other people dress. It tempts us to sin by remaining quiet and tolerating the flagrant unrighteousness of our sisters. When it comes to clothing and personal appearance, the dangers are many and varied. But Scripture gives us some clear advice on how to navigate our way through this quagmire.

To begin, the Lord wants His girls to be stunningly beautiful. But He repeatedly stresses that a woman's beauty—and her beautification—is something that primarily happens on the inside. "Do not let your adoring be external . . . but let your adorning be the hidden person of the heart" (1 Peter 3:4). The heart is where we put on Christ and the clothing of Christ. A wise woman commits more time and energy dressing herself up on the inside than on the outside. She is like the Proverbs 31 woman, who makes strength and dignity "her clothing" (31:25). The Girl-Gone-Wise *puts on* the new self (Ephesians 4:24). She *puts on* compassion, kindness, humility, meekness, patience, forbearance, forgiveness, love (Colossians 3:12–13). She *puts on* "the whole armor of God" (Ephesians 6:11). She *puts on* a gentle and quiet spirit (1 Peter 3:4). She clothes herself with these garments of Christ, "so that the shame of [her] nakedness may not be seen" (Revelation 3:18).

Spiritual adornment is the reality. Physical adornment is the symbol of that reality. The external clothing we wear is of secondary importance. But it is important nonetheless. In 1 Timothy 2:9, the Lord provides three critical guidelines that help Christian women figure out what and what not to wear. "She adorns herself with *respectable* apparel, with *modesty* and *self-control*." The three guidelines are:

1. Is it becoming or unbecoming? (*respectable*)
2. Is it decent or indecent? (*modest*)
3. Is it moderate or excessive? (*self-controlled*)

The word *adorn* (Greek: *kosmeo*) can also be translated as "to decorate" or "to beautify." It means "to put in order, arrange, make ready." Elsewhere, Jesus' parable talks about wise bridesmaids "trimming" (adorning) their lamps—ensuring that they are in good order, properly set up, and ready for the Bridegroom (Matthew 25:7). Women are to adorn their bodies in the same way. The three guidelines help us ensure that our looks are in good order, properly arranged, and ready to display Christ.

WHAT AND WHAT NOT TO WEAR

It appears that some of the wealthy women in the church in Ephesus were adorning themselves inappropriately—and very likely, quite provocatively. The way they dressed presented a problem. Their clothing was opulent, their jewelry was excessive, and their hairstyles were extravagant. Braided hair was considered a work of art and was very popular among Greek and Roman women. They intertwined elaborate braids with chains of gold or strings of pearls, and piled them high above their heads. Their big hair, low-cut togas, and mounds of tinkling gold bracelets were likely distracting fellow worshipers and setting apart the haves from the have-nots. They were dressing "as a prostitute," to attract attention. The worshipers sitting behind them may have felt the same as I did sitting behind those six young women at the hockey game.

In his letter to Timothy, Paul encouraged these primped women to evaluate their wardrobe in light of the overall purpose of clothing. He counseled them to dress in a way that was in keeping with their Christian character and to concentrate on what was most important. While their inner heart attitude was Paul's primary concern, he did cite three Greek adjectives that would help them govern their choice of clothing: *kosmio*, *aidous*, and *sophrosunes*. The English Standard Version of the Bible translates these qualifiers as "respectable," "modest," and "self-controlled." Other translations use a variety of other words to translate the Greek. These three terms are related; their meanings are very rich and overlap in some ways. They give us some valuable insight about what and what not to wear.

Is It Becoming or Unbecoming?

Kosmio is the descriptive form of the Greek noun *kosmos* (to put in order, trim, adorn or decorate), which is related to our English word *cosmos*—the universe. The Greeks regarded the universe to be an ordered, integrated, harmonious whole. *Kosmos* is the opposite of *chaos*. So when Paul told the women that their adornment should be *kosmio*, he meant that like the universe, all the parts should be aptly and harmoniously arranged with the other parts. It should be "becoming"—that is, appropriate or fitting for someone and/or something. Given the context, I believe Paul was implying that our adornment ought to be *becoming* on a number of different levels.

First, and foremost, your clothing ought to be becoming, congruous with, fitting to, and consistent with your character as a child of God. It needs to "match" the clothing of Christ. But it also ought to be becoming to your body type, becoming to your femininity, becoming to your husband, becoming to the other clothes you are wearing, and becoming to the occasion and place you intend to wear it. There's a tremendous amount of guidance in that small word, *becoming*. There's a "cosmic" amount, because it challenges you to evaluate your clothes, shoes, purses, makeup, and hair from multiple angles, as part of the harmonious, integrated whole of your life—to line up the seen with the unseen and the temporal with the eternal. It challenges you to bring a cosmic perspective to bear on your everyday decisions.

I like the word Paul chose. It has enormous implications. *Kosmio* means that a Christian woman's "look" ought to be consistently put together, inside and out. This challenges those who put an undue emphasis on external appearance as well as those who neglect their personal appearance. It's a corrective to women who dress extravagantly like the ones in Ephesus. It's a corrective to those who dress seductively like hookers. But it's also a corrective to those who think that "holy" means frumpy, ugly, unfeminine, and out of style. *Becoming* indicates that running around in baggy jeans and T-shirts all the time is just as inappropriate as being obsessed with stylish clothing. It means that a woman's appearance ought to be put together nicely. It ought to be pleasant and attractive—on the inside and on the outside.

Say that you're trying to decide whether to buy a certain skirt. You try it on, look in the mirror, and ask yourself, "Is this becoming?" Most women will ask and answer that question on the superficial level of "Do I like it and does it fit?" But Paul appears to be challenging women to take the question a lot further. He wants you to consider:

• Does it fit with who I am as a child of God?
• Does it fit with Christlikeness?
• Does it fit and flatter my body?
• Does it fit and flatter my femininity?
• Does it fit my age and stage of life?
• Does it fit my wardrobe?
• Does it fit my budget?
• Does it fit my needs?
• Does it fit the occasion?
• Does it fit the place I intend to wear it?

You get the picture. It all needs to fit. All of it. If the skirt is "becoming" in all of these areas, then you might purchase it. If it's unbecoming, then you shouldn't.

Is It Decent or Indecent?

The second word, *aidous*, is based on the Greek term for shame and disgrace. The word is a blend of modesty and humility. *Modesty* is how it's most often translated. When I think about a word picture that personifies this concept, I think of approaching God with eyes that are downcast. It's timid respect in the presence of a superior, penitent respect toward one who has been wronged, or the diffidence of a beggar in the presence of one from whom he seeks help. It involves a sense of deficiency, inferiority, or unworthiness. It suggests shame, but also a corresponding sense of reverence and honor toward rightful authority. It's the opposite of insolence, imprudence, disrespect, or audacity. Downcast eyes are the opposite of defiant eyes.

So what does it mean to dress with your eyes downcast? Does it mean that you are self-conscious? No. It means that your clothing tells the truth about the gospel. Your clothing shows the world that Jesus covers your shame and makes you decent. Your clothes cover your nakedness as the clothing of Christ covers your sin.

Dressing "with eyes downcast" means that you are not defiant toward God. You choose clothes that are decent in His eyes . . . not clothes that are provocative, seductive, and that honor nakedness. When you dress decently, you recognize that God ordained clothes to cover, and not draw attention to, your naked skin. You cover up out of respect for Him, the gospel, your Christian brothers—and out of respect for who He made you to be. Decency means you agree with the Lord about the true purpose of clothing and set aside your self-interest to dress in a way that exalts Christ.

So in that dressing room, trying on that skirt, you need to sit, bend, and stretch in front of that mirror, and ask yourself, "Is this skirt decent? Does it do what it should do? Does it properly cover me up? Does it showcase my underlying nakedness—or exalt the gospel of Christ?"

Is It Moderate or Excessive?

The final thing you need to ask yourself about the skirt is whether it is moderate or excessive. Paul uses the Greek word *sophrosunes*. It means "of a sound mind, sane, in one's senses; curbing one's desires and impulses, self-controlled, temperate." The word indicates that our adornment should be reasonable and not crazy. We ought to rein in our impulses and avoid crazy extremes in fashion, hairstyles, and makeup. We also ought to avoid spending crazy amounts of money or stuffing our closets full of crazy quantities of clothing. We ought to govern our wardrobe choices with a sense of moderation, simplicity, and self-control. If the skirt is crazy extreme, crazy expensive, or if it's crazy for you to be buying another one, then you ought to pass it up. Christian women don't get extreme, outrageous, or exorbitant, like *Sex and the City*'s Carrie and her Manolo Blahniks.

Understanding the purpose of clothing and asking yourself the three questions, "Is it becoming?" "Is it decent?" and "Is it moderate?" will help you figure out how to dress. And don't forget to include your "Helper" in the process. The Holy Spirit is an invaluable source of assistance when it comes to figuring out whether or not your appearance glorifies God. He cares about your clothes. He has a big stake in making sure you adorn your body the right way. "Do you not know that your body is a temple of the Holy Spirit within you, whom you have from God? You are not your own, for you were bought with a price. So glorify God in your body" (1 Corinthians 6:19–20). If your heart is right, and you seek the Holy Spirit's guidance, He will be your personal wardrobe consultant and teach you what and what not to wear.

A Girl-Gone-Wise presents herself in a different manner than a Girl-Gone-Wild. Her appearance doesn't scream, "Look at me!" The way she styles her hair and does her makeup enhances her looks, but doesn't clamor for attention. Her clothing doesn't invite onlookers to see or imagine her nakedness. She adorns herself in a dignified, God-exalting way. Her appearance is pleasant and attractive. Proverbs 31 points out that the wise woman is "clothed in scarlet," that "her clothing is fine linen and purple," and that "strength and dignity are her clothing." The implication is that everything she wears—both inside and out—is beautiful. She doesn't dress *as a prostitute*, but in the way that is "proper for women who profess godliness" (1 Timothy 2:10).

Point of Contrast #8

BODY LANGUAGE
Her Nonverbal Behavior

Girl-Gone-Wild: **Suggestive**	Girl-Gone-Wise: **Demure**
She captures him with her eyelashes. (Proverbs 6:25) ". . . graceful and of deadly charms." (Nahum 3:4)	She does not resort to deceitful charm. (Proverbs 31:30)

S he had the *look*. You know the one I'm talking about. It wasn't her sparkly halter dress, her snappy sandals, her perfectly-sprayed-on tan, her incredibly white teeth, her false eyelashes, or her big hair. It was *the* look. The provocative, over-the-shoulder, chin-tipped, sultry-eyed, flirty, tantalizing one. Her mom was instructing her how to pose seductively, walk with a hand perched on her writhing hips, and act all sexy and playful for the judges.

My daughter-in-law and I gaped in disbelief. The girl was only five years old! But what really fascinated me was what happened next. My husband walked into the room. He came in humming a tune, carrying a massive mug of soda and a plate piled high with munchies in anticipation of the family movie we were about to watch. When his eye caught the image of the young beauty pageant contestant on TV, he stopped dead in his tracks. A look of fury I have rarely seen darkened his eyes. With teeth clenched, he grimly ordered us, "Turn that garbage off! How *dare* they do that to that little girl?!!"

As women, Jacqueline and I were morbidly amused and critical of the mom teaching her five-year-old daughter the body language that a girl does not normally learn until she is much older. But Brent, as a man, processed the body language of this little girl in an entirely different manner. Her nonverbal communication told him and every other watching male, "Come get me! I'm available." That's why he was overcome with righteous indignation and holy anger. The thought that anyone would teach a five-year-old girl to send such a message was absolutely reprehensible to him. His outrage and protective fatherly instinct was so strong that I'm sure he would have dropped the snacks and crashed his way through the TV screen and onto that stage if he could have, to halt the pageant and administer a severe tongue-lashing to all the adults in the theater.

The look. The tilt of the head. The flip of the hair. The sway of the hips. The deliberate caress of a curve. The cross of the legs. The leisurely forward lean. The titillating exposure of skin. The brush of the bottom lip. The catlike stretch. The lingering touch . . . By the time a woman reaches adulthood she has learned how to move and position her body in a provocative way. If she chooses, she can hit the "sexual charm" button and turn it on. When activated, her body sends out alluring nonverbal messages to entice her chosen prey. Women, you *know* what I'm talking about! I don't think men have any idea how calculating women are when they employ this strategy. As Jacqueline said, "Not every woman chooses to use that artillery. But we all have it, and we all know how to use it. We can turn it off, or we can turn it on."

A discussion about a woman's appearance isn't complete without a discussion of her body language. The Girl-Gone-Wild uses suggestive body language to attract the attention of men. Her counterpart, the Girl-Gone-Wise, is demure. She does not resort to deceptive charm.

CHARMED!

She's an assertive, self-assured woman, and she has perfected the subtle art of attracting men. She knows how to flirt with her eyes, seductively tilt her head, and position her body in a provocative way. She's a classy dresser who chooses her wardrobe carefully—curve-hugging clothes that reveal just the right amount of skin. Tempting, but not distasteful. High heels are a must. Especially with those tight designer jeans.

Her closet needs constant replenishment. Clothes, jackets, shoes, jewelry, accessories, handbags. And she doesn't neglect her beauty regime. Makeup, manicured nails, styled and highlighted hair, tanned skin, whitened teeth . . . creams, lotions, perfumes. Magazines keep her up to date with the latest advice on interacting with men. She's become an expert at provocative body language, playful banter, and innuendo. She goes to church and Bible study, but her commitment to God is superficial. Her deepest desire is to be sexy, powerful, and alluring.

Who is this woman? You might be surprised to learn that the description (with a few minor fashion updates) comes from the pages of Isaiah. And it may surprise you even more to learn that her behavior was so reprehensible to God that He punished her and her like-minded girlfriends.

> The Lord said: Because the daughters of Zion are haughty and walk with outstretched necks, glancing wantonly with their eyes, mincing along as they go, tinkling with their feet, therefore the Lord will strike with a scab the heads of the daughters of Zion, and the Lord will lay bare their secret parts.
>
> In that day the Lord will take away the finery of the anklets, the head-bands, and the crescents; the pendants, the bracelets, and the scarves; the headdresses, the armlets, the sashes, the perfume boxes, and the amulets; the signet rings and nose rings; the festal robes, the mantles, the cloaks, and the handbags; the mirrors, the linen garments, the turbans, and the veils. Instead of perfume there will be rottenness; and instead of a belt, a rope; and instead of well-set hair, baldness; and instead of a rich robe, a skirt of sackcloth; and branding instead of beauty . . . empty, she shall sit on the ground. (Isaiah 3:16–26)

The women in Isaiah's time were guilty of using their finery to charm men. Years later, another prophet, Nahum, noted that a Wild Thing is full of "deadly charms" (Nahum 3:4). In Assyrian and Babylonian culture, charms were magic formulas that women chanted or recited to get a certain desired result. They believed that love-charms, spells, and incantations to the goddess of love were very effective at helping them bewitch the man of their dreams. Often they wore an ornament—a gem, a stone, a bead, a plaque or an emblem—on a bracelet or chain to symbolize the charm. Sometimes the ornament or stone had an incantation inscribed directly on it. A woman could wear any number of charms. Charm jewelry was very popular and fashionable throughout the ancient Near East.

To charm a man is to affect him by magic or as if by magic. Spells, potions, and incantations are not necessarily involved. A charm is *any* method of enchanting and compelling him. It's obvious that the women in Jerusalem wore charm jewelry such as crescents, pendants, and amulets. But that wasn't the only way they tried to charm men. The passage indicates that these women also tried to charm them with their flashy clothing. They were shopaholics. Isaiah's extensive list indicates that they had stuffed their closets full of shoes, handbags, clothes, and jewelry. These women were also obsessed with primping—meticulously styled hair, perfume, and cosmetic boxes are a few clues. They also attempted to charm men in the way they carried themselves—with their body language. The passage provides details about how they walked. This indicates that they had perfected the feminine art of the *look*. They swayed their hips. They strategically moved and positioned their bodies. They allured and enticed men like charmers hypnotizing snakes.

The women in Jerusalem may have impressed the guys, but they certainly didn't impress the Lord. He was dismayed that they had neglected the most important aspect of womanhood—the beauty of a holy heart—and had attempted to seduce men with their deceptive charm. God called them to task, but His daughters didn't repent. So as predicted, He punished them by having the Assyrians and Babylonians invade and decimate Jerusalem. The women lost everything. "Empty, they sat on the ground."

It's evident that God wouldn't like His daughters wearing any type of jewelry that was thought to contain magical power or influence. But the jewelry wasn't the only charm the Lord viewed in a negative light. Something about the way the women in Jerusalem dressed and primped bothered Him. Based on what we learned in the last chapter, it was undoubtedly that their adornment was unbecoming, indecent, and excessive. However, the charm that topped His list, the one He mentioned first, was their body language—their outstretched necks, wanton looks, wiggling hips, and mincing feet. The Lord was highly offended by the provocative way these women moved their bodies and directed their eyes.

NOT A HINT

What was God's issue? Is it wrong for a woman to be attractive and beautiful to look at? Is He saying that a woman shouldn't be charming? What's the problem with flirting and showing off your womanly wares?

The Bible makes a clear distinction between women who are truly "charming" and those who deceptively try to charm. Women who are charming are gracious, full of favor and elegance. Their selfless goodness makes them attractive from the inside out. Women who seductively try to charm have an underlying selfish agenda. Their intentions are impure. That's why Proverbs 31:30 says, "Charm is deceitful." There's a huge difference between a Girl-Gone-Wise who looks and smiles at a guy to show that she likes him, and a Girl-Gone-Wild who looks and smiles at a guy to try to attract him.

A Wild Thing turns on her seductive charm in order to get a man to be turned on to her. The Sage Father warns his son about a woman like this: "Do not desire her beauty in your heart, and do not let her capture you with her eyelashes" (Proverbs 6:25). The father didn't want his son to be enticed by flirtatious, coy glances. He wanted him to be aware of the danger of women who used body language to seduce men. One ancient commentator suggested that the word translated *eyelashes* could also be "the nets of the eyes." A Girl-Gone-Wild uses her eyelashes to "capture" men as in a net.

You might defend your flirtatious behavior by claiming that you don't intend to seduce a man to have sex—you're just playing and are not really serious. But suggestive body language implies or hints at something improper. The Bible's perspective on the sin of seduction includes more than just the type of seduction that leads to illicit sex. Seduction is *any* behavior that purposefully leads another person in the wrong direction. It's *any* behavior that falsely hints that evil is desirable or exciting. It's *any* behavior that entices someone to think about something improper. Even if she's just playing, the woman who turns on her sexual charm clearly *wants* men to think that sex with her is an alluring idea. That's seduction. And that's sin.

The other day, I heard a female talent-show judge compliment a contestant on how enchanting her "naughtiness" was. As if just a little bit of naughtiness is cute and doesn't matter. Naughtiness might not be an offense on your radar, but it's a crime on God's. A woman who gives any man (other than her husband) a "come-and-get-me" look is in effect telling a lie. She is thumbing her nose at God by hinting that illicit sex is desirable and exciting. She is sinning by willfully enticing a man's thoughts away from the path of virtue. Body language that implies or hints at a wrongful sexual act is just as heinous to God as performing that sexual act. Jesus told men that looking at a woman lustfully was just as sinful as having sex with her. So I'm sure He would tell you that giving the look to the stranger across the room is just as sinful as jumping into bed with him.

Seductive body language may have been one of the sins Paul had in mind when he told the believers in Ephesus, "But among you there must not be even a hint of sexual immorality, or of any kind of impurity . . . because these are improper for God's holy people" (Ephesians 5:3 NIV). This certainly deflates the theory that a wee bit of naughty is OK. According to Paul, not even a hint of sexual immorality or impurity is appropriate among believers. *Not even a hint!* That means that even the tiniest allusion, suggestion, or whiff of sexual "naughtiness" is *not* OK. It means the "I'm just teasing" excuse is not acceptable. "Teasing" doesn't negate the fact that this type of behavior is sin.

Nowadays, Christian teachers routinely address the problem of sexual sin in regards to men looking at porn and lusting after women, but they rarely address the problem of women inviting men to lust. Let me say this loud and clear to all you women: Suggestive dress and suggestive body language is sin. There's no getting around it. The woman who sends the invitation to look is just as guilty as the man who accepts it.

WANT-ON EYES

The Bible describes "the look" as wanton. (Not to be confused with the small round dumpling floating in your Chinese soup. Not *wonton—wanton*.) Just divide the word into syllables and you'll get the gist of the meaning. Want-on is someone whose attitude is, "I want (to get it) on." A woman who is wanton will come on to men. Wanton is lacking appropriate restraint or inhibition, especially in sexual thought and behavior.

The corresponding New Testament sin is *sensuality* (lasciviousness; Greek: *aselgeia*). The sin of sensuality appears in numerous lists of vices. The following verses demonstrate that sensuality is an evil from which all believers ought to flee:

"Now the works of the flesh are evident: sexual immorality, impurity, sensuality . . ." (Galatians 5:19)

"Let us walk properly . . . not in orgies and drunkenness, not in sexual immorality and sensuality." (Romans 13:13)

"Evil thoughts, sexual immorality, theft, murder, adultery, coveting, wickedness, deceit, sensuality, envy, slander, pride, foolishness. All these evil things come from within." (Mark 7:21–23)

"For the time that is past suffices for doing what the Gentiles want to do, living in sensuality, passions, drunkenness, orgies, drinking parties, and lawless idolatry." (1 Peter 4:3)

"Many . . . have not repented of the impurity, sexual immorality, and sensuality that they have practiced." (2 Corinthians 12:21)

If you take the Bible seriously, you have to admit that sensuality is a sin. Sensuality can be (a) characterized by lust, (b) expressing lewdness or lust, and (c) tending to excite lust. Provocative body language falls into one or more of these three categories. If you typically act like a vamp, then your body language is characterized by lust. If you come on to a man because you yearn for him, then your body language is expressing lewdness or lust. If you intentionally broadcast provocative sexual signals, then you are tending to excite lust. Whenever you hint or playfully suggest that you want to get it on with anyone other than the man you are married to, you are probably guilty of the sin of sensuality.

The definition of sensuality provides three essential questions you can ask yourself about your body language:

1. Is my body language characterized by lust?
2. Does my body language express lewdness or lust?
3. Am I intentionally inciting lust with my eyes or the way I move my body?

A Girl-Gone-Wise does not engage in inappropriate, sexually charged nonverbal communication. Her body language is demure. That means that she keeps her body language in check: modest, reserved, and free of impure sexual undertones. She takes God's disdain for sensuality seriously. She doesn't shrug off the Bible's warnings as outdated and prudish. The Wise Woman refuses to resort to any behavior that might lead her brother in the wrong direction. She does not hint, by way of innuendo, that evil is desirable. She is very, very careful to avoid any look or behavior that sends this ungodly message.

DANCING TO THE BEAT OF A DIFFERENT DRUM

Several years ago, my son and I were in a mall and walked past a seductively dressed young woman. I noticed that she gave him "the look" as she brushed by. So I asked him, "What do you think when a woman dressed like that comes on to you?" (My poor sons—I ask them such piercing questions.)

He thought for a long moment and then replied, "Well . . . I would have to say that it excites the male in me, but it doesn't attract the man in me."

Read that again. It's a pretty profound answer for a seventeen-year-old. And one that women of all ages should sit up and take note of. It's not very difficult to use sexual charm to pique the sexual interest of a male. But provocative dress and body language won't attract the heart of a godly man. Your provocative body language might get you some attention, but it won't get you the kind of love relationship you yearn for. And even more serious than that, it will interfere in your relationship with the Lord.

Body language is part of any romantic "dance" between a couple. The glances, the smiles, and the playful interaction are important elements that signal interest and move the relationship along. Nonverbal communication is an important part of all face-to-face interaction. Some psychologists say that it conveys 55 percent of the overall message. The point of paying attention to our body language is not to get rid of body language, but to make sure that our nonverbal communication is holy.

I hope you'll take an honest look at what your body language says and whether you are guilty of the sin of sensuality. If you are unmarried, I challenge you to stop reverting to deceptive charm in an attempt to attract men. In the way you dress and act, do not hint at any kind of sexual impurity. Do not resort to seductive flirtation. If you are married, I challenge you too, to stop using seductive flirtations to attract attention from men. I also challenge you to *increase* your sexually inviting body language toward your husband. The Lord gave you the capacity for that "come get me" look for a reason. Your body language toward your husband *ought* to be alluring and sexually playful.

Today, females learn to be sexually flirtatious at a very young age. This chapter about body language is radical stuff. It's extremely countercultural. It flies in the face of how popular media has taught this generation of women to interact with men. Truth may be grating, but only because it cuts away at the restrictive entrapping of sin. The disciples were once aghast with a standard that Christ presented as the ideal. Initially, it seemed far too radical and unattainable to accept (Matthew 19:6–12; Mark 10:9–12). You may feel the same way about some of the ideas in this book. I challenge you to think about them nonetheless. Wrestle with them. Study the Scriptures to see if what I am saying is true.

By now, you're getting the idea that Scripture's portrait of a Girl-Gone-Wise is radically different than culture's norm. As my one son exclaimed after encountering a truly godly young woman, "All those other girls are cut out of the same cloth. She's different. Everything about a woman who loves God is different." He meant it in an admiring way. The Girl-Gone-Wise is exceedingly attractive. Her attractiveness relies on the imperishable beauty of her inner self and not on seductive charm. She knows that "charm is deceitful, and beauty is vain, but a woman who fears the Lord is to be praised" (Proverbs 31:30).

Point of Contrast #9

ROLES
Her Pattern of Interaction

Girl-Gone-Wild: **Inclined to Dominate**	Girl-Gone-Wise: **Inclined to Follow**
"She seizes him. . . . He follows her." (Proverbs 7:13, 22)	Like Sarah, she submits to her husband, and to God's beautiful design. (I Peter 3:4–6)

The phone was ringing. Katy was calling for the eighth time that evening. She had called five times the evening before and nine times the evening before that. I knew what this seventh grader wanted . . . to speak to my youngest son, Jonathan. Instead of beckoning him to the phone, I normally took a message, so he could call her back at his leisure. My standard reply to her inquiry if she could speak to him was, "I'll give him the message and have him call you back."

Which he did. When it suited him. But that wasn't good enough for Katy. She was getting irritated that I was interfering with her desire to cajole my son into jumping through her hoops. Jonathan wasn't at home that particular evening, so I told her, "I'm sorry, he's not available."

Katy sarcastically snapped back, "Well . . . when *will* he be *'available'?"*

That was it. Enough. Enough Katy. I wouldn't tolerate disrespect from a cheeky twelve-year-old. So I called the phone company and blocked her number. And my husband and I challenged Jonathan to step up and refuse her advances.

The incident happened just before the era of students routinely using cell phones. I remember thinking about how aggressive young girls had become. It used to be that the girls waited for the guys to call them. A female phoning a male was very forward and inappropriate. Social etiquette stipulated that the male was the pursuer. But the feminist movement changed all that. Women became the pursuers. More recently, my sons have dealt with girls who text them every two minutes every waking hour of every day (and several times during the night), girls who ask them out, girls who stalk them on Facebook, and girls they have to block because "the woman won't take 'no' for an answer." (And these were "Christian" girls!) Females have morphed into hawkish predators. For a mom trying to raise godly sons, it's scary out there!

The rules have changed. Social convention now stipulates that women can and ought to be initiators in male-female relationships. They can take the lead. This may sound good in theory, but it doesn't work very well in practice. I constantly see the carnage resulting from this approach. I think of Heidi, a Christian woman who bought into the "roles don't matter" paradigm. She saw a guy she liked. She asked him out. She insisted on paying for half their dates. She called him. She kissed him. She brought up the subject of marriage. She negotiated the terms. She insisted on a hyphenated name. She made him give up his job and move because of hers. She made more money, so she made him stay home with the kids. OK. Now fast-forward ten years into their relationship: Heidi hates her husband. Her complaint? He's unmotivated. A deadweight. She has to beg him to do anything. He doesn't initiate. He's wimpy, whiny, and disgusting. She's the only one contributing. And she's exhausted.

Wait a minute, Heidi. Let me get this straight: You asked him out. You pursued him. You took the lead. You dominated the relationship.

Like putty in your hand, you molded him into what you wanted him to be . . . and now you hate him for it? What's more, you expect him to go against years of emasculation and suddenly become a man? Why should he? You're the "man" in your house—or at least you pretended that you could be.

Details differ, but I can't tell you how many "Heidis" have ended up crying on my shoulder, dismayed that their husbands are wimps and not men—that they are passive and won't lead. Inevitably, it only takes a few pointed questions to discover why. It's usually because, right from the start, the woman "wore the pants." That was the pattern of their relationship. She was the pursuer. He was the pursued. It doesn't take a rocket scientist—or a social scientist—to figure out that once established, this relationship pattern is difficult to change.

A major notion of this generation is that gender roles are insignificant and irrelevant. It doesn't matter who pursues. It doesn't matter who wears the pants. In fact, it's good if women take the wheel. Men have had their turn, and for far too long! While it has made for an interesting—though tragic—social experiment, this theory neglects to take the created design of male and female into consideration. It assumes that we get to decide for ourselves what manhood, womanhood, and male-female relationships are all about. However, according to Scripture, we don't. Our text in Proverbs reveals that a Girl-Gone-Wild "seizes" a man and compels him to "follow her." A Girl-Gone-Wise knows that this pattern goes against God's created design.

BACK TO THE DRAWING BOARD

Let's go back to the drawing board—not to take pen in hand and try to redraw the image of womanhood, like the generation of the sixties did, but to take a look at the model God drew. Genesis lays out His blueprint. The first chapter gives a zoomed-out view of the big picture. It displays the profound dignity of the human race and shows how the creation of humanity fits into the overall story of creation. It reveals that men and women are more like God than anything else in the universe, and that they share this status equally. Genesis 2 zooms in to capture the spectacular details. It reveals that God created each sex to be unique. Each has a distinct significance and function. Each perfectly complements the other.

The truth that God wanted to display through male and female was of paramount importance. So it stands to reason that He was highly intentional when He created them. Every action was significant. That's why Genesis 2 is so careful to provide a detailed, frame-by-frame rendering of the creation of mankind. God could have made men and women at the exact same time and in the exact same way. But the fact is, He didn't. The blueprint displays twelve markers that show how male and female roles are complementary, but not identical. Let's have a look and see, starting with what makes the male uniquely male.

UNIQUELY MALE

The Male Was Firstborn

> "Then the Lord God formed the man of dust from the ground and breathed into his nostrils the breath of life, and the man became a living creature." (Genesis 2:7)

The first thing to note about the creation of the sexes is that God created the male first. You might think that this fact is trivial or inconsequential, but the Bible teaches otherwise. The firstborn son held a unique role and position in the Hebrew family. He ranked highest after his father and carried the weight of the father's authority. He was responsible for the oversight and well-being of the family. He also served as the representative of all the other family members. This wasn't just a cultural quirk that the Hebrew people dreamed up. God gave them these directions. Their family structure followed the pattern He gave.

We can tell that the position of firstborn son was important to God, because He called Israel His firstborn son (Exodus 4:22). Adam was God's firstborn human being, but Israel was the first nation He adopted as His own. When Pharaoh stubbornly refused to release the Israelites from bondage, the Lord sent the angel of death to kill all the firstborn sons of all the families in Egypt. Those oldest brothers were the family representatives. As such, they were destined to die to pay for Egypt's sin. But the Lord graciously made a provision to save them. If they smeared lambs' blood on the doorposts of their houses, the firstborn sons wouldn't die. The lambs bore the punishment in their stead. The

Hebrew people followed God's direction and sacrificed lambs. Their firstborn sons were saved. The Egyptians didn't. Their firstborn sons died.

After this momentous event, God instructed the parents of every Hebrew family to redeem all their offspring by sacrificing a lamb at the birth of their oldest son (Exodus 11:4–7; 13:11–15). The oldest brother represented all his brothers and sisters. His redemption signified the redemption of them all. Conversely, his disgrace signified the disgrace of all.

God made Adam first. He was the firstborn—the head of the human race. He carried the weight of responsibility for the oversight and well-being of the human family. So when the human race fell, God held Adam responsible, even though Eve sinned first. The New Testament bluntly states, "In Adam all die" (1 Corinthians 15:22). The Lord held Eve personally responsible for her sin. But He held Adam responsible for smearing the entire human race with his.

Are you beginning to see the significance of Adam's position? The Old Testament sketches the outline, but the New Testament colors it in. The position of firstborn is all about Jesus Christ, the firstborn—the only begotten Son of God. He is firstborn among many brothers, firstborn of all creation, firstborn from the dead (Romans 8:29; Colossians 1:15, 18; Hebrews 1:5–6). His divine authority is greater and higher than every human authority, and the model on which all human authority rests. Jesus Christ is "the Last Adam" (1 Corinthians 15:45). He was the lamb that died to take the place of the first Adam and the human family he heads. "For as in Adam all die, so also in Christ shall all be made alive" (1 Corinthians 15:22).

So what does all this have to do with male and female roles, and young Katy aggressively stalking my son? It has a great deal to do with them. The New Testament says that Adam's position has ongoing implications for male leadership in male-female relationships. The responsibility that God put on the shoulders of Adam extends—in one way or another—to the shoulders of all other males. Paul tells Timothy that the reason males bear responsibility for spiritual leadership in God's family is that "Adam was formed first" (1 Timothy 2:13). He also teaches that every man bears responsibility for the oversight of his own individual family unit (Ephesians 5). What's more, this charge appears to extend to a general responsibility of all men to take the initiative and look out for the welfare of the women around them. Exercising godly initiative and oversight is a big part of what manhood is all about.

That leaves us with one of three possibilities concerning the fact that God created the male first. Take your pick:

a. God was crazy—His decision was arbitrary. It meant nothing. The position of firstborn means nothing.

b. Paul was crazy—he hated women. He egotistically tried to seize power for men. He was wrong to draw any significance from the fact that God created Adam first. He was wrong to suggest that Adam's position had ongoing implications for manhood and womanhood.

c. People who reject the idea of God giving men a unique responsibility to take initiative are crazy—they presumptuously think they know more about manhood and womanhood than God or His apostle Paul.

God made the male first. That *doesn't* mean he made the male better. But it *does* mean that He created him to bear a unique responsibility that differs from the female. (I suppose there's a fourth option you could add to the list—"Mary is crazy, and this book is crazy." Please don't pitch it across the room quite yet—there are eleven markers to come . . .)

The Male Was Put in the Garden

"The Lord God took the man and put him in the garden . . ." (Genesis 2:15)

The second observation we can make about Genesis 2 is that God took the man and "put" him in the garden. God created the male out in the wild, from the dust of the open desert. Then He led His firstborn male away from his place of creation and put him in a garden, in Eden. Why is this significant? Because later in the chapter we see that when a man gets married, he leaves the place where he was created in order to initiate a new family unit ("A man shall leave his father and his mother and hold fast to his wife," Genesis 2:24). It is as though God "puts him" in a new position of responsibility. What's more, the image seems to foreshadow Christ forsaking the home of His Father in heaven in order to pursue His bride, the church.

God put the male in the garden in Eden. The Hebrew word for "garden" indicates an enclosure, a plot of ground protected by a wall or hedge. It's an area with specified boundaries. The garden was a specified place in the land of Eden. It wasn't the entire land of Eden. It was more like a designated homestead within that land. Eden means "pleasure" or "delight." The Lord took the male to the land of delight and set him up in his own place, to be the head of a new family unit. But before the Father presented him with a wife, He took some time to teach him the specific roles and responsibilities of a man.

The Male Was Commissioned to Work

> "The Lord God took the man and put him in the garden of Eden to work it . . ." (Genesis 2:15)

The word translated as *work* (Hebrew: *abad*) is the common word for tilling soil or for other labor (Isaiah 19:9). It contains the idea of serving someone other than oneself (Genesis 29:15). What's more, it frequently describes the duties of the priests in worship (Exodus 3:12). The man's life in the garden was not to be one of idleness. God's plan, from the very start, was that the man worked to provide for his family's needs. He was supposed to work to provide for them— physically as well as spiritually. God created men to be the providers. That doesn't mean that women don't contribute. But it does indicate that the primary responsibility for provision for the family rests on the man's shoulders.

The Male Was Commissioned to Protect

> ". . . and keep it." (Genesis 2:15)

God also wanted the man to "keep" the garden. The Hebrew word for *keep* translates as a verb meaning "to be in charge of." It means to guard, to protect and look after, to provide oversight. It involves attending to and protecting the people (Genesis 4:9; 28:15) and property (Genesis 30:31) under one's charge. It also extends beyond the physical to include a spiritual component of protection (Numbers 3:7–8). The Lord created men to be physically stronger than women are. Men are the protectors, more suited for a fight. The physical protection mirrors the spiritual protection that God wants men to provide for their families. Again, this doesn't exclude women from contributing. It simply indicates that if a robber crawls in through the window, the man is the primary protector. He's the first one to jump up and take the bullet.

The Male Received Spiritual Instruction

"And the Lord God commanded the man, saying, 'You may surely eat of every tree of the garden, but of the tree of the knowledge of good and evil you shall not eat, for in the day that you eat of it you shall surely die.'" (Genesis 2:16–17)

Before the woman arrived on the scene, God explained the rules of the garden to the man. It was up to him to pass on this spiritual instruction to his wife. That's not to say that the man interacted with God on her behalf. No. She had a personal relationship with the Lord. But it does indicate that as leader of his newly minted household, the man had a special responsibility to learn and understand the ways of the Lord. This was so that he could fulfill his commission to provide spiritual oversight and protection.

The Male Learned to Exercise Authority

"Now out of the ground the Lord God had formed every beast of the field and every bird of the heavens and brought them to the man to see what he would call them. And whatever the man called every living creature, that was its name. The man gave names to all livestock and to the birds of the heavens and to every beast of the field." (Genesis 2:19–20)

I smile when I think of what it must have looked like when the Lord brought the animals to the man to name. It seems to me that besides serving the purpose of making the man yearn for a suitable mate, this was a type of training exercise. To name something is to exercise authority over it (Genesis 5:2; Daniel 1:7). The Lord wanted the male to learn how to exercise authority in a godly manner. His firstborn had a unique responsibility to govern. And the Lord wanted him to govern well. That's why the Lord closely supervised and mentored him through the naming process. The Lord wanted the male to learn to exercise his delegated authority with gentleness, kindness, wisdom, and much care.

The first chapter of Genesis indicates that "dominion over the earth" extends to women as well as men. God gave *both* dominion. So God's excluding the female from the process of naming the animals doesn't indicate that she lacks God's authority to govern. But it does indicate that the Lord does not view her authority to govern as interchangeable with the authority of His firstborn male. A man's authority is unique to what it means to be a man. A woman's authority is unique to what it means to be a woman.

The man was firstborn, but had no kin. He was head of a new household, but his were the only feet that trod within the walls. God commissioned him to work, but there was no one for whom to provide. He knew his mission was to guard and protect, but there was no one to look after. He had thought of new ideas, but had no one to discuss them with. He was bursting at the seams with the desire to love and serve, but as the day wore on and he named animal after animal, it became painfully obvious that no creature had anywhere near the capacity to receive what he so deeply wanted to give.

The Lord knew it. He could read it on Adam's face. It was the only thing in creation that was not good. But for the time being it was necessary. It was part of the man's training. Part of his preparation. The Lord wanted him to catch a glimpse of the full import of God's final and most magnificent work. He wanted the man to feel the longing intensely—to love and want a soul mate with such passion that he was willing to pay the ultimate price to win his bride. God knew that He had to wound His firstborn to create woman. It would draw blood. Having a bride would cost the man dearly. When the man named the last animal and turned back to his Maker, the Lord knew it was time. Time to make "her"—the one who would captivate the man's heart as completely as the vision of the Lord's coming heavenly bride had captivated His.

"Sleep." The man sank down as if dead, on the soft carpet of moss. The Lord extended His hand and pierced the side of his firstborn to extract a bloody mass of bone and flesh. I wonder if a lump formed in His throat as He saw the future toward which the image pointed. I wonder if His hand trembled as He began to shape and form. I wonder what thoughts flew through His mind as He carefully sculpted each soft curve. This final masterpiece tipped the scales and set it all in motion. When He was finished, He stepped back to look. He glanced past the flesh He had just formed to peer into eternity future at *her* and softly sighed. It was good. Yes! It was *very* good!

UNIQUELY FEMALE

God created woman from the side of man, so she's made of the same stuff—equal to man. But He didn't create her at the same time, place, or from dust, so she's also different. Male and female are equal and different. God made them to complement each other. We've already looked at six markers of complementarity that can be observed in the creation of the male. Six more markers appear in the creation of the female.

The Female Was Created from the Male

> "So the Lord God caused a deep sleep to fall upon the man, and while he slept took one of his ribs and closed up its place with flesh. And the rib that the Lord God had taken from the man he made into a woman." (Genesis 2:21–22)

In our culture, "Remember where you came from!" is a common admonition not to look down on one's beginnings. It's a warning to avoid pride and an overinflated sense of self-importance. We intuitively know that it's inappropriate to regard that from which we were made as lesser than us. We know that we are obliged to honor and respect our origins.

The same sort of idea is present in the creation of the female. Because woman was drawn from man's side, it was appropriate for her to have an attitude of respect toward him. He was the firstborn. In the New Testament we see that the fact that she was created from him—and not the other way around—is the basis of a wife honoring the authority of her husband. "For man was not made from woman, but woman from man. . . . That is why a wife ought to have a symbol of authority on her head" (1 Corinthians 11:8–10).

The Female Was Made for the Male

> "Then the Lord God said, 'It is not good that the man should be alone; I will *make him* a helper fit *for him*.'" (Genesis 2:18, italics added)

The second chapter of Genesis tells us that the female was created "for him"—that is, on account of the male. First Corinthians 11:9 reinforces that man was not created "for the woman;" rather the woman was created "for man." He explains that this is the basis for a wife respecting the authority of her husband.

For most of us, the idea of woman being created "for" man sounds somewhat negative, since it appears to imply that he has license to use and abuse her at will. But the Hebrew preposition carries no such overtones. It simply denotes direction. She was created for—that is, toward or with reference to him, or on account of him. She was created *because* of him. His existence led to hers. It didn't happen the other way around. Our adverse reaction to the idea that we were created "for man" serves to underline how very far we've fallen from the original created order. When the first bride was presented to her husband, her heart was undoubtedly bursting with joy to have been created for him. She was thrilled that his existence led to hers.

There's another important point here. Being created for someone indicates that God created the female to be a highly relational creature. In contrast to the male, her identity isn't based on work nearly as much as on how well she connects in her relationships. Woman is the relater-responder who is inclined toward connecting with others.

The Female Enriched the Male

> ". . . a helper fit for him." (Genesis 2:18)

God created woman to be a helper. "Helper" is another word that begs explanation. It's not a term that indicates a lesser status or the type of help that assists in a trivial way. The Hebrew word (*ezer*) is a very powerful one. It's most often used with reference to the Lord being our helper (Psalm 33:20; 72:12). An *ezer* provides help that enriches and makes the recipient more fruitful than he would be without that help.

God created the woman to enrich the man by providing invaluable support that without her he would not have. What the man lacks, the woman accomplishes. She makes it possible for them to receive the blessing that he could not achieve alone. Woman plays an integral part in the survival and success of the human race. Without her, man could not be fruitful—physically or metaphorically.

So does that mean that women exist to serve the selfish ends of men? Absolutely not. The phrase "fit for him" in Hebrew literally means "like opposite him"—like an image in a mirror. The term is unique to Genesis. It expresses the notion of complementarity. She's not exactly like him. She's like-opposite him. Corresponding. Harmonized. Suitable. An exact fit. She's a "helper," but more importantly, she's a helper "alongside."

The *alongside* part is extremely important. The purpose of woman helping man isn't about exalting the man. It's not about him. Her help contributes to the both of them achieving a greater, nobler, eternal purpose that is far bigger and more significant than their own existence. She struggles alongside for the same purpose for which he struggles. And what is that? The glory of God. The Lord says that He formed and created sons and daughters to magnify His glory (Isaiah 43:6–7). A woman helps a man achieve the purpose of exalting and displaying the jaw-dropping magnificence of the gospel of Jesus Christ and the glory of God. That's what she helps him do.

The Female Deferred to the Male

"The Lord God . . . brought her to the man. Then the man said, '. . . she shall be called Woman, because she was taken out of Man.'" (Genesis 2:22–23)

I think that the first male and female intuitively knew how to behave. He knew what it meant to be a man. She knew what it meant to be a woman. So when the Lord presented the bride to the groom, the man spontaneously broke into a poem that expressed ecstatic love and delight, and at the same time demonstrated his intuitive grasp of the nature of their relationship. He named her—thus fulfilling his responsibility to initiate and lead. She joyfully responded with deference. For both of them, it was the natural and beautiful thing to do.

When God presented Eve to Adam, you don't see Eve taking charge and saying, "Wait a minute, Adam, I'm going to name myself—thank you very much! In fact, I'm going to be the one doing the naming around here. I've thought of a great name for you!" No. That's not what happened. Adam and Eve acted according to their God-given bents. He initiated. She responded. The pattern of their relationship reflected who God created them to be.

The Lord created woman with a bent to be amenable, relational, and receptive. He created man with a bent to initiate, provide, and protect. As we talked about in an earlier chapter, Genesis 3:16 indicates that sin severely damaged the God-given inclination of both. Sin twisted the positive desire of woman to respond amenably to man into a negative desire to resist and rebel against him. It twisted the positive drive of man to use his strength to lead, protect, and provide for woman into a negative tendency to abuse or refuse that responsibility.

When a girl goes wild, she's overcome by the sinful desire to go against the created order and selfishly dominate a man. Like the Proverbs 7 woman, she becomes the one who does the pursuing—she "seizes him" and demands that he follow her lead. A Girl-Gone-Wild is inclined to dominate. Her counterpart, the Girl-Gone-Wise, is inclined to joyfully defer to and give the man the opportunity to set the pace in the relationship.

The Female Was the Male's Perfect Counterpart

> "She shall be called Woman [*Isha*], because she was taken out of Man [*Ish*]." (Genesis 2:23)

In Hebrew, the name with which the male identified himself was *Ish*, while his name for woman was *Isha*. As discussed previously, *Ish* comes from the root meaning "strength" while *Isha* comes from the root meaning "soft." The idea goes beyond the mere physical difference between men and women to encompass the totality of their essence. The man was created to joyfully and actively initiate and give strength. The woman was created to joyfully and actively respond and receive it. Each was created with a unique role and responsibility to be the perfect counterpart to the other.

The Female Was Created in the Garden

"Therefore a man shall leave his father and his mother and hold fast to his wife, and they shall become one flesh." (Genesis 2:24)

A final but highly significant observation is that the female—the softer, more vulnerable one—was created in the garden, in a place of safety. She was created in a place that was already under the protective authority of her husband-to-be. The male leaves the protective sphere of his household of origin to become the protector of a new household (Genesis 2:24). The woman doesn't "leave." She's the constant beneficiary of protection from the authorities God has put in her life. The Lord wanted to ensure that woman, His final delicate masterpiece of creation, would always be loved, cherished, and kept safe.

The fact that woman was created within the boundaries of a household also implies that women are to have a unique responsibility in the home. This is consistent with the idea that a woman metaphorically keeps her feet (and heart) centered in the home, rather than outside of it. For the woman, nurturing her relationships and keeping her household in order takes priority over other types of work.

LET HIM DRIVE

The Lord evaluated his equal-yet-different creation of male and female as, "Very good! Spectacular! Outstanding!" Do you agree with Him? Do you feel the same way? Do you try to bring your life in line with God's beautiful, unique design for the woman He created you to be? Or do you defiantly take pen in hand and scribble over His blueprint?

When we think about roles, we often make the mistake of thinking that they are primarily about what we do. Roles influence what we do, but the role defines the behavior, and not the other way around. People miss the point when they engage in endless debates about specific behavior, like whose job it is to take out the trash. Everyone wants a list of dos and don'ts, but the Bible does not provide such a list. Roles speak to *who we are* more than they speak to *what we do*. Roles are about who God created male and female to be. The Lord knows that we'll figure out what we ought to do when we figure out who we ought to be.

Let's think about how all this relates to junior high Katy chasing my son. Setting aside the fact that she was young and the fact that her calls were excessive, do you think that Katy pursing boys was healthy and appropriate behavior for a young woman? If Katy (who is now twenty) continued this pattern of relating to boys, what kind of a relationship do you think she would end up in? Do you think her style of relating supports who God wants her to be as a woman? Do you think it will result in Katy having a husband who assumes his God-given responsibility to be a man? Or will Katy likely end up crying on someone's shoulder in the future, because she'll eventually be clued in to the fact that her husband is a wimp? And that her effort to wear the pants in her house has become exhausting and frustrating, because it doesn't fit with who God created her to be?

Is it wrong for a woman to phone a man? No. Is it wrong for her to initiate from time to time? No. But if her habitual pattern of behavior is that she is the pursuer and he is the pursued, this is unlikely to change if and when the couple get married. When we were talking about it last week, my daughter-in-law astutely said, "I tell my girlfriends that the right roles start right at the start of a dating relationship. I rarely called Clark. Only if he called me, did I call him back, or only if there was a really good reason for me to call him. I didn't text him very much. I waited for him to ask me out. I waited for him to declare his love before I declared mine. I waited for him to give me a kiss. I waited for him to bring up the idea of marriage. I waited for him to propose. I held back so he could lead. I wanted a man who would be a man in our marriage." Smart girl!

So here's my advice to you—unmarried or married—who want to

be Girls-Gone-Wise: Let him drive. Wait for him to pick up the keys (physically and metaphorically). Hold back. Don't rush in. Give him a chance to initiate. Welcome his leadership. I know that nowadays men are plagued with the sin of passivity. This is primarily due to their sin nature, but also in part because women have shoved them out of the driver's seat and brashly taken the wheel. I know that many women ache for their men to step up and be men. What I advise all the Heidis crying on my shoulder is this: "Reclaiming your womanhood is the best way to help a man reclaim his manhood." We live in a world broken by sin. So this isn't easy. But a Girl-Gone-Wise inclines her heart to embrace her role as a woman and follow God's design.

You'll find videos, a forum, and many other resources to help you learn how to walk wisely on the GirlsGoneWise.com website. And make sure to follow Gorls Gone Wise on Facebook (facebook.com/girlsgonewise) and Twitter (twitter.com/girlsgonewise) tool.

Point of Contrast #10

SEXUAL CONDUCT
Her Sexual Behavior

Girl-Gone-Wild: Impure and Dishonorable	Girl-Gone-Wise: Pure and Honorable
"... and kisses him." (Proverbs 7:13)	She controls her body in holiness and honor, and does not wrong her brother. (I Thessalonians 4:4–6)

S ex. Sex. Sex. Sex is everywhere. Movies, sitcoms, soaps, reality TV, news stories, commercials, talk shows, billboards, magazine ads, and MTV. Sex sells everything from travel to telephones to toothpaste. This current generation has more sex education, sex books, sex columns, sex therapists, sex supplements, sex talk, sex techniques, and sex toys than any other in the history of mankind. Sex is the topic of Internet chatter, locker-room gossip, and watercooler banter. We live in a sex-saturated world.

Given the modern-day obsession with sex, I'm going to say something that may sound radical: *We don't make as much of sex as we should*. Oh, most women are overwhelmingly eager to indulge. They partake in worldly sexual pleasures like revelers greedily snatching up beads at a Mardi Gras carnival. They hang them up as cheap trophies to collect dust on the edge of their vanity mirrors and eagerly wait for the next big parade. Others scorn the festivity. They think the beads are tawdry. They were once mesmerized and collected a few strands, but the sparkle has worn off. Now the trinkets hang tarnished and neglected in the back of their closets. Been there. Done that. Got the necklace.

The problem is not that we value sex too much—but that we don't value it enough. We fool about with lust, sensuality, seduction, glossy-magazine titillation, movie-screen romance, illicit sex, obligatory sex, or boring sex, when divine pleasure is offered us. We are like a senseless child who refuses to trade in her dollar-store baubles for a gold locket. We don't make nearly as much of sex as we should. We are far too easily pleased.

Sexual conduct is one of the major differences between a Girl-Gone-Wise and a Girl-Gone-Wild. The sexual behavior of the former is holy and honorable, whereas the sexual behavior of the latter is not. The Wild Thing thinks that the way she conducts herself sexually is her own business—whether or not she collects sexual baubles is a personal matter and not all that important. The Girl-Gone-Wise realizes that her sexual conduct, both inside and outside of marriage, *is* important. What she does sexually is much bigger than her own personal life. It has meaning that connects to the cosmic, unseen, eternal realm. The Girl-Gone-Wise understands that sex is a big deal to God—and that He wants her to know and experience what great sex is all about.

It's my aim, in this chapter, to help you understand, from a biblical perspective, what great sex is all about. I believe that this understanding is necessary for both single and married women. Knowing what sex is all about will motivate a single woman to delight in sexual continence. She will understand that restraint is as much and as valid of an expression of the meaning of sex as the sexual act itself. Her sexual chastity contributes to the cosmic story. It testifies to the astonishing meaning of it all—and glorifies God.

Understanding what sex is all about will motivate a married woman to delight in having sex with her husband—to have a strong, "till death do us part," pure, unwaning desire to make love to him and to honor the exclusivity of their union. She will understand that sex is a God-given, delightful act that is, among other things, a testimonial act of worship. It is a means whereby a married woman glorifies God.

Most Christian discussions about sex and sexuality put the emphasis in the wrong place. They spend a whole lot of time focusing on what constitutes improper sexual conduct. They draw lines and boundaries that delineate pure from impure behavior. It seems to me that coming up with a list of "don'ts" somewhat misses the point. It tackles the issue from the wrong side. We can't hope to know which behaviors we should avoid until we understand the reason that we ought to avoid them. What's more, this approach lopsidedly focuses on behaviors to avoid, rather than attitudes and behaviors to cultivate. It can result in a pharisaical sense that we're getting our sexuality right, when in fact, we're getting it very wrong. Many married Christian women are guilty of wrongful sexual conduct, even though they may not technically be transgressing a specific biblical boundary. For example, a woman who is frigid toward her husband dishonors God's pattern for sexuality as much as the one who commits adultery does. A married woman who uses sex to punish or reward her husband is as wrong in her thinking about sex as an unmarried woman who hooks up with a guy just for the thrill of a fleeting night of pleasure.

The Bible's principles for sexual conduct take the issue of sex a lot further than a written list of dos and don'ts. They emanate from the heart of God. He wants us to cherish and value our sexuality as much as He does. He wants us to understand the cosmic, amazing meaning of sex and to honor that meaning with all our hearts. He wants us to delight in sex. Honor it. Think His thoughts about it. He wants us to live in such a way that our sexuality puts His glory on display. He wants us to be so familiar with the awesome meaning of sex that we will be able to spiritually discern whether any thought or behavior contradicts or detracts from that meaning. The more we embrace *why* God created sex, the more readily apparent it will become *what* constitutes appropriate sexual conduct. Understanding the reason for this amazing gift will help us honor and enjoy it in the right way.

SEX IS A BIG DEAL

To figure out what sex is all about, we need to look again at the creation of man and woman and the first marriage. In the previous chapter, we talked about the twelve markers of complementarity evident in Genesis 2. We discovered that God created man and woman to be equal, yet different. The difference in our anatomy mirrors our difference in makeup. What it means to be a man is different from what it means to be a woman. The question we're going to explore right now is *why*. Why did God create male and female? Why did He create marriage? Why did He create sex?

The meaning of sex can't be addressed outside of the context of what it means to be a man or a woman—nor can it be addressed outside of the context of marriage. Manhood, womanhood, marriage, and sex are indivisibly connected. Their meaning intersects. As you'll soon see, the meaning is a mystery that God hinted at from the beginning of time, but did not reveal until the death and resurrection of Jesus Christ.

Did you know that the Father had the death and resurrection of Jesus Christ in mind before He created the world or anything in it? Before He created male and female, He had a plan to redeem them. Paul makes this clear in Ephesians 1:4–11. He points out that God planned to display His glorious grace by adopting us into His family. He planned to accomplish this through the death and resurrection of Jesus Christ, "the Beloved." This was God's plan "before the foundation of the world." When God set about creating man and woman, He already had in mind the marvelous plan of Jesus dying to redeem His church-bride. He already had in mind the marriage that will take place between Christ and the church at the end of time.

In the first chapter of Genesis, we see the Creator reflectively pause before His final and greatest creative act. There was no question in His mind about what He was going to do. He had settled on His plan long before the foundation of the world. It was already in motion. At His word, the galaxies and planets, sun and moon had all formed and aligned. The earth had ripened with life: The ground had sprouted vegetation; the sky, sea, and land teemed with every sort of living creature. Everything was in place. Everything was ready. It all led up to this moment—and this moment pointed to another moment far off in time but eternally present in the mind of God. The significance of what He was about to do was deeper and more profound than even the angels could fathom. He was about to make man—and to make him male and female.

> Then God said, "Let us make man in our image, after our likeness. And let them have dominion over the fish of the sea and over the birds of the heavens and over the livestock and over all the earth and over every creeping thing that creeps on the earth." So God created man in his own image, in the image of God he created him; male and female he created them. (Genesis 1:26–27)

Take note of the language. It's significant. God said, "Let *us* make man in *our* image, after *our* likeness," and then He created man in His own image—male and female He created them. The discussion about the creation of male and female took place between members of the Godhead. It may have been between all three: Father, Son, and Holy Spirit. But at the very least, it involved the Father and his Son, as Scripture draws parallels between that relationship and the relationship of a husband and wife. When God created man and woman, He had the dynamic of His own relationship in mind. God created the two sexes to reflect something about God. He patterned the male-female relationship ("them") after the "us/our" relationship that exists within the Godhead. He used His own relationship structure as the pattern.

Paul confirms, in 1 Corinthians 11:3, that the relationship between a husband and wife is patterned after the relationship between God the Father and His Son. "The head of a wife is her husband, and the head of Christ is God." God purposefully created marriage to reflect the headship structure that exists within the Godhead. But He also created marriage and sex to reflect some other truths about the Trinity.

Jesus confirmed what Genesis says about marriage: "From the beginning of creation, 'God made them male and female.' 'Therefore a man shall leave his father and mother and hold fast to his wife, and they shall become one flesh.' So they are no longer two but one flesh. What therefore God has joined together, let not man separate" (Mark 10:6–9). Marriage is about union, communion, commitment, and family—and these things all point to the character and nature of God.

Marriage is about *union*—It's about the "oneness" of two individuals. Two become one. The word *one* stresses unity while recognizing diversity within that oneness. The same word is used in the famous Shema of Deuteronomy 6:4: "Hear, O Israel . . . the Lord is One." Jesus used the same language: "I and the Father are one" (John 10:30). The oneness of male and female in marriage is an earthly picture that helps us understand the oneness of God.

Marriage is about *communion*—husband and wife become "one flesh" through the physical union of their bodies. The physical act consummates their emotional and spiritual intimacy. The Old Testament expression for sexual intercourse is that a man "knows" his wife. Sexual intercourse equals knowing. Covenant love is all about "knowing" someone. It's communion of the most intimate kind. It's the deepest love that is humanly possible. "One flesh" expresses the idea that within the marriage covenant, husband and wife get to know each other intimately, in every possible way.

When Jesus talked about the divine love between Himself and His Father, He used the language of communion: "The Father knows me and I know the Father" (John 10:14). "The Father has loved me" (John 15:9). "The Father is in me and I am in the Father" (John 10:38). "I am in my Father, and you in me, and I in you" (John 14:20). John described the intimacy between God the Father and Son this way: "The only begotten Son, who is in the bosom of the Father" (John 1:18 NKJV). The terms "know," "in," and "in the bosom" indicate that the Father and Son experience a divine intimacy. Their relationship is one of closest communion. Communion in marriage bears witness to the spiritual, divine intimacy between the members of the Trinity.

Marriage is about *commitment*—the man commits to forsake all others and "hold fast" to his wife. The word means to permanently adhere oneself to. The Hebrew word refers to permanently soldering one piece of metal to another. It's used in Job 41:15–17 to describe how tightly a crocodile's scales are joined together. This joining of husband to wife is a permanent covenant, orchestrated by God. He joins two individuals together indivisibly. The indivisibility of husband and wife is to bear witness to the fact that Father and Son are indivisibly one (1 Corinthians 8:4–6). and that Christ is indivisibly one with His church (Colossians 1:18).

Marriage is about *family*—a husband and wife establish a new family unit. Their union produces children. The family relationship is a symbol that teaches us a lot about God. It teaches us about the relationship a father has to his children. It helps us understand the relationship between God the Father and His only begotten Son, the enormousness of what it meant for the Father to sacrifice His Son, and what it means for Him to adopt us as His children (Romans 8:29; Galatians 4:5–6).

In Romans 1:20, Paul sheds more light on why God created men, women, marriage, and sex. He says, "For his invisible attributes, namely, his eternal power and divine nature, have been clearly perceived, ever since the creation of the world, in the things that have been made." What does this tell us? It tells us that when God created male and female, sex and marriage, He put two very important truths about Himself on display: (1) His divine nature (the glory of who He *is*) and (2) His eternal power (the glory of what He *does*).

God created male and female in His own image. We don't fully understand what the image of God is all about, but two things are clear. First, being created in His image gives us enormous dignity, privilege, and responsibility. He has crowned us with honor and glory and given us authority over the earth. It's a breathtaking charge to go about the business of daily life and all the while reflect the image of the Almighty. And that leads to the second thing: what a mess we've made of this awesome dignity! The image of God in man is badly marred, sometimes even beyond recognition. It begs for redemption. Transformation. A type of re-creation. And stunningly enough, God stamped this vision and hope onto human beings in the very beginning, before they had even sinned.

When God created male and female, He provided an object lesson—a parable, as it were—of his entire redemptive plan. Manhood, womanhood, marriage, and sex are mini-lessons that proclaim the gospel (Colossians 1:23). They tell the cosmic story about the Bridegroom who loved His bride so much that He died to redeem her, and about how wonderful their wedding and union will one day be.

Throughout the Old Testament, God used the image of marriage to teach His people about the nature of His relationship to them. He was the husband; Israel was His wife. "For your Maker is your husband" (Isaiah 54:5). God likened their spiritual infidelity to a wife whoring around with other men (Ezekiel 16). Old Testament marriage imagery foreshadowed the mystery that remained hidden until the time of Christ. "In that day, declares the Lord, you will call me 'My Husband' . . . and I will betroth you to me forever. I will betroth you to me in righteousness and in justice, in steadfast love and in mercy. I will betroth you to me in faithfulness. And you shall know the Lord" (Hosea 2:16, 19–20).

Paul connects all the dots in Ephesians. In chapter 3, he explains that the mysterious plan came to light through the work of Jesus Christ (vv. 9–10). In chapter 5, he links the mystery of redemption (Christ loving and dying for the church) to male-female sexuality and marriage. "Husbands, love your wives, as Christ loved the church. . . . 'Therefore a man shall . . . hold fast to his wife, and the two shall become one flesh.' This mystery . . . refers to Christ and the church" (Ephesians 5:25, 31–32).

When God described the work of His Son as the sacrifice of a husband for his bride, He was telling us the ultimate reason why he made us male and female, and why He created marriage and sex. Christ and His bride are the reason. Sexuality is a parable—a testimony to the character of God and to His spectacular plan of redemption through Jesus. This spiritual truth is so magnificent that God chose to put it on display permanently. Everywhere. Men were created to reflect the strength, love, and self-sacrifice of Christ. Women were created to reflect the character, grace, and beauty of the bride He redeemed. He created marriage and sex to display the joining of Christ and the church in an indivisible covenant. History started with the covenant wedding and sexual union of a man and woman because it will end with the covenant wedding and spiritual union of Christ and His bride.

Manhood, womanhood, marriage, and sex exist to tell the story of Jesus, the Bridegroom who loved and gave His life for His bride. What is manhood about? Displaying the glory of Jesus Christ. What is womanhood about? Displaying the glory of Jesus Christ. What is marriage about? Displaying the glory of Jesus Christ. What is sex about? Displaying the glory of Jesus Christ.

Sex is the act that defines marriage. It consummates (completes) the marriage covenant. It is the act of ultimate significance because it represents the essence of what covenant is all about. Sex confirms that covenant means union, communion, intimacy, commitment, exclusivity, satisfaction, delight, and fruitfulness. God created sex so that a husband and wife might display, confirm, and enjoy their union—so that their physical bodies bear witness to the spiritual, supernatural, and legal joining that has taken place. Physical intimacy reinforces the fact that God has joined two individuals together in covenant commitment.

Through sex, a husband and wife affirm in the private realm what has taken place in the public and heavenly realm. They tell and retell the story to each other. Sex is the testimony. Sex bears witness that God has made two one. That's why God restricts sex to marriage. If unmarried individuals are physically intimate, they tell a lie with their bodies. They testify that a joining has taken place, when in fact it hasn't.

God created manhood, womanhood, marriage, and sex because He wanted us to have symbols, images, and language powerful enough to convey the idea of who He is and what a relationship with Him is all about. Without them, we would have a tough time understanding concepts such as desire, love, commitment, fidelity, infidelity, loyalty, jealousy, unity, intimacy, marriage, oneness, covenant, and family. We would have a hard time understanding God and the gospel. God gave us these images so that we have human thoughts, feelings, experiences, and language adequate and powerful enough to understand and express deep spiritual truths. The visible symbols display and testify about what is unseen. That's why the symbols are so very important.

Scripture is emphatic that who we are as male and female has very little to do with us and very much to do with God. The Lord says, "Bring my sons from afar and my daughters from the end of the earth, everyone who is called by my name, *whom I created for my glory*, whom I formed and made" (Isaiah 43:6–7, italics added). The storyline of gender and sex is ultimately not about us. It's about displaying the glory of our Creator and His spectacular redemptive plan. So when my husband and I make passionate love, we bear witness to the glory of the gospel of Jesus Christ. Our sex bears testimony to it. If my heart wanders and I lust for a man who is not my husband, I bring disgrace on the gospel of Jesus Christ.

Any violation of the exclusivity of the marriage covenant throws mud at God's beautiful parable. Given the powerful symbolism of gender, marriage, sex, and family, is it any wonder that Satan tries to destroy the image? Is it any wonder that these symbols are at the forefront of the spiritual battle? Is it any wonder that they are at the heart of so much brokenness, dysfunction, and pain?

NO MESSING AROUND

I hope you can see how understanding the "why" directs the "what" of our sexual conduct. Understanding that marriage and sex go hand in hand, and that the image is all about the covenant commitment, love, unity, permanency, and exclusivity of Christ's relationship to the church, answers a whole lot of questions about what and what isn't appropriate sexual behavior.

In the spiritual realm, would it be appropriate for Christ's bride to "mess around" with anyone other than her Bridegroom? Even just a little bit? On the other hand, would it be appropriate for her to shun her Bridegroom, refuse His approaches, or give Him the cold shoulder? The answer is simple. No. And I believe the answer is almost as simple when it comes to sex in the physical realm. We honor God with our sexuality by restricting physical, sexual expressions of intimacy to the confines of marriage, and by delighting in the joy of marital sex. Keeping sex exclusive to the marriage covenant and having great sex with one's spouse, is the right way for Christians to display the purity, unity, and fidelity of the church's relationship to Christ. It's the way we tell the story.

Physical intimacy is the sign of covenant commitment. The covenant is what changes the traffic light from red to green. *Sex testifies to the fact that a union has taken place.* So what are the implications for physical intimacy between unmarried couples? The simple answer is that it's wrong for two people to act as if they are married when they are not married. Our sexual behavior in the physical realm is to mirror the purity and faithfulness of Christ's bride in the spiritual realm. Therefore, if the behavior is inappropriate between a *married* woman and a man who is not her husband, then it is just as inappropriate between an *unmarried* woman and a man who is not her husband.

Would it be appropriate for a bride to seek to give or receive sexual pleasure outside of the confines of her marriage bed? Would it be appropriate for her to sleep over at a male friend's apartment? Would it be appropriate for her to passionately kiss anyone other than her husband? I think the answer is obvious.

Does this mean that couples should refrain from kissing or holding hands until they are married? The Bible doesn't say. And I don't think it's wise for us to enforce a set of rules and boundaries. That misses the point. But honoring the meaning of marriage definitely means bridling our passions and confining sex to marriage. Outside of the covenant relationship, the traffic control light is red. This is the standard for those who are married as well as those who are single. Unmarried individuals respect the meaning of sex by restraining their sexual appetites and saving most—if not all—expressions of physical intimacy for the covenant context for which God designed it.

Arguing that "just a bit" of messing around outside of the covenant of marriage is OK is as logically indefensible as justifying that it's OK for Christ's bride to mess around on Him "just a bit." Christ gave His life for the new covenant—it was bought by His blood. Faithfulness to the covenant is supremely important to Him. It is impossible and utterly unthinkable that He would ever be unfaithful to His bride. That's why Christ's standards for the covenant of marriage are so shockingly high. To those who don't grasp the significance of sex and marriage, they sound totally unreasonable. Christ's view on the exclusivity and permanency of the marriage relationship shocked His disciples. Jesus saw the marriage covenant as so binding, and its symbolic significance so profound, that in His mind, divorce and remarriage were out of the question. His perspective left His disciples gasping. His claim that lust is as sinful as adultery undoubtedly left the crowd gasping. Christ's ideal for covenant commitment and absolute sexual purity is radical.

Married or unmarried, a woman's sexual behavior is to present an image of the purity, faithfulness, and exclusivity of the church-bride to her one and only beloved Bridegroom. God takes marriage and sex very, very seriously. The Bible teaches that God intends sex to consummate the marriage covenant, and *not* to precede marriage. The Lord wants us to cherish and set apart sex to bear testimony to this exclusive, till-death-do-us-part relationship. This honors what sex is all about.

Hang in there. Keep reading. I think things will become even clearer when we unpack a passage that Paul wrote to new believers who lived in a sex-saturated culture not unlike our own.

UNCOMMON, SET-APART SEX

The moral climate within the Roman Empire was not healthy. Sexual promiscuity was common. People got divorced on a whim. The Roman philosopher Seneca observed, "Women were married to be divorced and divorced to be married."[1] Romans traditionally identified the years by the names of their consuls—but fashionable Roman women identified the years by the names of their husbands. One historian quotes an instance of a woman who had eight husbands in five years. Promiscuity and adultery also saturated Greek culture. One writer admitted, "We keep prostitutes for pleasure; we keep mistresses for the day-to-day needs of the body; we keep wives for the begetting of children and for the faithful guardianship of our homes."[2] There was no shame whatsoever in extramarital relationships.

It was to new believers in this sex-crazed Roman and Greek culture that Paul wrote the following passage:

> Finally, then, brothers, we ask and urge you in the Lord Jesus, that as you received from us how you ought to walk and to please God, just as you are doing, that you do so more and more. For you know what instructions we gave you through the Lord Jesus.
>
> For this is the will of God, your sanctification: that you abstain from sexual immorality; that each one of you know how to control his own body in holiness and honor, not in the passion of lust like the Gentiles who do not know God; that no one transgress and wrong his brother in this matter, because the Lord is an avenger in all these things, as we told you beforehand and solemnly warned you.
>
> For God has not called us for impurity, but in holiness. Therefore whoever disregards this, disregards not man but God, who gives his Holy Spirit to you. (1 Thessalonians 4:1–8)

The young believers in the church in Thessalonica were trying to figure out what their new faith meant. Some undoubtedly had promiscuous sexual histories and were carrying around all kinds of sexual baggage. They reasoned that they ought to be able to indulge their passions and pursue sexual pleasure, and that it was completely acceptable to do so outside the confines of marriage. Though they had accepted Christ, they still had a very ungodly perspective on sex. Paul challenges them to bring their thinking and behavior in line with the gospel of Jesus Christ. He reminds them of five things the Lord wants believers to do: (1) abstain from sexual immorality, (2) aim for increased sexual purity, (3) control your body in holiness and honor, (4) don't sexually defraud others, and (5) don't disregard the importance of sexual conduct.

Abstain from Sexual Immorality

Immorality translates as the Greek word *porneia*, from which we get our English word *pornography*. It means sexual unfaithfulness. It refers to any type of illicit sex that takes place outside of a marriage covenant. Paul tells the believers to abstain from sexual immorality. In other words, he says, "Christians don't sleep around outside of marriage! Staying out of bed with someone you aren't married to is the bare minimum, Christianity 101, baseline sexual standard for followers of Jesus. If you've been sleeping around, stop sleeping around. Abstain. Give it up. That's what Jesus expects you to do."

Aim for Increased Sexual Purity

The Lord doesn't just ask us to refrain from illicit sexual intercourse. He asks us to aspire to increasingly higher standards of sexual purity. That's why "How far is too far?" really isn't the right question. He doesn't want us to ask how close to immorality we can get without crossing the line. He wants our sexual conduct to become more and more holy. Paul encourages the Thessalonians to pursue sexual purity—and to "do so more and more."

Sexual impurity is a sin that the Lord often lists alongside the sins of immorality and sensuality. The word *impurity* literally means "uncleanliness." It means dirty, common, and ordinary. *Purity* is the exact opposite. It means clean, uncommon, and extraordinary—set apart. As we grow in Christ, our understanding of and desire for sexual purity will also grow. It won't happen overnight, but as we are sanctified to become more like Jesus, our sexual conduct will become

147

increasingly clean, extraordinary, and set apart for Him. The Lord doesn't want you to settle for dirty, common, ordinary sex. He wants you to reach higher. He wants you to nudge the bar up from where it is now. He wants you to constantly aim for increased sexual purity and increasingly higher standards.

Control Your Body in Holiness and Honor

Sexual purity takes self-control. It requires that we don't mindlessly follow our sexual passions, like people who don't know God. The Lord wants us to control our sexual impulses. He wants us to intentionally rein them in and submit them to Him. He has bestowed His Holy Spirit upon us—the Spirit of power, love, and self-control—to help us discipline ourselves and control our bodies and sexual passions in a holy and honorable way (2 Timothy 1:7).

Don't Sexually Defraud Men

Paul advises the Thessalonians to ensure "that no one transgress and wrong his brother in this matter." The Greek word used here for "transgress" is also translated as *defraud*. It means to overreach or overstep; to go beyond. It carries the implication of selfish personal gain. Defrauding a brother is overstepping the line to take something that is not yours to take. The Girl-Gone-Wild of Proverbs 7 defrauded the young man. She seized him and kissed him when she had no right to. His compliance or approval is inconsequential. She still wronged him. She wronged him when she overstepped *God's idea* of what was appropriate sexual behavior. Whenever you interact with a man who is not your husband in a way that you should only interact with your spouse, you not only sin against God, you also wrong your brother.

Don't Disregard the Importance of Sexual Conduct

Sex is a big deal to God. Paul warns the new believers not to underestimate or disregard the importance of their sexual conduct. He told the believers in Corinth the same thing:

> The body is not meant for sexual immorality, but for the Lord, and the Lord for the body. . . . Do you not know that your bodies are members of Christ? Shall I then take the members of Christ and make them members

of a prostitute? Never! Or do you not know that he who is joined to a prostitute becomes one body with her? For, as it is written, "The two will become one flesh." But he who is joined to the Lord becomes one spirit with him. Flee from sexual immorality. Every other sin a person commits is outside the body, but the sexually immoral person sins against his own body. Or do you not know that your body is a temple of the Holy Spirit within you, whom you have from God? You are not your own, for you were bought with a price. So glorify God in your body. (1 Corinthians 6:13–20)

Wrongful sexual conduct violates your covenant relationship with Jesus. It's serious stuff. It has serious consequences. Paul implies that it has greater consequences than other types of sin. Over my years of ministering to women, I have found this to be the case. Because sexual immorality is an assault on your personhood and a severe violation of covenant, it damages you in a way that other sins do not. When you sin sexually, you sin against your own body. You fracture your God-given identity. There is always great hope in the power of Christ's redemption. But those who engage in sexual sin dig themselves into a very deep pit from which it is often exceedingly difficult to climb out. In my experience, Satan capitalizes on sexual sin and establishes spiritual ties, footholds, and strongholds that require extensive spiritual warfare to overcome. So if you haven't wandered down the path of sexual sin, please don't. If you have, realize that God has the power to heal, and that He will fight with you to redeem what you have lost. But realize, too, that the scars will remain for some time, and that you will face battles that you would not have had to face if you had remained sexually pure.

FOR THE SAKE OF SEX

Some will claim that narrowing and confining physical intimacy to marriage will decrease the pleasure of sex. But quite the opposite is true. Narrowing the boundary to its God-given parameter increases the power, passion, and pleasure of sex. It allows sex to be everything God created it to be. The boundary creates the beauty. The following illustration captures the idea:

The pleasures and goodness of sex are heightened, not lessened by proper restraint, in the same way the Colorado River is made more powerful by the walls of the Grand Canyon. The very narrowness of the river's channel there makes for a greater river. Farther south, as the river flows through the deserts of California and Arizona, it is shallow, wide, and muddy, even stinky in spots. Wider boundaries diminish the river; sharper, stronger, and narrower boundaries strengthen it. Less is more. The boundaries and proscriptions of sex in the Bible are for the sake of sex. Again, less is more— at least less as understood by one man and one woman together exclusively till death parts them.[3]

God wants Christians to experience great sex. We haven't even brushed the surface of what that looks like. God is so supportive of good sex that He devoted an entire book of the Bible, the Song of Solomon, to the joy of passionate sex between a husband and wife. Make sure to read it sometime. I hope that this chapter has given you a vision of sex that is bigger and more wonderful and more astonishing than anything you have ever dreamed. I hope that it inspires you to give up the cheap sexual trinkets of a Girl-Gone-Wild and open your hands to reach for God's pure, solid gold locket of uncommon, set-apart sex. Don't settle for less.

Watch the *Girls Gone Wise* DVD and do the study quetions in the *Girls Gone Wise Companion Guide.* They'll help you evaluate whether your outlook on sex is the one God wants you to have.

Point of Contrast #11

BOUNDARIES
Her Hedges
and Precautions

Girl-Gone-Wild: **Leaves Herself Susceptible**	Girl-Gone-Wise: **Safeguards Herself**
". . . in the twilight, in the evening, at the time of night and darkness." (Proverbs 7:9)	She foresees danger and takes precautions. (Proverbs 22:3)

E spresso macchiato. Extra foamy." That's what Kyle ordered the day he came into the college coffee shop where Jennifer worked. He came back the next day. And the next day after that. For their first date, they went to a movie. For their second, Kyle took her on a long walk through the autumn leaves in the river valley. Jennifer was smitten. He was handsome. Funny. Engaging. He made her feel special. They had known each other a scant two weeks when Kyle invited her to a party at a club. She had never been to one, but he assured her it would be a lot of fun. He'd teach her to dance. Jennifer didn't normally go to such places, but Kyle was so kind and sweet. What harm could it do? She'd make an exception —just this time. It would be a great opportunity to witness to him some more.

The morning after the big party, Jennifer woke up in her apartment with a smashing headache and aching all over. She remembered having a drink, but little else. She couldn't shake the gnawing, dark suspicion that something bad had happened. She was too confused and embarrassed to confront Kyle when he dropped by the coffee shop later that day with a bouquet of flowers. She could tell that something had changed between them. He came by a couple more times, and then his visits abruptly stopped. Several weeks later, a pregnancy test confirmed her deepest fear. Kyle had drugged and date-raped her.

Jennifer couldn't bring herself to tell her parents. Her pregnancy would bring shame and embarrassment on her family, who were prominent in the church and community. She couldn't tell any of her friends. She was the Bible study leader—the one who challenged them to follow God's ways. How could she face them? How could she face the whispers and stares and all the other consequences of an unplanned pregnancy? Overcome with shame, Jennifer quietly went for an abortion. When I met her—five years later—she had undergone counseling and had dealt with the emotional aftermath of the rape. But she still hadn't told anyone about the baby. Her guilt over aborting the baby had emotionally crippled her. She couldn't accept God's forgiveness. Her walk with God, her desire to talk to others about Jesus, and her hope for the future had all but shriveled up. She asked me to pray to help lift the dark cloud that had settled over her life.

Sarah was a thirtyish single woman who inadvertently fell in love with a coworker, Paul. The only problem was that Paul was married. Their relationship had started innocently enough. Their boss had assigned them to work together on a project. At some point their e-mails, lunchtime meetings, and backroom network programming took a romantic turn. They crossed all boundaries one weekend, in a hotel room in California, when they attended the computer analyst conference together. The affair had been going strong ever since. Sarah wanted Paul to leave his wife. But they had three children, and he was reluctant to break up his home. He was beginning to waver. Sarah was turning into an emotional wreck. It was an impossible, no-win situation. With tear-filled eyes, she wondered, "How could this have happened to me?"

To her credit, Amanda could see it coming. She had gone to talk to her pastor, Mike. He was such a good listener and empathized with the struggles in her marriage. She was surprised to learn that his marriage wasn't as wonderful as it appeared on Sundays. He, too, felt deeply alienated from his spouse. Their "counseling" sessions ignited a spark between them. Amanda started thinking and daydreaming about Pastor Mike. At church, their looks grew deeper and their touches started to linger. He was finding reasons to call and ask if she could volunteer in the office. She could feel the chemistry intensify. They had already crossed many small boundaries. The ball was rolling downhill and gaining speed. Against such strong momentum, the remaining barriers provided little resistance. She could already imagine them giving way. Amanda came for prayer because she knew that if she didn't turn back immediately—and rebuild some stronger hedges—she would ruin two marriages, destroy a church, and bring scandal to the community. She knew what she needed to do, but didn't have the desire or the strength to do it. I prayed with her, but had the uneasy feeling that Amanda was more enthralled about the prospect of intimacy with Pastor Mike than she was about her relationship with Jesus Christ. She was holding the forbidden fruit up to her mouth, ready to bite.

What do these stories have in common? All three of these women went off track because they crossed proper boundaries. They experienced difficulties they would have avoided had they faithfully observed the boundaries. Minding them would have protected them from harm.

In Jennifer's case, the sin was not her "fault." That is, she was not complicit to it. Kyle committed a criminal offense against her. But by failing to maintain protective boundaries, Jennifer increased her vulnerability to this type of attack. Please don't misunderstand me. I am not saying she asked for what she got. The crime was heinous and unjustified and deserving of punishment. Leaving your car door unlocked doesn't justify the theft of the laptop you left on the seat. The person who steals it from an open vehicle is just as guilty as one who steals it from a secured one, and ought to receive as severe a sentence. But if you had hidden the laptop in your trunk and locked your vehicle, chances are you would not have become the victim of theft.

Failure to safeguard yourself increases your vulnerability. If Jennifer had observed the boundaries of not going out with unbelievers and not going to a place conducive to sin, she would have avoided or at least minimized the opportunity for Kyle to sin against her.

Sarah and Amanda, on the other hand, were complicit to sin. They progressed down the road of immorality of their own free will. Each did so by failing to put up hedges to protect her sexual purity. In the absence of protective boundaries, they became more and more vulnerable to sin. It probably happened the same way for the Wild Thing of Proverbs 7. She likely didn't begin her marriage planning to commit adultery. But bit by bit, she got to that point. One small compromise led to another until finally she ended up in an immoral situation that she would have never envisioned at the start.

Proverbs says the woman came out of her house to meet the young man "in the twilight, in the evening, at the time of night and darkness." The author implies that she shouldn't have been out at that time of night. It was inappropriate. In being out that late, her behavior crossed the boundary between appropriate to inappropriate conduct. You couldn't exactly call it sinful conduct—there are no "thou shall not go out after midnight" directives in the Bible. But it was definitely unwise. It opened the door to sin. If she had had a policy about not going out late and had abided by that policy, she would not have continued down the track of compromise. After she crossed the first boundary of going out late at night and the second boundary of secretly meeting the young man alone, she crossed the boundary of appropriate touch—by kissing him. She crossed another boundary when she engaged in inappropriate flattery and flirtation, and another when she invited him over to her place. Before she knew it, she had violated all the boundaries she should have observed.

A Girl-Gone-Wild disregards boundaries and leaves herself susceptible to the danger of sexual sin. Her counterpart, the Girl-Gone-Wise, safeguards herself. Her hedges are appropriate, clear, definitive, and strong.

HEDGING YOUR PURITY

When you hear the word *hedge*, you might imagine a row of shrubs that form a boundary around a yard. Hedges marked off several boundaries of the yard of my childhood home. They lessened the risk of us six kids wandering out and of big dogs wandering in. In a figurative sense, the word *hedge* refers to a protective method that lessens the risk of something negative happening. In the financial world, a hedge is a strategy to minimize exposure to an unwanted business risk. It defends against loss. And that's exactly what a clear boundary for sexual purity does. It protects against sexual injury and loss. For our purposes, a hedge is a personal rule that minimizes a woman's exposure to an unwanted sexual risk. It's a boundary that helps her protect her own sexual purity as well as the sexual purity of the men around her. It's a strategy whereby she lessens the opportunity for sin.

The Sage Father instructed his son that a sensible person "sees danger and hides himself, but the simple go on and suffer for it" (Proverbs 22:3). He repeats the exact same warning in Proverbs 27:12. "Danger" is literally the threat of evil. It's anything that could be a potential source of injury or harm. "Hides himself" means that the person takes action to guard from danger, or to escape or avoid it. This foresight is contrasted with the stupidity of those who ignore potential dangers and who end up getting themselves in trouble because of their lack of caution.

The father voices a similar sentiment in Proverbs 14:16: "One who is wise is cautious and turns away from evil, but a fool is reckless and careless." To be cautious is to be "careful," "alert," "on guard." It means to be apprehensive about the potential for sin. A wise person takes precautions to avoid being entrapped by sin. A fool doesn't take precautions. This person is reckless and careless. The Hebrew has connotations of arrogance, overconfidence, and throwing off restraint. The Latin translation uses the image of a person who overconfidently neglects and "leaps over" restrictions, thinking he won't get hurt.

A Girl-Gone-Wild crosses boundaries and plunges ahead with reckless confidence. She scoffs at the danger, believing that she's in control of the situation. A Girl-Gone-Wild doesn't believe that she's vulnerable to falling ("It won't happen to me!") or that the danger is substantial ("It can't hurt!"). So she doesn't put up hedges and precautions to safeguard her sexual purity.

TEN TYPES OF HEDGES

How can a woman keep her way pure? By "guarding" (hedging) it according to God's Word (Psalm 1 19:9). Practically, this means that we identify the common pitfalls of sexual sin and guard ourselves from stepping into those traps. We save ourselves "like a gazelle from the hand of the hunter, like a bird from the hand of the fowler" (Proverbs 6:5). We stay far away from the "thorns and snares" that entangle sinners (Proverbs 22:5). The Proverbs 7 woman did not do this. She did not establish hedges to protect herself from sexual sin. She overstepped ten boundaries that any woman who wishes to keep her way pure ought to hedge.

I. Location Hedges: Unhealthy Versus Healthy Environments
A Girl-Gone-Wise avoids unhealthy environments.

It always amazes me that women think they can expose themselves to immoral ideas, go to immoral environments, and constantly hang out with immoral people and suffer no ill consequence. The Sage Father asks, "Can a man carry fire next to his chest and his clothes not be burned? Or can one walk on hot coals and his feet not be scorched?" (Proverbs 6:27–28). A wise woman is not deceived. She recognizes that "bad company ruins good morals" (1 Corinthians 15:33). She resolves that she will not go to places that will potentially harm her. She puts up hedges such as these:

- I will not go to bars, lounges, or clubs.
- I will not go to strip shows or lewd bachelorette parties.
- I will not go to any parties that involve heavy drinking, drugs, or sex.
- I will not go to X-rated movies.
- I will not go to restaurants that encourage servers to dress and act provocatively.

- I will not go to comedy clubs that feature foul language and crude sexual humor.
- If I find myself in an unhealthy environment, I will quickly leave.

2. Pairing Hedges: Dual Versus Group Interaction
A Girl-Gone-Wise avoids inappropriately pairing herself with men.

The Wild Thing of Proverbs 7 was a married woman. She shouldn't have socially paired up with the young man. It was inappropriate for her to hang out with a man who wasn't her husband. If either individual in a male-female combination is married, then it is unwise for them to interact on a "paired-up" basis. It's also unwise for unmarried individuals to unreservedly pair off with each other. Scripture warns us, "The righteous should choose his friends carefully, for the way of the wicked leads them astray" (Proverbs 12:26 NKJV). Group interaction, involving three or more people, is a hedge that protects a pair from sexual temptation. Here are some suggested pairing hedges:

- I will interact with men in a group rather than one-on-one situations.
- I will not meet up, dine, or travel alone with a man if one of us is married.
- I will try to avoid being paired up with men in work projects, school assignments, or volunteer work. If pairing up is unavoidable, I will strengthen and emphasize other hedges to compensate for this.
- As an unmarried woman, I will not pair off with an unmarried man (one-on-one) until I have had ample opportunity to get to know him in a group context.

3. Seclusion Hedges: Private Versus Public Venues
A Girl-Gone-Wise avoids being in private, secluded places with men.

The Wild Thing of Proverbs 7 had no business inviting the young man into her home while no one else was there. It's inappropriate for a man and woman who are not married to each other to be together in a private, secluded place. That privilege belongs to married individuals. Men and women who desire to guard their sexual purity interact in places that are open to the view of others. Here are some suggested hedges that protect a woman from the sexual temptation and dangers of seclusion:

- I will not be alone with a man in a bedroom, an apartment, a house, a hotel room, a cabin, or any other place that is cut off from public view.
- I will interact with men in places where other people in the vicinity can potentially observe our interaction.
- If I am meeting alone with a man in a business context, I will ensure to keep the door of the room open or to meet in a room with glass walls or windows.
- If I am meeting with a man by webcam (e.g., Skype), I will observe these same precautions.

4. Communication Hedges: Inscrutable Versus Open Interaction
A Girl-Gone-Wise avoids secret communication with men.

Sin loves to remain hidden. It flourishes under the cover of secrecy. Do you think the Proverbs 7 woman would have said the same words to that young man if her husband had been standing there? Of course not. Today, many women get themselves into trouble by engaging in chat, e-mail, and text messages that are inappropriately personal or sexual in nature. They send secret messages that they would be ashamed to have others see. Girls-Gone-Wise hedge themselves by avoiding "for your eyes only" communication. They keep their communication with men as "above board" as possible. They do not keep secrets from spouses or send messages that they would be embarrassed about if intercepted. Here are my suggestions for some communication hedges:

- I will keep my electronic communication clean and pure, and free of all sexual flirtation, innuendo, and other sexual content.
- I will copy my spouse, the recipient's spouse, or other recipients if e-mails contain interaction of a personal nature.
- I will not communicate anything verbally or in writing that I would be hesitant to share with my spouse or a godly mentor.
- If I receive an inappropriate message, I will forward the message to my spouse or godly mentor and copy him or her on my response.

5. Contact Hedges: Copious Versus Controlled Contact
A Girl-Gone-Wise controls the frequency and amount of contact with men.

The more contact a man and woman have with each other, the more careful they need to be to guard against sexual impropriety. The "pull" to be together goes hand in hand with the "pull" toward sexual intimacy. Limiting contact goes a long way to diminishing the chance of falling into sexual sin. Here are some hedges that might help. Some are for married women, and some relate to interaction between unmarried couples.

- I will not initiate or reciprocate inappropriate contact with a man if one of us is married.
- If I feel "pulled" toward an adulterous relationship, I will immediately pull back and break off, or minimize contact with him.
- Before I am married, I will resist the pull to spend time with a guy as though I were married to him. I will resist the pull to be constantly together just as I resist the pull toward sexual intimacy. (You may want to limit the number of times you are together each week, based on what's appropriate for your age and circumstance.)
- I will not monopolize a guy's time or attention.

- I will not clamor for a guy's attention by sending him excessive texts or messages.
- I will not needlessly interrupt and distract him by calling and texting him when he is busy.
- I will not allow a guy to monopolize my time or attention.
- I will not neglect my obligations, responsibilities, or ministry opportunities.
- I will encourage him to attend to his obligations, responsibilities, and ministry opportunities.
- I will not neglect my family relationships or other friendships.
- I will encourage him not to neglect his family relationships or other friendships.

6. Curfew Hedges: Cover of Night Versus Light of Day Parameters
A Girl-Gone-Wise abides by curfew and nighttime boundaries.

Last summer, a female acquaintance of my son proudly told me, "I hardly ever get to bed before three!" All kinds of red flags went up in my mind. Really? I was thinking what is it that you do every night until three? I suspect it isn't anything healthy, like reading your Bible. I suspect that you're getting physical with someone you shouldn't be getting physical with, surfing to Internet sites you shouldn't visit, having conversations you shouldn't have, watching things you shouldn't watch, thinking thoughts you shouldn't think, and wasting time you shouldn't waste. Can you look me in the eyes and tell me that you do a good job of avoiding sexual sin—immorality, impurity, sensuality—in those hours between midnight and three?

My editor, who assures me she is a "chaste, middle-aged single woman," laughed when she read this passage at 2 a.m. and reminded me that some people are simply "night owls" by the way their body clocks naturally operate. If this describes you, you still need to be aware of whether the night hours induce you to sin and change any habits that you need to change.

My mom once told me, "Nothing good ever happens after midnight." I'm sure it's not literally true, but the point is well taken. The later it gets, the more tired we get, and the more we drop our guard. The more our guard drops, the more susceptible we are to sexual sin. The Bible draws a very strong connection between night, darkness, and sin. It warns us to shun darkness and love the light. This means that we must be very careful to hedge our purity by abiding by curfew and nighttime boundaries like this:

- I will keep the lights on when I am in a room with a man I am not married to.
- I will not sleep over at a man's apartment or house.
- I will be home before . . . (11 p.m., midnight, 1 a.m., etc.).
- I will turn off my computer by . . . (10 p.m., 11 p.m., midnight, 1 a.m., etc.).
- I will not send texts after . . . (9 p.m., 10 p.m., etc.).
- I will get to bed by . . . (10 p.m., 11 p.m., midnight, 1 a.m., etc.).

7. Disclosure Hedges: Deep Versus Casual Disclosure
A Girl-Gone-Wise doesn't inappropriately confide in men.

For most women, emotional intimacy precedes physical intimacy. The more emotionally connected a woman feels to a man, the greater the chance that this emotional intimacy will lead to physical intimacy. In order to guard against inappropriate sexual conduct, it's important that a woman hedges herself against deep, personal disclosure. Before marriage, she will resist disclosing too much, too soon. After marriage, she will resist disclosing her inner self to a man other than her husband. I suggest the following disclosure hedges:

- I will not disclose my inner self to a man when it is inappropriate to do so or (in the case of unmarried individuals) premature to do so.
- If I feel an emotional pull toward an illicit relationship, I will confess that pull to a trusted godly friend or mentor, so she

can pray for me and hold me accountable to maintain boundaries.

- Unless there is another person present, I will not allow a man to confide in me about difficulties he is having with his wife.
- I will not offer a man the emotional support he ought to receive from his wife.

(The following hedges are specific to married women.)

- I will only express admiration or compliments for a man in a group setting, where others can hear my remarks.
- Unless there is another person present, I will keep conversations with men on a superficial level.
- If I need to talk about struggles in my marriage, I will seek out a godly female friend or mentor and will not speak of them to another man.
- I will not seek from another man the emotional support I ought to receive from my husband.
- If I feel an emotional connection with a man that tempts me to cross any boundaries, I will immediately pull back, and tighten and strengthen the boundaries.

8. Encroachment Hedges: Wide-Open Versus Guarded Demeanor
A Girl-Gone-Wise doesn't leave herself open and unguarded.

To encroach is to exceed the proper limits of something. An encroachment hedge ensures that a woman does not invite a man to encroach on her purity. She sends the message with her appearance and body language that sexual sin is off limits. She guards her purity by the way she dresses and acts. Here are some ideas:

- I will not sit or stand too close to men.
- I will not provocatively position my body.
- I will not tease men with provocative body language.

- I will not wear revealing clothing.
- I will physically distance myself from men who encroach on my personal space.
- I will distance myself from men who fail to respect me or my standards for purity.

9. Touching Hedges: Improper Versus Proper Physical Contact
A Girl-Gone-Wise maintains strict boundaries of physical contact with men.

In the last chapter, we spent a lot of time discussing appropriate boundaries of extramarital physical contact. It's important for you to establish and maintain hedges that will help you honor those boundaries. The hedges that you decide on will help protect you when your emotions are screaming to take things further. I'm going to give you a variety of suggestions for hedges. You might come up with more on your own. Some of my suggestions relate only to unmarried women; others relate to married ones. Some are more and some are less restrictive. Some are more protective and closer to the heart of purity than others are. I hope you will aim for increasingly higher standards of purity. I challenge you to take God seriously and seek the desire of His heart. But if you disagree with the standard we discussed last chapter, or can't or won't attain it, I challenge you to put up hedges that will at the very least protect you from completely crossing over from impurity to immorality or adultery.

- I will restrict my physical contact with men to socially appropriate forms of greeting such as a handshake, hug (from the shoulders up), or, in the case of close friends or family, a peck on the cheek.
- I will not allow a man to touch parts of my body other than my hands, arms, upper back, and shoulders.
- I will dress modestly and always keep all of my clothes on when I'm with a man.

- I will not allow a man to touch parts of my body that I have covered with clothing. (Note that in Ezekiel 23:21, the Lord identifies pressing or touching breasts as lewd conduct.)
- I will not unbutton or unfasten articles of clothing and expose my nakedness to a man.
- I will not allow a man to look at or touch my private parts.
- I will not allow a man to kiss me anywhere except on the face and lips.
- I will not look at or touch a man's private parts.
- I will not lie down on a couch or bed with a man.
- I will not lie under or on top of a man, or position myself against him in any way that mimics the posture of sexual intercourse.
- I will only hold hands, kiss, and hug (from the shoulders up).
- I will save my first kiss for marriage.
- I will not touch a man in private in any way that we would not touch in public.

10. Covenant Hedges: Dishonoring Versus Honoring Marital Unions
A Girl-Gone-Wise does everything she can to honor and affirm marriage covenants.

The final type of hedge affirms and honors the sacredness of the covenant of marriage. It helps you interact with men in a way that acknowledges and affirms the vows that each of you have made. These hedges show that you have the same sort of value and respect for marriage that God does, and that you will never say or do anything to dishonor this holy institution. Here are a few, final suggestions for some covenant hedges you can establish. Again, some will apply to married, and some to unmarried women.

- I will always wear my wedding ring.

- I will reinforce the fact that I am "one" with my husband by mentioning him and by using inclusive words like "we," "us," and "our" when I talk about my personal life.
- I will affirm and support the marriage of others by inquiring about their spouses and acknowledging them in verbal and written conversation.
- I will try to get to know the wives of men I interact with and, whenever possible, relate to the husband and wife together, as a couple.
- I will never say or do anything to threaten or diminish the sanctity of marriage.

A GOLD RING IN A PIG'S SNOUT

Miguel De Cervantes, the author of the classic novel *Don Quixote*, once said, "No padlocks, bolts, or bars can secure a maiden better than her own reserve."[1] He lived in the 1500s, when society expected fathers to guard the purity of their unmarried daughters. Cervantes argued that the personal hedges a woman puts up around her sexual purity protect her far more effectively than her father or anything else ever would or could. That was certainly in line with the thinking of King Solomon, the Sage Father. He said that people fall into sin because they don't take the necessary personal precautions to avoid it. They lack discretion.

Discretion is exercising good judgment and foresight to avoid danger and do the right thing. Solomon told his son that a beautiful woman without discretion is like a gold ring in a pig's snout (Proverbs 11:22). Given that the Jews regarded pigs as filthy, unclean animals, this is a shocking image. It implies that women who lack discretion are shameful. Solomon wanted his son to avoid them at all costs. In essence he said something like this, "Son, a woman may be exceedingly beautiful, but if she lacks discretion, she'll pull you down in the mud where you'll wallow like disgusting pigs. Be on guard against beautiful women who fail to discern and maintain proper boundaries."

When you establish a hedge, you choose, ahead of time, to live by that protective policy. You choose to exercise discretion. Knowing what your hedges are will help guide you when you encounter a potentially compromising situation. For example, if a male colleague asks me to lunch, I might say, "Can Susan join us? I have a policy that I don't do lunch alone with men." The hedge gives me the freedom to relate to the colleague within appropriate boundaries. It helps keep the relationship pure. It honors my marriage and my colleague's too. It keeps the relationship on track and prevents it from taking a wrong turn.

I've suggested numerous ideas for ways you can hedge your sexual purity. If you have a few years of womanhood under your belt, you've probably already figured out that you need to have hedges. If you're like me, you figured it out by bumping your nose against situations where someone misunderstood your intent or where you naively left yourself in an exposed position by not having a clear hedge. It took me quite a while, as a newlywed, to figure out that I couldn't hang out and be friends with guys in the same way I did before I was married. Other than the general encouragement to remain a virgin until marriage and not to cheat on my husband after marriage, no one ever sat me down and challenged me to think through and establish clear protective hedges in my relationships with men. So now that I've figured some things out, that's what I am challenging you to do. Far too many women are careless and overconfident, and foolishly leap over restrictions. I think of the untold pain and heartache that women I've ministered to would have saved themselves if only they had exercised discretion and guarded their sexual purity. So I challenge you to come up with a list of personal hedges. Write them down. Have a friend hold you accountable.

I'll borrow the words that the Sage Father spoke to his son and speak them as though I were a sage mother: "My daughters, do not lose sight of these—keep sound wisdom and discretion" (Proverbs 3:21). "Discretion will watch over you, understanding will guard you, delivering you from the way of evil" (Proverbs 2:11–12). Hedge your sexual purity. Be a Girl-Gone-Wise.

(Do you have a comment or question about boundaries? You can visit the website GirlsGoneWise.com and post it there.)

Point of Contrast #12

AUTHENTICITY
Her Public Versus Private Persona

Girl-Gone-Wild: **Two-Faced**	Girl-Gone-Wise: **Genuine**
"With bold face she says to him, 'I had to offer sacrifices, and today I have paid my vows.'" (Proverbs 7:13–14)	"She who walks in integrity walks securely." (Proverbs 10:9)

M r. Facing-Both-Ways. His name says it all. This allegorical character in John Bunyan's classic book, *Pilgrim's Progress*, was two-faced. One face pointed toward the Celestial City, and the other pointed toward the City of Destruction. Scripture talks about people who have a double heart, and are double-minded, double-tongued, and double-faced. The Proverbs 7 woman is a prime example of this kind of individual. As the story unfolds, the narrator tells us that she seizes and kisses the young man, "and with bold face she says to him, 'I had to offer sacrifices, and today I have paid my vows.'" The face she showed when she worshiped together with people at church wasn't the same brash face she showed after church, on that back lane, hidden in the shadows. She was duplicitous. A hypocrite. Ms. Facing-Both-Ways.

Authenticity is another point of contrast between a Girl-Gone-Wise and a Girl-Gone-Wild. A Girl-Gone-Wise is genuine. Her public persona is congruent with her private one. The outside matches the inside—the visible matches the unseen. She is a woman of integrity. Her counterpart, the Girl-Gone-Wild, is two-faced. She wants people to think she is something that she is not. She puts on a religious face to impress, but secretly behaves in a way that is totally at odds with the faith she professes. She's the type of girl who religiously attends Saturday-night service with her boyfriend, sings on the worship team, and then sleeps with him in the back of the car after the church parking lot has emptied.

TWO-FACED HYPOCRISY

The rendezvous between the Proverbs 7 woman and the young man took place in the evening. She tells him that she had "paid her vows" earlier that day. Paying vows indicates that she had asked God for something and had promised to express her gratitude when He answered her prayers. She obviously got whatever it was she asked for, because on the day they met up, she fulfilled her promise. She went to the temple to offer a special kind of sacrifice to God—a vow offering (Leviticus 7:16).

The vow offering differed from other offerings in several ways. First, unlike a sin offering, a vow offering wasn't required. It was a voluntary offering, which an Israelite could offer at virtually any time. Second, the giver was to bring loaves of freshly baked leavened bread, unleavened pastries, and cakes to accompany the meat sacrifice. Third, while some offerings belonged completely to God and others were apportioned to the priests, the vow offering was a fellowship offering that everyone shared. The Lord got the inner, fatty portions of the animal, the priest got the breast and right thigh, and the person offering the sacrifice got the rest of the meat to take home. Each party also received loaves, pastries, and cakes.

Finally, this type of offering was unique in that there was a celebratory meal associated with it. The entire family joined in eating it.

The communal feast symbolized fellowship with God and with one another. Since the meal was holy, the guests had to be ceremonially holy in order to partake. They had to clean themselves up, and wash and change their clothes and dress up for the occasion. Impurity excluded them from participation. The celebration could last a couple of days, but the rules stipulated that on day three, all leftovers had to be burned (Leviticus 7:11–21; 19:5–8; 1 Samuel 20:26).

The vow offering was supposed to be a holy symbol of communion with God, but this woman used it as a crafty ploy to entice the young man over to her house. I suspect she let him know ahead of time that she was going to make this type of sacrifice. Perhaps she flattered him by telling him that his friendship was the answer to her prayers—*he* was the reason for her vow offering. She probably informed him that if he didn't join her, she would be left to celebrate the feast alone, and the food would go to waste. She likely pressured him by implying that if he didn't help her fulfill her obligation to partake in a communal meal, her hopes would be dashed, all her work would be for naught, and her offering would be ruined.

It's quite obvious that the woman's sacrifice was motivated by her desire to fellowship with the young man more than her desire to fellowship with God. Her husband was gone, so why else did she choose that day to make the type of sacrifice that required a communal meal? Why would she go to the trouble of preparing the bread, pastries, cake, meat, and other delicacies for the feast if she was the only one who would partake? Why go to the temple that day if she didn't already have the seduction in mind? And why did the young man wander over to her neighborhood on that particular night if she hadn't made the invitation clear? When she saw him, why did she confirm that the fellowship meal was waiting on her table? It didn't all happen by chance. It's clear to me that the sacrifice was part of her crafty, manipulative plan.

The Proverbs 7 Wild Thing was a hypocrite. Her religious behavior was a farce. A hypocrite is a person who deliberately and habitually professes to be good when she is aware that she is not. The word itself is a transliteration of the Greek word *hypokrites*, which means *play actor* or *stage player*. In ancient Greek comedies and tragedies, *hypokrites* wore masks. The mask was the most essential part of the *hypokrite's* costume. The *hypokrite* hid behind the mask, and the mask projected the necessary image. Hiding their true selves behind a mask is what hypocrites do.

SIGNS OF HYPOCRISY

Jesus had an ongoing conflict with His two-faced religious opponents, the scribes and Pharisees. He repeatedly called them to task for their hypocritical behavior. His run-ins with them demonstrate how much the Lord hates it when people playact at loving God. Their interactions with Christ reveal seven signs of hypocrisy, many of which are evident in the life of the Wild Thing of Proverbs 7.

Contradiction

The first sign of hypocrisy is contradiction. A hypocrite is a pretender who honors the Lord with her lips, but her heart is far from Him (Matthew 15:8). There's a fundamental contradiction between who she is when people are looking and who she is when they aren't. Jesus said:

> Woe to you, scribes and Pharisees, hypocrites! For you are like whitewashed tombs, which outwardly appear beautiful, but within are full of dead people's bones and all uncleanness. So you also outwardly appear righteous to others, but within you are full of hypocrisy and lawlessness. (Matthew 23:27–28)

This type of incongruence is evident in the Proverbs 7 woman. She knew that partaking in a vow offering demanded that she be outwardly and inwardly clean. She pretended to be pure, but all the while was planning that night's illicit encounter. Her words and behavior didn't match up. There was a contradiction. Just like Melissa, the young woman who had a long chat about sexual purity with her boyfriend's mother, Nicole. Melissa feigned concern that the girls in her class were losing their virginity, but just a few hours later, she stripped down naked on screen for her boyfriend in their nightly sex-video encounter. The contradiction mortified Nicole when she took a load of laundry into her son's bedroom and happened upon the scene.

What Melissa said didn't add up with what she did. Her life was a contradiction.

A wild, two-faced woman is extremely clever at deception. She is often successful in keeping the contradiction hidden. But someone who is discerning can usually sense that things in her life aren't quite right. She is not who she makes herself out to be. She acts like a good girl, but a naughty bad-girl streak percolates under the surface. The double-minded woman is actually dishonest with herself and others. She uses truth and lies in whatever way they will best benefit her. Godly people who interact with her have the uneasy feeling that she's not being totally honest and up front. Incongruities exist.

Although a two-faced woman is usually an excellent pretender, the Lord won't tolerate her behavior forever. At some point in time, He'll expose her—just like He exposed Melissa's true nature to her boyfriend's mother, Nicole. Jesus warned, "Beware of the leaven of the Pharisees, which is hypocrisy. Nothing is covered up that will not be revealed, or hidden that will not be known. Therefore whatever you have said in the dark shall be heard in the light, and what you have whispered in private rooms shall be proclaimed on the housetops" (Luke 12:1–3).

A Girl-Gone-Wise isn't afraid of being found out. She's authentic. She's honest about her struggles, and does not try to hide. Who she is in public is the same as who she is in private. There is no deceit and no contradiction.

Self-Indulgence

The second sign of hypocrisy is self-indulgence. Jesus said, "Woe to you, scribes and Pharisees, hypocrites! For you clean the outside of the cup and the plate, but inside they are full of greed and self-indulgence" (Matthew 23:25). A hypocrite is a lover of pleasure rather than a lover of God (2 Timothy 3:4–5). She treats God like a vending machine. She puts her coins of religious conduct into the slot and expects Him to dispense the goods she wants. The Proverbs 7 woman fulfilled her vow to God, because in her opinion, He was giving her exactly what she wanted to get. The problem is, she expected God to do what she wanted, but didn't have any intention of doing what He wanted.

According to Scripture, this self-indulgent vending machine perspective is common among double-minded people. They constantly ask the Lord for things, but they ask for the wrong things, to indulge their worldly passions. They also have a wrong perspective about God. They suspect that He's stingy, vengeful, and withholds from them the very things that would bring them happiness. They question whether He really has their best interests at heart. A double-minded person "must not suppose that [she] will receive anything from the Lord" (James 1:7). This isn't because God doesn't want to give—but because she doesn't want to receive what He wants to give. She doesn't want to change her sinful behavior and desires. James explains:

> You ask and do not receive, because you ask wrongly, to spend it on your passions. You adulterous people! Do you not know that friendship with the world is enmity with God? Therefore whoever wishes to be a friend of the world makes himself an enemy of God. . . . Draw near to God, and he will draw near to you. Cleanse your hands, you sinners, and purify your hearts, you double-minded. (James 4:3–4, 8)

Focus on Externals

The third sign of hypocrisy is a focus on externals. The scribes and Pharisees "do all their deeds to be seen by others" (Matthew 23:5). They draw people's attention to their "goodness" so that "they may be praised by others" (Matthew 6:2). Two-faced people want others to think that they are very spiritual and have enviable morals. They are very concerned about outward appearances—how they look to others and what people think about them.

The Proverbs 7 woman was concerned about appearances. Otherwise, she wouldn't have bothered going to the temple that day. The priests and the other people milling around probably thought she was very devout. And from all outward appearances, she was. She was careful to draw attention to the good things she did in order to cultivate her "good girl" image.

Partial Obedience

Jesus criticized the scribes and Pharisees for partial obedience. They did some small things right—like tithing everything, down to mint and dill and cumin—but "neglected the weightier matters of the law: justice and mercy and faithfulness" (Matthew 23:23–24). Because they didn't wholeheartedly obey the Lord, their religious behavior was worthless. They totally missed the point.

The Proverbs 7 woman missed the point when she got the particulars of her vow offering right, but failed to address the glaring sin in her heart. Outwardly, she was clean—but because she neglected the weightier matter of inner purity, she totally missed the point. Two-faced people are very selective about which parts of Scripture they choose to obey.

Rationalization

Rationalization of sin is the fifth sign of hypocrisy. The scribes and Pharisees were masters at rationalizing sin. They came up with elaborate loopholes and arguments to justify disobeying God. Jesus accused them of "void[ing] the word of God" with their clever rationalizations (Matthew 15:3–6).

Over the years, I've heard innumerable rationalizations for immorality and impurity: "If God is love, how can our love be wrong?" "My husband doesn't love me." "We're going to get married anyway." "I prayed about leaving my husband." "God made us with sexual needs that must be fulfilled." "It isn't wrong if we don't go all the way." On and on the rationalizing goes. Hypocrites always find a way to justify their two-faced behavior. The Proverbs 7 woman undoubtedly rationalized her behavior. The Sage Father said, "This is the way of an adulteress: she eats and wipes her mouth and says, 'I have done no wrong'" (Proverbs 30:20).

Contempt

Hypocrites are full of contempt. They look down on others (Luke 18:11–12). They see the "speck" in another person's eye, but fail to notice the log in their own (Matthew 7:5). They have unrealistically high expectations of what other people should do, but aren't willing to apply that same standard to themselves (Matthew 23:4). They are highly critical when other people fail. They self-righteously think that they are beyond such weakness (Matthew 23:29–30). They feel malice toward anyone who tries to teach or correct them (Matthew 22:18). They easily take offense (Matthew 15:12).

Chameleon-Like Conduct

Hypocrites are like chameleons. They change color depending on which environment they are in. My friend Nate said of a common friend, "The Krista you get at a party is different than the Krista you get at church. She's only as spiritual as the people she's with." The scribes and Pharisees were like that. They were different people when they were out in public than they were at home (Luke 13:15). Their conduct changed depending on their environment. The Proverbs 7 woman was also guilty of chameleon-like conduct. Like Krista, she was only as spiritual as the situation demanded. The woman the worshipers saw at church in the light of day presented herself in a much different way than the woman who emerged dressed like a prostitute to seduce her prey at night.

ABOUT FACE

Two-Face is a fictional DC Comics super villain who first appeared in the classic Batman comic book series in 1942. He goes insane and becomes the crime boss Two-Face after sulfuric acid hideously disfigures the left side of his face. Two-Face does not consistently do evil. Every time he contemplates a crime, he flips his two-headed coin. If the coin lands unmarred side up, he refrains from evil and resigns himself to doing good. He turns his good face to the world. If it lands defaced side up, he boldly goes ahead and commits the crime. The Girl-Gone-Wild is like that. She flips the coin of public opinion to determine what she should do. If the situation demands that she show a good face, she displays that side of her persona. But if it doesn't, she boldly goes ahead with the sinful desires of her heart.

The Lord despises hypocritical behavior. He says, "I cannot endure iniquity and solemn assembly" (Isaiah 1:11–17). For Him, an unrepentant heart and religious behavior don't mix. Do you recognize any of the signs of hypocrisy in your life? If you are honest, I think you'll be able to identify tendencies toward contradiction, self-indulgence, focus on externals, partial obedience, rationalization, contemptuousness, or chameleon-like conduct in yourself. At least I hope you do. I can certainly see some of those sins in my life. The problem is not when we fight against hypocrisy in our lives—but when we don't. All of us have a long way to go when it comes to true authenticity.

The passage in James 4:3–8 explains that the way to combat double-mindedness is to draw near to God, to examine our lives constantly for sin, and to humbly repent. "Cleanse your hands, you sinners, and purify your hearts, you double-minded." A Girl-Gone-Wise is concerned about keeping the inner, hidden parts of her life just as pure as the outer, visible ones. She fights against hypocrisy in her life. She knows that the two-faced woman will be found out, but one who walks in integrity walks securely (Proverbs 10:9).

Point of Contrast #13

NEEDINESS
Whom She Depends on to Fulfill Her Longings

<table>
<tr><td>Girl-Gone-Wild:
Depends on Man</td><td>Girl-Gone-Wise:
Depends on God</td></tr>
</table>

"So now I have come
out to meet you,
to seek you eagerly,
and I have found you."

(Proverbs 7:15)

She delights in the Lord,
and He will give her her
heart's desires.

(Psalm 37:4)

He's out with a terrible case of CGS." That's what my son's twenty-year-old neighborhood friend, Warren, said, dropping himself into a wing chair in the family room. Jonathan sighed and nodded his head knowingly, disappointed that their friend had to miss the evening's planned activities.

"CGS?" I asked, alarmed, "What's CGS?" I had visions of their friend lying quarantined in a hospital room, hooked up to a respirator, with tubes sticking out from all over his body, surrounded by masked doctors and nurses talking in hushed tones. I asked, "Is it serious? Is he going to be OK?"

Warren looked at me with a deadpan expression and explained, "CGS—Clingy Girlfriend Syndrome. It is serious, and *no*, he's not OK. He's suffocating to death." I just about fell out of my chair laughing. I knew exactly what he was talking about. And so do you. Some women are so needy for attention and affirmation that they cling to men like plastic wrap to a piece of raw meat. The young man couldn't come to his scheduled outing because his girlfriend didn't want to spend the evening alone. She insisted that *her* needs take precedence over his wanting to spend time with his friends.

As the Proverbs 7 narrative unfolds, we see the woman expressing her ardent desire to be with the young man. She hopes and expects that he will come to her house and meet her needs. She's spent the whole day preparing for this possibility. She says, "So now I have come out to meet you, to *seek you eagerly*, and I have found you." She strokes the young man's ego by emphasizing his importance to her: "I have come out to meet *you*, to seek *you* eagerly . . . *You* are the man of my dreams! *You* are so amazing, so strong, so handsome, so right for me! *You* are the only one who can help me! *You* are the one I've been waiting for! I'm so glad that I found *you*!" She puffs up the young man's head to think that he is the only one who can rescue her from her loveless plight. He's her knight in shining armor, her savior. But the truth is, her flattery has very little to do with him being sensational and very much to do with her being needy. He is merely a means to a perceived end. She's only interested in him because she thinks he will satisfy her desires.

A Girl-Gone-Wild looks to men to fulfill the deep longings of her heart. She relies on them for her sense of self-worth. She is needy and dependent. A Girl-Gone-Wise knows that no man on the face of earth could ever fill the God-shaped vacuum in her heart. She doesn't depend on men for her sense of self. She delights in the Lord and depends on Him to give her the desires of her heart.

LOOKING FOR LOVE

The prophet Jeremiah tells the story of a woman desperate for love. As a young bride, she loved her husband—she delighted in him as he delighted in her. Then, her commitment was tested. Other men enticed her with the passion, thrill, and adventure of illicit sex. She took the bait. Lover after lover passed through her arms. With each one, her level of satisfaction decreased, and her level of desperation increased. She ended up so needy and so skilled in the art of pursuing illicit love, that even the most experienced whore could learn new secrets of seduction by observing her tactics. "How well you direct your course to seek love! So that even to wicked women you have taught your ways" (Jeremiah 2:33).

Who is this needy woman? It's God's bride, the nation Israel. In Jeremiah's time, she turned her back on her exclusive devotion to God and made alliances with the surrounding nations, embracing their morals and their gods. She played the whore by forsaking His love and pursuing relationships with them. She looked to them instead of Him to meet her needs. But the meaning of this allegory is much broader than that particular historical situation. It's also a lesson for women today.

Martin Luther once said, "Whatever your heart clings to and confides in, that is really your god."[1] Most women yearn to find love in the arms of a man. Their heart yearns for earthly romance more than it yearns for the reality to which it points. Romance is the hope they cling to and confide in. Romance is their god. Jeremiah's narrative portrays their story. It speaks to all of us who "direct our course to seek love"—and who turn to men rather than God to find it. It tells the parable of every woman who feels deep desires, longings, and needs, and tries to fulfill them in the wrong place and in the wrong way.

The tragedy in Jeremiah's tale is that the woman foolishly turned her back on the true lover who could meet her needs and embraced false lovers, who couldn't possibly satisfy the desires of her heart. The Lord told His bride that it was as though she had spurned a natural spring of pure, fresh water and sought instead to satisfy her thirst with the stagnant water from a self-made, leaky cistern. He says, "My people have committed two evils: they have forsaken me, the fountain of living waters, and hewed out cisterns for themselves, broken cisterns that can hold no water" (Jeremiah 2:13). Later He even curses those who would make such a choice:

> Cursed is the man who trusts in man and makes flesh his strength, whose heart turns away from the Lord. He is like a shrub in the desert, and shall

not see any good come. He shall dwell in the parched places of the wilderness, in an uninhabited salt land.

Blessed is the man who trusts in the Lord, whose trust is the Lord. He is like a tree planted by water, that sends out its roots by the stream, and does not fear when heat comes, for its leaves remain green, and is not anxious in the year of drought, for it does not cease to bear fruit. (Jeremiah 17:5–8)

The most reliable and refreshing sources of water in the land of Israel were its natural springs. This water was dependable, and its clear, cool consistency was satisfying. In contrast, the most unreliable sources of water were cisterns. Cisterns were large pits dug into porous limestone rock and coated with plaster, to prevent leakage. These pits gathered rainwater. The water was brackish and stale, and if the rains didn't come, they could dry up. Worse yet, if a cistern developed a crack, it wouldn't hold the water. The water leaked through the plaster into the limestone beneath. To turn from a dependable, pure stream of running water to a broken, briny cistern was idiotic. Yet this is exactly what the woman in Jeremiah's account did. She turned away from what would undeniably quench her thirst to what could undeniably not.

This text presents a picture of the contrast between a Girl-Gone-Wise and a Girl-Gone-Wild. A Girl-Gone-Wild relies on her own devices to quench her thirsty heart. She hews out a relationship and expects that it will meet her needs. She scoops out as much water from the leaky cistern as she can, but at some point, realizes that she's still not satisfied, and that the water she has greedily sipped has left a bitter taste in her mouth. Her heart feels parched—like a dry, brittle bush in a desolate desert. She has no roots. She feels her spirit wither up. But instead of planting herself next to the stream, she desperately tries to suck more water from her cistern, or she hews out another cistern with the unrealistic hope that there she will find water that is plentiful and sweet.

The Girl-Gone-Wise does not "trust in man and make flesh her strength." Her heart relies on the Lord. She is "like a tree planted by water, that sends out its roots by the stream, and does not fear when heat comes, for its leaves remain green, and is not anxious in the year of drought, for it does not cease to bear fruit."

The image is a powerful one. It's not that the wise woman never experiences pressure-cooker "heat" in her relationships—or that she never faces a year of relational drought. But she withstands those tough times. She doesn't get fearful or anxious when they come, because her relationship with the Lord nourishes and sustains her. She doesn't rely on the cistern. She doesn't dry up spiritually or emotionally when a man disappoints her. She doesn't have to hew out cistern after cistern after cistern, desperately trying to find the water she needs. Her roots go deep. If the love of her life disappoints, betrays, and wounds her—or even if she never marries—she will not dry up. Her leaves will remain green, and she will not cease to lead a spiritually productive and satisfying life. Her well-being does not depend on a man.

The passages in Jeremiah (2:13; 17:5–8) demonstrate that looking for love the wild way differs substantially from looking for it the wise way. Here are two lists that summarize how:

LOOKING FOR LOVE THE WILD WAY

- She forgets or neglects her relationship with God ("whose heart turns away from the Lord").
- She thinks that a relationship with a man will (or ought to) meet her emotional needs ("trusts in man and makes flesh her strength").
- Her heart feels lonely and needy ("uninhabited salt land," "parched places").
- She hacks and digs at the relationship, and makes demands of her man to get him to fill her perceived need ("hew[s] out cisterns for [herself]").
- She demands that the relationship provide her with something it cannot possibly provide ("cisterns that can hold no water").
- Her relationship repeatedly disappoints her ("broken cisterns").

- She feels anxious and afraid when the relationship falters ("fears when heat comes," "anxious in the year of drought").
- Her heart slowly shrivels and dies ("like a shrub in the desert").

- Her life is spiritually barren and unproductive ("shall not see any good come").

LOOKING FOR LOVE THE WISE WAY

- She faithfully pursues a relationship with God. (She "trusts in the Lord." She has not "forsaken" Him.)
- She knows that only a relationship with God can meet her deepest needs. She does not depend on men to do this ("whose trust is the Lord").
- Her relationship with God nourishes her spirit ("like a tree planted by water").
- She sends her roots deep into God's stream to meet her emotional needs. She does not demand emotional satisfaction from people ("sends out its roots by the stream").
- She knows that the Lord will sustain her if a love relationship goes through difficult times or in the absence of such a relationship ("does not fear when heat comes"; "is not anxious in the year of drought").
- Her heart remains alive and grounded in God's love, regardless of the state of her earthly relationships ("leaves remain green").
- Her life is spiritually fruitful and productive, regardless of the state of her earthly relationships ("does not cease to bear fruit").

Which way best characterizes the way you look for love? The Girl-Gone-Wild puts her trust in man—she looks for some guy to be her savior. She tries to monopolize his time and attention and makes demands to try to get what she wants. The Girl-Gone-Wise trusts in the Lord. She has a Savior, so she doesn't need or expect a guy to meet her deepest needs. She is not desperate for a man. It's not that she wouldn't enjoy a healthy relationship. She would. But she draws her identity and strength from a much more reliable source.

DESPERATE GIRLFRIENDS— DESPERATE HOUSEWIVES

To introduce a talk, I once showed the classic Walt Disney clip of Snow White singing "Someday My Prince Will Come" to a roomful of college-aged girls. Their response was dramatic. Many raised arms in the air and shouted, "Yes!" Some stood on their chairs with their hands clasped over their hearts. Some whooped. Some cheered. Some hollered. Some pretended to swoon. One or two had tears streaming down their cheeks.

The response when I showed the same clip to a room full of mostly married middle-aged women, several weeks later, could not have been more different. Most looked disinterested. Many laughed and sneered. Some rolled their eyes. Some shrugged a shoulder and went back to having conversations with their girlfriends. Not one woman pumped her arm and shouted, "Yes!" Not one.

The reactions were telling. The college girls had hearts filled with hope of meeting their Prince Charming and living happily ever after. They eagerly anticipated that marrying Mr. McDreamy would fulfill their desire. The middle-aged women had hearts filled with cynicism because their Prince Charming hadn't delivered the happily-ever-after ending they had hoped for. Mr. McDreamy had turned into Mr. McDreary and Mr. McDumpy. They had the gut-wrenching suspicion that no one would ever meet the longings of their hearts. The nods, tears, and "yeses" for these women came when I talked about the pain of disappointment. It's not that their desire had died. It's just that they were wearied and wounded from all the years of hoping and yearning. They were tired of trying to squeeze water out of a broken, empty cistern. They still hadn't found what they were looking for.

So what are we to make of all the longing? To quench their thirst, many women spin themselves around in endless circles of desire, dissipation, and disappointment. I think of my high school girlfriend, Michelle, who has experienced numerous failed relationships: two or three serious boyfriends, two common-law relationships, one broken engagement, and one failed marriage. When we had dinner several years ago, her desire and desperation had reached a frenzied level. This forty-year-old was dating and sleeping with three different guys at the same time. "I just wish I could find someone to love me," she lamented, with eyes brim-full of tears.

C. S. Lewis once wrote, "What does not satisfy when we find it, was not the thing we were desiring."[2] He suggested that we can best describe the restless desire that exists in the human heart with the German word *Sehnsucht*. My parents were German immigrants, and my first language was German, so let me try to explain the word. There really is no adequate English equivalent. It's a quasi-mystical term that melds ardent inner longing or yearning (*das Sehnen*) with obsession or addiction (*die Sucht*). *Sehnsucht* is a deep, driven, inconsolable inner longing for something of monumental importance.

Sehnsucht compels us to reach for an ultimate answer that remains just beyond our reach. Some people experience it as a type of nostalgia, others as a type of homesickness. Others think that it's a longing for someone they have not yet met or something they have not yet attained. They think that if they only meet that "someone" or get that "something," their desire will be satisfied. The majority of people who feel *Sehnsucht* are not conscious of who or what the longed-for object might be.

King David knew. He said, "As a deer pants for flowing streams, so pants my soul for you, O God. My soul thirsts for God, for the living God. When shall I come and appear before God?" (Psalm 42:1–2). *Sehnsucht* is the deep, inner "panting" of our spirits for God. The human soul was made to enjoy something that is never fully given—that cannot even be imagined as given—in our present mode of existence. *Sehnsucht* is a longing for God that only God can fill, but cannot fill completely until we see Him face-to-face. Even the satisfaction and joy we can taste in His presence now is shot through with longing. It's like a woman enthralled to hear the voice of a distant lover, but craving the moment he will hold her in his arms. *Sehnsucht* beckons and whispers, points and draws us to the time when we will finally be united with the lover and redeemer of our souls.

When women feel *Sehnsucht*, many identify it as a desire to be the leading lady in a passionate romance. They think that finding a soul mate is the only thing that will fulfill their longing. That's what my friend Michelle thinks. In one sense, she's right. Her *Sehnsucht is* beckoning her to take part in a passionate romance—but not the one she's obsessed with finding. It's beckoning her to look past that image and reach for the reality it represents. Earthly romances are to the Cosmic One like sparkling reflections of light dancing on water are to the blazing sun. They are not the fiery light. They only reflect fleeting glimmers of it.

Michelle's neediness is not, in and of itself, a bad thing. She's just pinned it to the wrong hope. Looking to man to give what only God can supply is an exercise in futility, frustration, and pain. And it can lead farther and farther away from the place where that longing can truly be fulfilled. The Girl-Gone-Wise knows what the deep longing in her spirit is all about. So when she feels needy, she directs her longing and sighing Godward (Psalm 38:9). She understands that only as she delights herself in the Lord, will her needs be met. He is the One who gives her the desires of her heart.

Point of Contrast #14

POSSESSIONS
How She Handles Her
Money and Resources

Girl-Gone-Wild: Indulgent	Girl-Gone-Wise: Circumspect
"I have spread my couch with coverings, colored linens from Egyptian linen; I have perfumed my bed with myrrh, aloes, and cinnamon." (Proverbs 7:16–17)	"She opens her hand to the poor and reaches out her hands to the needy. . . . She makes bed coverings for herself . . ." (Proverbs 31:20–22)

S mart Girls Get More" is a wildly successful ad campaign that promotes the United Kingdom's bestselling young women's magazine, *More*. The message shouts from billboards, buses, TV commercials, radio spots, sponsorships, and competitions. It inundates British women with the idea that if they are smart, they will get more—more men, more sex, more celebrity gossip, more beauty, more fashion, more products, and, of course, more of the magazine that supplies all the latest and greatest information on these pleasures. "Cuz Smart Girls Get More!"

Although that particular ad campaign hasn't run in North America, it's the clandestine message of virtually all mass-marketing efforts. Merchandisers want to convince us that we need more of whatever it is they are selling. The Bible's perspective differs from the world's. Constantly buying more stuff isn't a trait of a woman who's smart; it's a hallmark of a Girl-Gone-Wild. The Wild Thing is an indulgent, voracious consumer who pursues pleasure through the purchase of material goods. A Girl-Gone-Wise thinks differently about the way she spends her money. She's circumspect. She understands that everything she has comes from God. She tries to honor Him by being a good steward of all her resources. She treasures the riches of the Kingdom more than the riches of the world.

DESIGNER LABEL DESIRE

As we rejoin the story of our Proverbs 7 woman, we see her trying to pique the young man's interest by describing her bedroom: "I have spread my couch with coverings, colored linens from Egyptian linen; I have perfumed my bed with myrrh, aloes, and cinnamon."

When the woman tells the young man about her couch and then later mentions her bed, she's not talking about two separate pieces of furniture. In Palestine, people commonly slept on the floor on mats that they could roll up and store during the day or they slept on multipurpose mud-brick benches. But if their beds were pieces of furniture with legs, they could also use the word *couch* to describe them (Job 7:13; Psalm 6:6). A couch was a specific type of bed—just like a recliner is a specific type of chair. The woman uses the word *couch* to let the young man know exactly what type of bed she has. Given the space restrictions of most homes, a couch-bed was an impractical extravagance that few could afford or would allow themselves to indulge in. She wanted to let him know that she didn't sleep on a pallet on the floor like a lowly commoner. Her bed was a couch. It was a luxury item.

The woman also makes sure to mention that she had spread her bed with coverings of delicate cushions and with linens imported from Egypt. Egyptian linen was the finest and most desirable cloth in the world. Its coolness, luster, softness, and strength set it apart from less expensive material. The woman emphasizes that her linens are colored—they're even more splendid and exclusive than uncolored ones. The dyes used in antiquity were costly, since artisans obtained them from the bodies of insects or mollusks, or from the petals and heads of flowers. Colored Egyptian linens were a particularly opulent indulgence.

The Proverbs 7 woman was undoubtedly trying to impress and allure the young man with the description of the exquisite designer label décor in her bedroom. I'm sure he was "wowed." His eyebrows probably rose even farther when he heard that she had perfumed her linens with myrrh, aloes, and cinnamon. Myrrh was a spice native to Arabia, aloe came from India or China, and cinnamon came from the east coast of Africa and Ceylon. These imported fragrances were exotic and pricey. She makes it clear that she spared no expense in preparing for their night of romance. She had prepared a sumptuous feast for his palate and for his senses, and was inviting him to indulge.

The fact that the woman takes such care to detail the extravagant luxury of her possessions gives us a clue as to her attitude toward them. It's clear she has an underlying attitude of self-importance and self-indulgence. She wants the young man to be impressed and to hold her in high regard. She wants him to admire her and desires to charm him with all her finery. She wants him to affirm that she is really something. She's like the harlot, Lady Babylon, who indulged in the "power of her luxurious living" and in the "passion of her sexual immorality," and seduced nations to "drink [her] wine" (Revelation 18:3).

The passage in Revelation informs us that Lady Babylon was a greedy consumer. She was a shopaholic who bought all sorts of exotic imported merchandise:

> gold, silver, jewels, pearls, fine linen, purple cloth, silk, scarlet cloth, all kinds of scented wood, all kinds of articles of ivory, all kinds of articles of costly wood, bronze, iron and marble, cinnamon, spice, incense, myrrh, frankincense, wine, oil, fine flour, wheat, cattle and sheep, horses and chariots, and slaves, that is, human souls.

She was extremely fond of these "delicacies" and "splendors." In her mind, they were status symbols—must-have items. The latest and greatest in Babylon's *More* magazine was "the fruit for which [her] soul longed" (18:12–14).

Nowadays, we've substituted designer jeans for purple cloth, satin sheets for fine linen, French perfume for frankincense, five-star restaurants for cattle and sheep, BMWs for horses and chariots, nannies and housekeepers for slaves, but we're just as greedy and self-indulgent. Like Lady Babylon and the Proverbs 7 woman, we're caught up in the endless quest for more. We spend and spend, even if we don't have the money.

A Girl-Gone-Wild is a voracious consumer. She treasures the things of this world more than she treasures Jesus Christ. She settles for fleeting pleasures that do not satisfy her deepest needs, and that, in the end, ultimately destroy her soul. The world tells us that smart girls get more. But Scripture says that if we're truly smart, we won't settle for the "more" the world can offer. We'll want immeasurably more than its cheap, temporary thrills. The problem is not that we desire beautiful and precious things, but that we have a faulty perception about what is most beautiful and most precious. We settle for treasures that wear out, break down, and can be stolen, when we ought to set our hearts on riches that last forever.

RESOURCE MANAGEMENT

Jesus told a parable in Luke 16 that illustrated what our attitude toward possessions ought to be. The story focused on a manager who was in charge of running a wealthy business owner's company. The owner heard that the manager was being irresponsible and reckless, wasting company resources. So the owner called him up, asked for a record of accounts, and gave him notice that his job would soon end. Upon hearing this, the manager decided he'd do his best to secure his future by doing a big favor for some of his boss's clients. The manager offered to write off a large portion of their debts if they immediately settled their accounts. He hoped that they'd remember the favor and be kind to him when he became unemployed. The business owner admitted that the manager was very shrewd in making sure he'd have friends after his job ended. Even though the manager was wasteful and irresponsible, the owner commended him for this. Jesus wraps up the story by saying:

> I tell you, use worldly wealth to gain friends for yourselves, so that when it is gone, you will be welcomed into eternal dwellings.

Whoever can be trusted with very little can also be trusted with much, and whoever is dishonest with very little will also be dishonest with much. So if you have not been trustworthy in handling worldly wealth, who will trust you with true riches? And if you have not been trustworthy with someone else's property, who will give you property of your own?

No servant can serve two masters. Either he will hate the one and love the other, or he will be devoted to the one and despise the other. You cannot serve both God and Money. . . . What is highly valued among men is detestable in God's sight. (Luke 16:9–13, 15 NIV)

Jesus' teaching contains several lessons for us about how we should manage our resources. The first lesson is about ownership. We often think that if we give the Lord a portion of our earnings, the rest of the money is ours to spend as we wish. But this parable teaches that everything we have belongs to God. Everything. Nothing is really "ours." We are just managers, not owners. And God doesn't like it when we're reckless and wasteful with His resources. We will answer to Him for the way we spend the money, time, talents, and gifts that He entrusts to us. So if I'm considering buying another cute skirt, one of the questions that ought to be at the forefront of my mind is, "Lord, is this the way You want me to spend Your money?"

The second lesson is about investment. The parable teaches that we ought to invest earthly resources—but not with a view to making more money. The owner commended the manager when he used money to gain friends for the future, for the time when his job would be over. Someday, our job on earth will end. Jesus' point is that we should invest our resources in heavenly things. The way we use our money on earth ought to help us gain friends who will join us in eternity. We should spend with a view to sharing the gospel and influencing people for the kingdom of God. The question for me is this: "Am I investing my money, time, talents, and gifts in eternal things?"

Third, the story contains a lesson about responsibility. Jesus said, "Whoever can be trusted with very little can also be trusted with much. . . . If you have not been trustworthy in handling worldly wealth, who will trust you with true riches?" In other words, the way you spend your money and resources is very, very important. The

Lord will not entrust you with handling the true riches of His kingdom until you've learned how to manage worldly wealth. The question is, "Am I being responsible with my money? Am I being careful not to waste it with costly, self-indulgent, or irresponsible purchases?"

The fourth lesson contained in Christ's teaching is about valuation. Valuation is the act of determining the value of something, established by appraising its quality, condition, and desirability. It answers the question, "What's it worth?" A woman in Scotland once bought an odd-looking vase at a sale for a pound (about a dollar). After the plant she kept in it died, she dumped it in the attic, and was about to throw it away when *Antiques Roadshow* came to town. On a whim, she took it for valuation. "The vase turned out to be a 1929 work—Feuilles Fougeres—by the renowned French designer and major Art Nouveau figure Rene Lalique." It sold at a Christie's auction for the equivalent of more than $50,000.[1]

The woman disregarded the vase until an expert told her the item's true worth. That's when she began to treasure it. The Lord wants to educate us about the true worth of earthly things. He gives us His expert valuation. He says, "What is highly valued among men is detestable in God's sight." He wants me to trust His valuation and esteem what He esteems. So what if I find a Feuilles Fougeres vase kicking around in my attic? Do I throw it in the garbage? No. I recognize its true eternal value. And I do my best to use its monetary value to invest in that which is of far greater worth in God's eyes. The question I need to ask myself is, "Do I treasure things based on God's assessment of their true worth? Is my valuation the same as His?"

The final lesson in the Luke 16 passage is about devotion. "No servant can serve two masters. . . . He will be devoted to the one and despise the other. You cannot serve both God and Money." How we spend our money indicates what's in our hearts. It reflects whether we're devoted to money or devoted to God. It reflects whether we've set our hearts on earthly goods or on Him. The rich man went away dejected when Jesus told him he would gain the kingdom if he gave away all his money (Luke 18:18–28). Jesus' challenge revealed what the young man truly treasured. If he had had the same perspective toward earthly riches that Jesus had, he would have gladly parted with what was less to gain what was more. As I consider the money and "stuff" that I have, I need to ask myself, "Is there anything that I would hesitate to give up for the sake of the kingdom? Is there anything that I'm clinging to more than I'm clinging to Jesus?"

RIGHT ON THE MONEY

You can tell a Girl-Gone-Wise from a Girl-Gone-Wild based on her attitude toward money and the way she manages resources. The Proverbs 7 woman was obsessed with spending her money on things that would make her desirable and enviable, and indulge her own senses and pleasures. The attitude of the Proverbs 31 woman was markedly different. She purchased quality goods like linen, but it wasn't so she could self-indulge. Her purchases were aimed toward best meeting the needs of those in her household and the needs of those around her.

In the narrative, we see the Wise Woman opening her hand to the poor, reaching out her hands to the needy, and making bed coverings for herself (Proverbs 31:20–22). She didn't buy exclusive, designer-brand, colored Egyptian linens like the Proverbs 7 woman did. She was much more careful and circumspect about the way she used her money. She probably could have afforded the same luxuries. If she had kept the money instead of giving it to the poor and needy, she likely could have bought the Egyptian linens for bed coverings instead of making her own. The problem is not that we have money, but that we use it for our own selfish ends, invest in worldly things, and neglect to invest in the kingdom. The Lord tells Israel, "Behold, this was the guilt of your sister Sodom: she and her daughters had pride, excess of food, and prosperous ease, but did not aid the poor and needy" (Ezekiel 16:49).

So what does this mean for you? It means that you should generously give money to your church, ministries, and missions to further the gospel of Jesus Christ. But it also means that you generously give your home, your food, your possessions, your time, your energy, your affection, and all the other resources God has entrusted to you. The Lord wants you to use all your resources to invest in the kingdom. The rich man Job is a good example. He tells his friends that he never "withheld anything that the poor desired," nor did he cause "the eyes of the widow to fail." His home was open to the needy. They always dined at his table. He says, "From my youth the fatherless grew up with me as with a father, and from my mother's womb I guided the widow." He fed the hungry. He warmed those who were cold with the fleece of his sheep. Whenever he saw a need, he generously used his resources to meet it (Job 31:16–21).

Job mentions that he was a "father to the fatherless and guided the widow" from the time he was very young. That indicates that what he provided the needy was much more than material goods. He provided spiritual oversight and guidance. You can follow his example by being a spiritual mother to your friends, relatives, neighbors, and work colleagues. Even if you are young, you can begin to spiritually parent girlfriends and to invest your resources in eternity.

The Bible teaches that what you do with money—or desire to do with it—can make or break your happiness forever. The Girl-Gone-Wild who makes material riches her goal in life has the wrong values. However wealthy she may appear, she is poverty-stricken in God's sight. In His economy, the truly rich woman is the one whose main aim in life is to serve Him as King. Her wealth lies in the currency of faith and good works, opening her hand to the poor, and reaching out her hands to the needy. She has a heavenly bank balance that no one can steal and nothing can erode. She lays up for herself treasures in heaven, "For where your treasure is, there your heart will be also" (Matthew 6:21). The Girl-Gone-Wise knows that heavenly treasure is the kind that smart girls get more of.

Point of Contrast #15

ENTITLEMENT
Her Insistence
on Gratification

Girl-Gone-Wild: Demands Gratification	Girl-Gone-Wise: Forfeits Gratification
"Come, let us take our fill of love till morning; let us delight ourselves with love." (Proverbs 7:18)	She denies herself and takes up her cross daily and follows Jesus. (Luke 9:23)

Last year, an Eritrean Christian woman, Azieb Simon, died of malaria in the Wi'a Military Training Center after being imprisoned and tortured for months. In Saudi Arabia, a member of the religious police cut his college daughter's tongue off and burned her to death for converting to Christianity. A twenty-year-old Christian Pakistani woman, Sandul, falsely accused of ripping pages from the Quran, was thrown into jail after an angry mob from the local mosque threw stones and set fire to her home. In Iran, thirty-year-old Marzieh and twenty-seven-year-old Maryam became very ill after languishing for months in a prison notorious for its harsh treatment of inmates. In the Shandong province of China, Christian youth camp workers, including a sixteen-year-old, were arrested, interrogated, threatened, beaten, and kept in detention.[1] All suffered greatly because they refused to recant their faith in Jesus.

At a conference for ministry women in Thailand, I met many such women. They came from all over Southeast Asia and the Middle East. One was deaf in her left ear because of a bomb that attackers had thrown into her house-church several weeks earlier. Her son had narrowly escaped death. They were still picking shrapnel out of his head. Another was weary from the police constantly harassing and threatening her children. Another, a former student of mine—a brilliant woman who was working on her doctorate in theology—was planning another move. Their names were on the Chinese government's wanted list. They had to move every three to four months when their evangelistic efforts alerted local police to their presence. They could have returned to North America, but chose not to. Another woman trembled as she worshiped, and tears poured down her face as she lifted her hands. At home, she was only able to whisper the name of Jesus, and it had been years since she was able to raise her voice and sing it aloud.

The most striking thing about all these women is not that they suffered for the name of Jesus—but that they suffered so gladly. They had the same attitude as the martyrs burned at the stake in the 1500s. When the sheriff put the rope about Ann Audebert, she called it the wedding-sash wherewith she would be married to Christ. With joy on her face she exclaimed, "Upon Saturday I was first married, and upon a Saturday I shall be married again." Or Elizabeth Pepper and Agnes George, who kissed and embraced the stake before they were burned. Or Elizabeth Folkes, who shouted, "Farewell all the world! Farewell faith! Farewell hope!" and taking the stake in her arms joyfully exclaimed, "Welcome love!" With fire licking and consuming her flesh, she clapped her hands for joy and raised her arms in exuberant praise.[2]

They were like the women in the Hebrews 11 faith hall of fame who "received back their dead by resurrection."

Some were tortured, refusing to accept release, so that they might rise again to a better life. Others suffered mocking and flogging, and even chains and imprisonment. They were stoned, they were sawn in two, they were killed with the sword. They went about in skins of sheep and goats, destitute, afflicted, mistreated—of whom the world was not worthy—wandering about in deserts and mountains, and in dens and caves of the earth. (Hebrews 11:35–38)

Or like the apostles, ten of whom, according to tradition, were martyred by various means, including by beheading, by sword and spear, and, in the case of Peter, reportedly by crucifixion upside down.

Entitlement is the next point of contrast between a Girl-Gone-Wild and a Girl-Gone-Wise. A Wild Thing is intent on immediate gratification. She feels she has a right to be comfortable, be happy, have fun, get what she wants, and indulge in all sorts of pleasures. Enjoyment, comfort, luxury, and ease are what she feels she deserves and what she constantly seeks and demands. A Girl-Gone-Wise, on the other hand, knows that the highest pleasure exists in denying self and willingly bearing the cross of Christ. She forfeits earthly gratification for the eternal joy that God has set before her. She sacrifices lesser joys for infinitely greater ones. She knows and accepts that on this side of heaven, Christian discipleship is a costly, uncomfortable, painful, and even bloody business.

INSTANT GRATIFICATION

The stage was set. She had primped herself to look provocative, seductively kissed him, told him about the sumptuous feast she had prepared, and described the lavish, sensual décor of her bedroom. She could tell he was tempted. Her subtle hints paved the way for her shameless proposition: "Come, let us take our fill of love till morning; let us delight ourselves with love."

"Take our fill" is literally "drink our fill." The Proverbs 7 woman was using a figure of speech that likened sexual relations to drinking from a fountain (Proverbs 5:15–19). The word signifies to drink something copiously in full draughts—to slurp it up without restraint. The verb in the second part of the sentence, *delight*, means to enjoy oneself fully, to "roll in" pleasure, or to give oneself up to it. She was brashly proposing, "Let's indulge. Let's make love all night. Let's play and pleasure ourselves to the max."

The Proverbs 7 woman was a "lover of pleasures." She was like the

Lady Babylon, whom Isaiah called to account for her attitude of entitlement:

> You said, "I shall be mistress forever," so that you did not lay these things to heart or remember their end. Now therefore hear this, you lover of pleasures, who sit securely, who say in your heart, "I am, and there is no one besides me; I shall not sit as a widow or know the loss of children": These two things shall come to you in a moment, in one day; the loss of children and widowhood shall come upon you in full measure, in spite of your many sorceries and the great power of your enchantments. You felt secure in your wickedness, you said, "No one sees me"; your wisdom and your knowledge led you astray, and you said in your heart, "I am, and there is no one besides me." But evil shall come upon you, which you will not know how to charm away; disaster shall fall upon you, for which you will not be able to atone; and ruin shall come upon you suddenly, of which you know nothing. (Isaiah 47:7–11)

The passage reveals that Lady Babylon had several faulty ideas about the things to which she was entitled. First, she assumed she was in control and had the right to do as she wished ("I shall be mistress forever"). Second, she felt entitled to self-indulge and put her own happiness first ("I am, and there is no one besides me"). Third, she considered her indulgence a private matter ("No one sees me"). And fourth, she denied that any harm could come of enjoying herself ("I shall not sit as a widow or know the loss of children").

The attitude of the seductress of Proverbs 7 was undoubtedly quite similar, and so is the attitude of a pleasure-seeking Wild Thing of this generation. The Girl-Gone-Wild thinks she is in control and can do whatever she wants. She denies that she is vulnerable to sin or accountable to anyone else for her behavior. She feels entitled to have fun and pursue her own happiness, feel good, gratify her desires, and indulge. She considers her sexual behavior a private matter. She rationalizes that it's no one else's business what she does behind closed doors. And she denies that any harm could come from enjoying herself. If it doesn't hurt anyone, what difference does it make? What's wrong with self-gratification?

The self-indulgence of the Girl-Gone-Wild isn't limited to illicit sexual affairs. A Wild Thing can self-indulge through emotional affairs, romance novels, fantasies, pornography, masturbation, sensuality, flirtation, and other types of sexual impurity. What's more, self-indulgence can, and usually does, show up in other areas too. The Proverbs 7 woman indulged in designer-label luxuries. The text implies that she indulged in her wardrobe, in food, in going out, in staying up late and sleeping in, and in neglecting her home. If she lived today, she'd probably indulge in beauty treatments, entertainment, fine dining, travel, and all sorts of luxury items. All of these indulgences point to an underlying attitude of entitlement. A woman indulges because she thinks, *I deserve this!*

Isaiah warns Lady Babylon that her sensual, self-gratifying behavior would only lead to disaster and ruin. The apostle Paul agrees that this is the case for all Christian women who have an attitude of entitlement: "She who is self-indulgent is dead even while she lives" (1 Timothy 5:6). He predicts that in the last days, self-indulgence will run rampant. People will be lovers of self, without self-control, "lovers of pleasure rather than lovers of God. . . . Avoid such people" (2 Timothy 3:1–5). James likewise condemns people who spend their time on earth luxuriating and self-indulging. He accuses them of foolishly fattening their hearts in a day of slaughter (James 5:5). The sarcastic illustration was vivid for Jewish believers who had seen many sheep and oxen happily fatten themselves on rich food, not knowing that their fatness singled them out as prime candidates for the butcher's knife.

RADICAL SELF-DENIAL

Do you remember what Peter did the night of Christ's arrest? Someone in the crowd recognized him as a friend of Jesus. Rather than suffer embarrassment, discomfort, harassment, or abuse, Peter denied it. Not once. Not twice. But three times he put his own comfort above his loyalty to Christ. The episode apparently taught him a thing or two about self-denial. At the end of a life of self-sacrifice, Peter paid the ultimate price when he refused to renounce Christ. Tradition says he was crucified upside down at his own request, as he did not feel worthy to die the same way as Jesus.

In his letter to the persecuted Christians dispersed throughout Asia Minor, Peter talked extensively about suffering and self-denial. As you read the following passage, notice how he suggests that a person's willingness to deny self and suffer like Jesus is a requisite for that person overcoming sins of sensuality, passions, and self-indulgence (debauchery):

> Since therefore Christ suffered in the flesh, arm yourselves with the same way of thinking, for whoever has suffered in the flesh has ceased from sin, so as to live for the rest of the time in the flesh no longer for human passions but for the will of God. For the time that is past suffices for doing what the Gentiles want to do, living in sensuality, passions, drunkenness, orgies, drinking parties, and lawless idolatry. With respect to this they are surprised when you do not join them in the same flood of debauchery, and they malign you. . . . Beloved, do not be surprised at the fiery trial when it comes upon you to test you, as though something strange were happening to you. But rejoice insofar as you share Christ's sufferings, that you may also rejoice and be glad when his glory is revealed. (1 Peter 4:1–4, 12–13)

Peter observes that refusing to gratify oneself with sinful, worldly pleasures often leads to suffering. People will malign and mock the one who refuses to self-indulge. Self-denial leads to suffering, which leads to a greater capacity to say no to sin, which leads to increased self-denial, which leads to more suffering. A Christlike mind-set toward self-denial and suffering causes sin to lose its power over us. But it also leads to more suffering. "Indeed, all who desire to live a godly life in Christ Jesus will be persecuted" (2 Timothy 3:12).

Peter says that those who are godly will share in Christ's sufferings. If a woman stands against the tide of popular opinion and boldly follows Jesus, she will suffer what He suffered. She will be despised and rejected, acquainted with grief and sorrow, insulted, scorned, mocked, ridiculed, afflicted, oppressed, humiliated, reproached, dishonored, deserted, estranged from friends and family. She will be stared at, gloated over, and be the object of gossip and slander. She will feel distressed, anguished, humiliated. Her heart will melt like wax. Her strength will dry up. She will be exhausted—utterly burdened beyond her own strength. She will weep and humble her soul with fasting to find the courage and strength to endure. In some hostile environments, opponents of Christ might physically attack and harm her, and in some cases, the Lord may ask her for the ultimate sacrifice of laying down her life for the sake of the gospel (Psalm 22:6–8, 13–18; 69:7–9, 19–21; Isaiah 53:2–5, 7–10; Matthew 10:22).

It costs to follow Jesus. Girls-Gone-Wise will pay a price for their obedience. In this culture, they will suffer for taking a stance on Christ's teaching about gender and sexuality. Like Amy, who endured stares, snickers, and whispers after she took a stand on morality in her social science class. Or Lisa, whose friend secretly dared three young men to enter a competition to get Lisa to lose her virginity. Or Samantha, who broke off her relationship with Jim because he didn't share her conviction on sexual standards. Or Christina, who was ostracized from her church group for having views that were far too radical. Or Kimberly, whose husband tried to force her to watch pornographic movies and relentlessly mocked her when she wouldn't. Or Alison, who lost her job because she refused her boss's advances. Or Rebecca, whose tires were slashed and house vandalized with graffiti when she said that homosexuality went against God's design. Or my fellow author who was stalked because she publicly took a stand on purity. Or Natalie, whose heart aches for a husband, but who refuses to settle for a man who isn't sold out to God. The price of obedience is suffering and self-denial. It's costly.

Christ's call for self-denial is radical. Jesus said, "If anyone would come after me, let him deny himself and take up his cross daily and follow me" (Luke 9:23). A Girl-Gone-Wise answers Christ's call to radical obedience. Every day, she takes up her cross and resolves to follow Jesus—no matter the cost.

FOR THE GREATER JOY

One of my favorite parables is the one about the pearl of great price. Jesus said that the kingdom of heaven is like a merchant in search of fine pearls, who, on finding one pearl of great value, went and sold all that he had and bought it (Matthew 13:45–46). He was so ecstatic about the prospect of getting the spectacular pearl that he gladly gave up everything else. It was worth more to him than the combined value of all his other possessions. That story pretty much sums up the reason that we ought to be willing to deny self and suffer for

Christ. It's not because we sadistically enjoy discomfort and pain, but because the treasure we've set our hearts on is worth the cost. The sufferings of this present time are nothing compared with the glory that we will enjoy in Jesus.

If there was ever a young man who knew how to indulge self, it was the first-century philosopher Augustine. He lived a hedonistic lifestyle, drinking, partying, and sleeping around with women. He felt himself drawn to the Lord, but hesitated to become a Christian because he thought he could never live a sexually pure life. He is famous for uttering the prayer, "Lord, grant me chastity and continence, but not yet."

Augustine was radically converted when he read Romans 13:13–14: "Let us walk properly as in the daytime, not in orgies and drunkenness, not in sexual immorality and sensuality, not in quarreling and jealousy. But put on the Lord Jesus Christ, and make no provision for the flesh, to gratify its desires." After he gave his life to Christ, he discovered, much to his surprise, that self-denial led to a far greater joy than self-indulgence ever did. The joy of Christ was sweeter than all other pleasures:

> How sweet all at once it was for me to be rid of those fruitless joys which I had once feared to lose! . . . You drove them from me, you who are the true, the sovereign joy. You drove them from me and took their place, you who are sweeter than all pleasure. . . . O Lord my God, my Light, my Wealth, and my Salvation.[3]

Do you believe it? Do you believe that treasuring Christ holds greater pleasure than sex, wealth, power, and prestige? Are you willing to forego worldly gratification? Are you willing to deny self and suffer so that the True and Sovereign Joy, "sweeter than all pleasure," can take the place of all lesser pleasures? It will cost you. For some, it will cost a great deal. But it's a price that a Girl-Gone-Wise is willing to pay.

Point of Contrast #16

RELIABILITY
Her Faithfulness
to Commitments

Girl-Gone-Wild: **Undependable**	Girl-Gone-Wise: **Dependable**
"For my husband is not at home; he has gone on a long journey; he took a bag of money with him; at full moon he will come home." (Proverbs 7:19–20)	"The heart of her husband trusts in her." (Proverbs 31:11)

Shibuya Station is located in the midst of one of the busiest and most colorful shopping and entertainment districts in Tokyo. If you were to visit, you'd see hordes of commuters bustling around a plethora of fashion stores, boutiques, nightclubs, and restaurants. The corner is lit up with neon advertisements and giant video screens—including one that covers half a skyscraper. But nestled among all the glitz, glamour, and movement is a simple bronze statue of a dog, Hachiko. Because of his loyalty, faithfulness, and love, little "Hachi" earned a place in the hearts of all Japanese people and has kept that place for the past seventy-five years.

Hachi used to accompany his Japanese master to the Shibuya Train Station each morning when he left for work. Upon returning, the master would find the dog with his tail wagging, patiently waiting for him. One day, the man died in the distant city and did not come back. That night and every night thereafter, Hachi went to the station and waited faithfully for him—sadly trotting home again when his friend didn't appear. The dog became a familiar sight to commuters as he kept up his vigil for more than ten years. On March 8, 1935, Hachi died on the very spot he last saw his friend alive. His loyalty so impressed the Japanese people that they erected a statue of the dog at the place where he had faithfully waited.

The story behind the statue is one that has endured. Though Hachi stood only two feet tall, the message he left is enormous. People yearn to have friends that are as loyal, reliable, and trustworthy. As the Sage lamented, "Many a man proclaims his own steadfast love, but a faithful man who can find?" (Proverbs 20:6).

Reliability is another point of contrast between a Girl-Gone-Wise and a Girl-Gone-Wild. The Wild Thing of Proverbs 7 wasn't loyal to her marriage vows—she wasn't a woman of her word. When her husband was out of town, she cheated on him. She betrayed her commitment. In the text, we see her enticing the young man with the fact that the coast was clear: "For my husband is not at home; he has gone on a long journey; he took a bag of money with him; at full moon he will come home" (Proverbs 7:19–20). In contrast to the untrustworthiness of the Girl-Gone-Wild, the Girl-Gone-Wise is faithful, loyal, and dependable. "The heart of her husband trusts in her" (Proverbs 31:11). She's a woman of her word. He knows that she will be true.

BREAKING FAITH

The husband of the Proverbs 7 woman appears to have been a merchant who often took long trips out of town, as was the custom of merchants those days. The woman assured the young man that there was no chance of him returning unexpectedly to catch them. Her choice of words is interesting. She literally says, "because the man is not in his house." She uses the impersonal "the man" instead of "my man" and "his house" instead of "our house." It's as though she's distancing herself from her husband, disparaging him, and making their relationship appear very cold and impersonal.

The indifferent, detached manner of referring to her husband is the only clue the woman gives about the state of their relationship. We can only speculate as to what it was like. Perhaps she felt trapped in a loveless marriage. Perhaps her husband was a rude, inconsiderate boor who constantly criticized and belittled her. Perhaps he was so busy in his business ventures and spent so much time out of town, that she felt ignored, isolated, and lonely. Maybe she suspected that he had been unfaithful too.

Earlier in Proverbs, the Sage tells us that this type of woman "forsakes the companion of her youth and forgets the covenant of her God" (Proverbs 2:17). The phrase "companion of her youth" indicates that the woman once loved her husband. When they first married, they were close confidantes, soul mates, and devoted companions. We don't know for sure what happened to contribute to the deterioration of their relationship. But whatever it was, I'm convinced the woman would have had a compelling story to justify why she was breaking her commitment. The young man probably empathized with her reasons. Her explanation would probably tug at our heartstrings too. But there's no reason that could ever justify her behavior in the eyes of God. Covenant unfaithfulness is reprehensible to Him. God expects that we will keep our word. When the woman cheated on her husband, she essentially abandoned "the covenant of her God."

Marriage is much more than a human covenant. It's a covenant with God. When a woman breaks faith with her husband, she doesn't just sin against her husband, she also sins against God and, as we'll soon see, against the entire covenant community of believers. She breaks and profanes covenant in multiple relationships and on multiple levels. Before we look at the passage that links all these covenant relationships together, I want to make sure that you understand what a covenant is.

A covenant is an arrangement between two or more parties involving mutual obligation. It's an agreement, a binding promise, or a standing contract that links or brings them together and unifies them in some way. Covenant is one of the central themes of the Bible, where some covenants are between humans and others between God and humans. The word *testament* is another word for *covenant*. Our Bible is divided into Old and New Testaments, which correspond to the old and new covenants that God made with humanity.

A covenant is essentially a mutual commitment. A variety of human relationships, from profoundly personal to distantly political, can be described as covenantal. Best friends David and Jonathan made covenant promises to each other (1 Samuel 18:3). A husband and wife enter into a covenant of marriage (Malachi 2:14). The elders of Israel made a national covenant with King David (2 Samuel 5:3). King Solomon entered into a covenant with Hiram, king of Tyre (1 Kings 5:12).

A covenant is an interpersonal framework of trust, responsibilities, and benefits. It stipulates that we have responsibilities to fulfill obligations toward others and to behave in a certain way toward them. The key word in Scripture to describe covenant responsibility is *faithfulness*. Faithfulness is maintaining faith or allegiance. It's being responsible to fulfill a commitment. It means that I do what I say I'm going to do and what our agreement obligates me to do.

Scripture emphasizes that faithfulness is an attribute of God. He always does what He says He's going to do. If He makes a promise, He keeps it. If He makes a commitment, He never turns His back on it. He is faithful to fulfill His responsibility. He keeps His word. He's totally and completely trustworthy. When He made a covenant with the Hebrew people, He told them, "Know therefore that the Lord your God is God, the faithful God who keeps covenant and steadfast love with those who love him and keep his commandments, to a thousand generations" (Deuteronomy 7:9). God remembers His promises forever (Psalm 111:5). He is never unfaithful. Not ever! "If we are faithless, he remains faithful—for he cannot deny himself" (2 Timothy 2:13).

The covenant-keeping nature of God is the foundation for faithfulness within human relationships. His faithfulness places a responsibility for faithfulness on our shoulders. He expects us to keep faith with Him, with our spouses, and with other people. He wants us to be as reliable to our commitments as He is to His. The prophet Malachi was upset that the people of Israel broke faith with each other. He claimed that when they broke their commitments, they profaned their covenant with God.

Have we not all one Father? Has not one God created us? Why then are we faithless to one another, profaning the covenant of our fathers? Judah has been faithless, and abomination has been committed in Israel and in Jerusalem. For Judah has profaned the sanctuary of the Lord, which he loves, and has married the daughter of a foreign god. . . .

You cover the Lord's altar with tears, with weeping and groaning because he no longer regards the offering or accepts it with favor from your hand. But you say, "Why does he not?" Because the Lord was witness between you and the wife of your youth, to whom you have been faithless, though she is your companion and your wife by covenant. Did he not make them one, with a portion of the Spirit in their union? . . .

So guard yourselves in your spirit, and let none of you be faithless to the wife of your youth. "For the man who does not love his wife but divorces her, says the Lord, the God of Israel, covers his garment with violence, says the Lord of hosts. So guard yourselves in your spirit, and do not be faithless." (Malachi 2:10–11, 13–16)

Let me give you a bit of background as to what was going on here. The Lord made a covenant with Abraham, his son, Isaac, and his grandson, Jacob—to whom He gave the new name "Israel." Israel had twelve sons, who became the heads of the tribes of the nation of Israel. These people were the covenant community of God. Soon after the death of King Solomon, infighting broke out, and the community split into two kingdoms: the northern kingdom, Israel (ten tribes), and the southern kingdom, Judah (two tribes). Instead of sticking together, the two groups began to make alliances with surrounding nations.

In the passage, Malachi condemns Judah for making such an alliance ("marrying the daughter of a foreign god"). Judah was "faithless" because it "cheated" on God by forsaking its covenant partner, Israel. What's more, the covenant breaking wasn't just a problem on the national level; it was a problem on the personal level too. Men were divorcing their wives to marry foreign women. The people were being unfaithful to their Jewish spouses as well as to the Jewish community. Malachi argued that this was a very serious matter. When they were unfaithful to each other, they were unfaithful to God and His covenant. Based on the Malachi passage, we can deduce some key concepts about covenants and faithfulness:

Covenants Are Based on the Character of God

God created the first covenant. He made a covenant with Adam, and then He performed a marriage ceremony to join Adam and Eve in covenant with each other. Malachi points out that bringing parties together and making them one is an act of God—"with a portion of His Spirit" in the union. There's something about the uniting of individuals that reflects God's nature. God, the united Three-in-One, created us in His image. A pure, faithful, unbreakable union is what He is all about. And that's what He wants us to image in our covenant relationships. When we are faithful to a covenant, we put God on display.

A Covenant Unites

A covenant connects or joins parties together in some sort of association. The purpose of a covenant is to unite. The language of "oneness" is foundational to the idea of covenant. The passage speaks of one Father. One God. One another. One flesh. One family. One nation. In the New Testament, the concept is enlarged. One Mediator. One faith. One baptism. One church. One body. One people. One heart. One soul. One mind. One Lover. One love.

Unfaithfulness to a Covenant Profanes God

The marriage covenant is a covenant of God, as is the covenant relationship between believers. When we are "faithless to one another," we violate our covenant. This isn't just an offense against an individual. It's an offense against the entire faith community. Even worse, it's an offense against the Lord. Malachi is emphatic that breaking faith in a human relationship damages a person's relationship to God and "profanes" His covenant.

Marriage Mirrors the Nature of God's Covenant

God is particularly disturbed by faithlessness in the covenant of marriage. He hates divorce. Why? Because marriage is a covenant of love. Marriage is the human relationship that most closely images God's covenant of love. Marriage best tells the story. When we are unfaithful in marriage, we tell a lie about the true nature of God's covenant. We misrepresent what it's all about.

Breaking Faith Rips Apart What God Has Joined

Faithlessness destroys unity. This is the case in all interpersonal relationships, but especially in marriage. Malachi says that those who fail to faithfully love a covenant partner "cover their garments with violence." They tear apart what God has joined.

Guarding against Faithlessness Is Critical

Being faithful to God requires that we be true to all our promises and commitments to one another. God is witness to all covenants. When we enter into a covenant, we are not only responsible to the other individual, we are also accountable to God. Malachi warns God's people to take care to guard their spirits against being unfaithful to each other. Faithfulness is critical, because it's the glue that makes a covenant work. Without faithfulness, a covenant relationship falls apart.

"I WILL . . . I DO"

When people get married, they make promises to each other with God, family, and friends as their witnesses. The difference between an ordinary promise and an oath is that, with an oath, a person appeals to or acknowledges a sacred witness. To take an oath before God is a very serious matter. A person who does this says, "I want you to know I'm telling the truth, I want God to witness I'm telling the truth, and I want God to punish me if I'm not telling the truth." The Jews understood that it was a very solemn thing to call God to witness a covenant. They knew that if they defaulted on the promise, He would punish them. That was part of the deal. Once they made an oath before God, breaking their commitment was out of the question. The promise was binding. For this reason, God warned them to be very careful about taking oaths, and to be very careful to do all that they promised to do (Numbers 30:2; Deuteronomy 23:21–23).

The Jews of Jesus' day put an interesting twist on the matter of covenants, oaths, and promises. They realized that if they swore before God to do something and then didn't do it, they'd be in a lot of trouble. Wanting to avoid this, they began swearing oaths by everything except God. They wanted to add some kind of force to their promises to make their words more credible, but they didn't want to incur the judgment of God by swearing something in His name, especially when they didn't fully intend to keep their word. So they swore oaths on heaven, on earth, on Jerusalem, on their own heads, and on all sorts of other things (Matthew 5:34–36). Apparently, it got pretty silly. For instance, the Pharisees argued that if you swore by the "the Temple," your word was not binding, but if you swore by the "gold of the Temple," you had to fulfill your obligation. If you swore by the altar, it was like having your fingers crossed behind your back, but if you swore by the offering on the altar, you had a duty to do what you said (Matthew 23:16–22).

Jesus chided the Pharisees for thinking they could get away with being unfaithful to their word. He pointed out that each of the items they were swearing by ultimately belonged to God. So in essence, they were still calling God as their witness. If they defaulted on their promises, they'd still fall under condemnation. God was a silent witness to every word they spoke. Jesus challenged them to stop using oaths to indicate when they were telling the truth, and to start telling the truth all the time. "Let what you say be simply 'Yes' or 'No'" (Matthew 5:37; James 5:12). He wants His followers to be people whose words are so characterized by integrity that others need no formal assurance of their truthfulness in order to trust them. He wants you to be as reliable with your word as He is to His (Ecclesiastes 5:4–5).

Last Thursday, my husband asked me to call someone and stressed how important it was that I do so that day. I said I would. But I procrastinated and didn't make the call until Sunday. I broke faith. I didn't do what I said I was going to do. I sinned, and needed to apologize to Brent for letting him down. I could write it off as "not a big deal," but faithfulness to my word *is* a big deal. Faithfulness is the foundation of my marriage covenant and of all my other relationships too. Being faithful in "little things" is extremely important. Jesus said, "One who is faithful in a very little is also faithful in much, and one who is dishonest in a very little is also dishonest in much" (Luke 16:10).

The Wild Thing of Proverbs 7 cheated on her husband. She was unfaithful to the solemn covenant promise she made. But I think it's fairly safe to assume that she broke faith with him, and others too, in many little ways every day. She was unreliable. She was the type who thought that going back on a promise or commitment, or failing to do what she said she would do, was "no big deal." It didn't matter if she said she would be there, and then wasn't. Or if she said she'd do it, and then didn't. Or if she said she wouldn't, and then did. Or if she said she was in, and then backed out.

How about you? Are you reliable to your commitments? Like the faithful dog, Hachiko, do you show up and continue to show up, even if the other person doesn't? Do you take your covenants and commitments as seriously as God does? The Wild Thing of Proverbs 7 felt justified in breaking faith. But the Girl-Gone-Wise knows that God is witness to the commitments she makes. Keeping faith with Him means keeping faith with others. His trustworthiness obliges her to be trustworthy. In a world where people continually break faith, her yes is yes, and her no is no. She is totally and utterly dependable.

 You'll find videos, a forum, and many other resources to help you learn how to walk wisely on the GirlsGoneWise.com website. And make sure to follow Gorls Gone Wise on Facebook (facebook.com/girlsgonewise) and Twitter (twitter.com/girlsgonewise) tool.

Point of Contrast #17

SPEECH
Her Speech Habits

Girl-Gone-Wild: **Excessive, Duplicitous, Manipulative**	Girl-Gone-Wise: **Restrained, Sincere, Without Guile**
"With much seductive speech she persuades him; with her smooth talk she compels him." (Proverbs 7:21)	She keeps her tongue from evil and her lips from speaking guile. (I Peter 3:10)

She could see the hesitation in his eyes. He knew it wasn't a good idea. Even though her husband was out of town, the thought that she was married reminded the young man that a liaison with her was terribly wrong. She could see him begin to waver, so she pulled out all the stops. If her provocative appearance, body language, kiss, and scintillating invitation weren't enough, she'd use her last and most powerful weapon—verbal arsenal. "With much seductive speech she persuades him; with her smooth talk she compels him."

The way a woman uses her mouth is the next point of contrast between a Girl-Gone-Wise and a Girl-Gone-Wild. A wise woman is very careful about what she says. She ensures that her speech is restrained, sincere, and without guile. Cultivating godly speech is a challenge. I've written an entire Bible study and book to help women develop some "Conversation Peace." Visit GirlsGoneWise.com, take the twenty-question "Conversation Peace Quiz," and evaluate how your speech measures up to the Bible's standard. I think you'll see that when it comes to speech, "we all stumble in many ways" (James 3:2).

Controlling our tongues and learning to speak in a godly manner are things that virtually all of us need to work on. It would be impossible to address the topic of godly communication adequately in one short chapter, so we're just going to discuss the three types of sinful speech that this passage identifies as characteristic of a Wild Thing. Her speech is excessive ("much"), duplicitous ("smooth"), and manipulative ("seductive").

UNZIPPED LIPS

Have you ever heard the statistic that a woman uses about twenty thousand words per day while a man uses about seven thousand? Some researchers claim that this commonly cited figure is inflated and is not based on proper scientific research. Nevertheless, the perception of most people is that women talk more than men do. I just asked my husband whether he believed this to be true. He thought for a moment, and then answered my question with a question.

"If I had three or four of my buddies over and we were outside in the hot tub, and you walked outside and noticed we were sitting in silence, would you think something was wrong?"

"No. I wouldn't. That wouldn't surprise me at all." I smiled. I thought I knew where he was going.

Brent continued, "If you had three or four girlfriends over and you were outside in the hot tub, and I walked outside and noticed you were sitting in silence, would I think something was wrong?"

The answer was self-evident. He would think something was terribly wrong if a group of women was sitting together in silence.

"So," he concluded triumphantly, "that should tell you something!"

I don't know if Brent's little parable demonstrates that the quantity of words men and women speak is different, but it does seem to indicate that there's a difference in the way we use words. For women, intimacy is the fabric of relationships, and talk is the thread from which it's woven. Women regard conversation as the cornerstone of friendships. The bonds between men are based less on talking, and more on doing things together and on common shared experiences.

Women are generally more adept at using language in interpersonal communication. They're better at discerning emotions, reading body language, interpreting nonverbal cues, and expressing thoughts, impressions, and feelings. In male-female interpersonal relationships, the woman is usually the one who has a higher threshold for verbal interaction. If she wants to, she can talk circles around the man. Linguistically and emotionally, he can rarely keep up. A woman will often use this to her advantage. She'll talk and talk until the guy gets overwhelmed, thrown off balance, befuddled, frustrated, or discombobulated, and agrees with her or gives in to her demands. Like Delilah, who cajoled Samson with her incessant yapping. "When she pressed him hard with her words day after day, and urged him, his soul was vexed to death. And he told her all his heart" (Judges 16:16–17).

The Proverbs 7 woman was a talker. When she wanted to bag the young man, she resorted to "much" seductive speech to overcome his resistance. Toward her forbidden lover, her many words were sweet. Her lips "drip[ped]" honey (Proverbs 5:3). But toward her husband, her incessant talk had probably morphed into constant nagging and criticism. Her speech still "dripped," but instead of honey, it was like the annoying drip of a leaky roof on a rainy day. "A continual dripping on a rainy day and a quarrelsome wife are alike; to restrain her is to restrain the wind or to grasp oil in one's right hand" (Proverbs 27:15–16).

The Sage says that trying to restrain the incessant "dripping" words of a contentious woman is an exercise in futility. It's like trying to restrain the wind or grab a handful of oil. Her words are many, and they're extremely slippery. He can't seem to pin down exactly what she means. And he can't stop the verbal barrage. The Bible is clear that excessive speech is usually sinful speech. "When words are many, transgression is not lacking, but whoever restrains his lips is prudent" (Proverbs 10:19). When words constantly drip out of a woman's mouth, chances are she's guilty of some sort of sin: misleading, corrupting, criticizing, gossiping, slandering, feuding, exaggerating, deceiving, clamoring, or a host of other speech sins.

A Wild Thing talks "much." She doesn't exercise restraint. She makes sure the guy is the constant beneficiary of her flattery, her opinion, and her attempts to influence and control him. The Proverbs 7 woman convinced the young man to sin with all her sweet talk and gabbing. The Sage says that the woman who multiplies words is a fool, but the one who restrains words has knowledge (Ecclesiastes 10:14; Proverbs 17:27). A Girl-Gone-Wise doesn't yap. She bridles her mouth and restrains how much she speaks and what she says.

Restraining words means that you don't have to have an opinion on everything. You don't have to comment on everything that happens. You don't have to answer every question. You don't have to constantly make your thoughts known. You don't have to be proved right. You don't have to show off your superior knowledge. You don't have to constantly offer advice. You don't have to nag. Restraining words means that you carefully weigh an answer before you speak, and that you hold back from constantly weighing in. It means that you are quick to listen, but slow to speak (James 1:19).

LIP GLOSS

The second quality of the Wild Woman's speech is that it is smooth. She compels the man with her "smooth talk" (Proverbs 7:21). The Sage warns his son several times about smooth-talking women. He wants to preserve him from the "smooth tongue of the adulteress"—from the woman whose speech is "smoother than oil" (Proverbs 6:24; 5:3).

Smooth talk is conversation that sounds sweet, pleasant, and affirming but is actually slippery, deceitful, and hypocritical. It's dishonest and insincere. It uses flattery, praise, adulation, and gentle pressure to manipulate a person into giving what the talker wants to get. People love to be praised and held in high esteem. They like compliments. They enjoy hearing good things said about themselves. They feel good when people stroke their egos. As a French author once said, "A man finds no sweeter voice in all the world than that which chants his praise."[1] People are much more inclined to respond favorably to those who make them feel good about themselves. A smooth talker takes advantage of this basic fact of human nature. Women are particularly good at sweet talk.

We've all heard the old saying, "Flattery will get you nowhere." But the truth is, flattery works, and works remarkably well. Call it what you will—apple-polishing, boot-licking, back-scratching, soft-soaping, currying favor, toadying, candy-talking, buttering up, kissing up, or managing up—smooth talk can and often does pay off. In the hands of someone who knows how to use it, it can be a dangerous manipulative weapon. Just think of the salesperson who offers a prospective customer profuse compliments on how good an expensive outfit makes her look. Or the subordinate who ingratiates herself to her boss to obtain a promotion or raise. Or villains like Grima Wormtongue in Tolkien's *The Lord of the Rings*, or Iago in Shakespeare's *Othello*, who flatter, deceive, and manipulate their superiors. Or the woman who uses sweet talk and flattery to charm, ensnare, and control a man.

Last week, my son expressed his disgust at the behavior of a girl in his class who was in the habit of apple-polishing the professor. What bothered him most was that everyone in the class could see through her scheme. Everyone, that is, except the professor. He seemed enamored and delighted by all her effusing. Smooth talk is often obvious to everyone except its target. Have you ever seen a man taken in by the smooth talk of a deceptive woman? Did you wonder how he could be so blind to what his family and friends could clearly see?

Flattery characteristically deceives. That's exactly what it's supposed to do. The apostle Paul maintained that those who resort to these tactics "do not serve our Lord Christ, but their own appetites, and by smooth talk and flattery they deceive the hearts of the naive" (Romans 16:18). He and the other apostles were extremely cautious never to resort to flattery when they interacted with people (1 Thessalonians 2:3–4). They did not want to use this deceptive tactic—even for a purpose as noble as furthering the gospel.

Smooth talk is deceptive talk. The Bible equates flattery with lying (Psalm 12:2). Flattery is dishonest because it masks a hidden agenda. It lies about a person's true intent. It glosses over the truth. A smooth talker doles out compliments and strokes a man's ego for personal gain. She butters him up so she can "take" something from him. William Penn, the Quaker colonizer and founder of Pennsylvania, once said, "Avoid flatterers, for they are thieves in disguise."[2] A smooth-talking seductress "lies in wait like a robber" (Proverbs 23:28).

The difference between a legitimate compliment and flattery is accuracy and motive. A legitimate compliment is not false, exaggerated, or motivated by self-interest. It's simply intended to encourage and give credit where credit is due. Flattery is self-serving and insincere. "Sincere" implies an absence of deceit, pretense, or hypocrisy, and an adherence to the simple, unembellished truth. It's derived from the Latin *sine ceras*, which means *without wax*.

When artisans in ancient times made a clay pot, it sometimes cracked due to the heat. Dishonest tradesmen disguised their inferior pots by covering the cracks and blemishes with beeswax before selling them. Picking out a good-quality clay pot wasn't an easy task. On the outside, a patched-up pot looked perfect. A woman wouldn't find out just how flawed it was until she tried using it. As soon as she poured in hot water, the wax melted and the pot began leaking. Honest artisans began labeling their pottery with the words *Sine Ceras*, without wax. A woman who bought a *Sine Ceras* pot knew that the clay had no hidden faults. If there were any imperfections, the artist left them visible. To be sincere is to be genuine, honest, and authentic—without pretense or disguise.

The Girl-Gone-Wild subverts her words. She speaks with flattering lips and a double heart. She's perfected the art of "sweet-talking him" and habitually uses this tactic to get what she wants. The Girl-Gone-Wise does not resort to flattery. Like Lady Wisdom, she can say, "Hear, for I will speak noble things, and from my lips will come what is right, for my mouth will utter truth; wickedness is an abomination to my lips. All the words of my mouth are righteous; there is nothing twisted or crooked in them" (Proverbs 8:6–8).

LIP STICK

We've covered the first two characteristics of the Wild Thing's speech—it is "much," and it is "smooth." The third descriptor the Sage mentions is that her speech is "seductive." To seduce is to win somebody over, to persuade or manipulate someone into agreeing. In this instance, her seductive talk persuaded and compelled the young man to have sex. But she could have used it to get him to agree to something else. Seductive speech is manipulative speech. It's wily speech. It seeks to control another person's behavior—it carries a hidden "stick." Seductive speech includes smooth speech, but it's much broader than that. It can also include criticism, put-downs, and all sorts of subtle innuendo and threats. It uses whatever type of speech is necessary to force the other person to comply with the hidden agenda.

For example, a woman might pout, "You're the only man who hasn't disappointed and hurt me. I put my trust in you. How can you be so selfish as to not give up your football tickets to go to my friend's party? You've been so dependable. You're not going to let me down like those other jerks, are you?" Her lip "stick" strokes his ego, stabs him in the back, and backs him into a corner, and all at the same time. Why? So she can seduce him into doing what she wants. She bombards him with all sorts of slippery talk so that her opinion and desires will prevail.

The Psalmist said this about seductive talkers, "Everyone utters lies to his neighbor; with flattering lips and a double heart they speak. May the Lord cut off all flattering lips, the tongue that makes great boasts, those who say, 'With our tongue we will prevail, our lips are with us; who is master over us?'" (Psalm 12:2–4). If this passage were personalized and paraphrased for a Wild Thing, it might say, "She is conniving and insincere. Her smooth talk masks a deceptive heart. May the Lord slice the lips off her face—pull from her mouth the bragging tongue that says, 'I have the power of persuasion. I can talk anyone into anything. I'm in control.'"

The Wild Thing is skilled at using smooth talk to seduce. She talks a lot. She sweet-talks, criticizes, coaxes, and cajoles. She says whatever is necessary so that her wish will "prevail." She's a control freak. She's determined to get what she wants. On the surface, she seems all sweet and nice, but cross her and she'll start to show her true colors. The Sage says that her lips drip honey, and her speech is smoother than oil, but in the end she is bitter as wormwood, sharp as a two-edged sword (Proverbs 5:3–4). She's like David's friend, whose "speech was smooth as butter, yet war was in his heart; his words were softer than oil, yet they were drawn swords" (Psalm 55:21).

What if the young man had resisted the woman's advances? What if he had said, "Listen. This is a really bad idea. I'm not going through with it. I'm going to stand firm and do what's right. Please take your hands off me. I'm going home now"? How do you think she would have responded? Would she have hung her head in shame and said, "Yeah, you're right! I'm so sorry!"? I doubt it. My guess is that she would have thrown a hissy fit. Her sweetness would have quickly transmogrified into bitter venom. She'd drop the verbal candy jar, pull out the daggers, and viciously attack. Instead of flattery, he'd be hit with a sharp barrage of accusing, scoffing, mocking, deriding, scorching, demeaning, angry, abusive words.

The Wild Thing uses words to control and manipulate. But the Bible says that whoever desires to love life and see good days will keep her tongue from evil and restrain her lips so that they speak no guile (1 Peter 3:10 KJV). *Guile* is an old-fashioned word that means deceit. It's cunning, tricky, crafty, or wily speech. The Greek word meaning *guile* translates as *bait for fish*. Like an angler baits a hook to catch a fish, so a guileful woman hangs her words to bait a man. She conceals her true thoughts and intentions while trying to hook him into doing what she wants. A Girl-Gone-Wise does not do this. Her speech is not cunning, tricky, crafty, or wily. She examines it and rids herself of all insincerity and guile (1 Peter 2:1; Psalm 34:13).

MIND YOUR MOUTH

How's your speech? Is it more wise or more wild? Do you talk lots? Are you insincere with compliments? Do you use flattery, smooth talk, or sweet talk to ingratiate others to you? Do you use words to manipulate or control? Cultivating godly speech is one of the biggest challenges for women today. Pop culture encourages us to sin with our speech. It encourages us to talk lots and loudly, to speak up and make ourselves heard, to gain favor with flattery, to be cunning, to manipulate, to be brazen, and to demand that others give us what we want. But the Bible says that excessive, duplicitous, and manipulative speech only leads to strife, iniquity, ruin, and trouble (Psalm 55:9–11). God's way is very different from the world's way and, paradoxically, much more effective. Do you want to enjoy life and see good days? Then work at restraining your words, and at speaking with sincerity, clarity, and honesty. Rid yourself of all insincerity and guile. Mind your mouth, and exchange your wild speech habits for those of a Girl-Gone-Wise.

Point of Contrast #18

INFLUENCE
Her Impact on Others and Their Impact on Her

Girl-Gone-Wild: Negative Influence	Girl-Gone-Wise: Positive Influence
"She persuades him. . . . She compels him. All at once he follows her, as an ox goes to the slaughter. . . . He does not know that it will cost him his life." (Proverbs 7:21–23)	"Whoever walks with the wise becomes wise, but the companion of fools will suffer harm." (Proverbs 13:20)

S he's so good for him. He's more 'Ryan' than ever before!" More Ryan? What did the mom of this twenty-three-year-old young man mean?

"More kind. More considerate. More gentle. More strong. More responsible. More good-humored. More focused. More all the good things that make Ryan, Ryan. More of the man God made him to be," she explained. "She brings out the best in him and makes him 'more.' I think she's *the one*."

I'd say that's a fairly high commendation from a potential mother-in-law! The godly influence his girlfriend exerted on her son convinced my friend that this young woman was pure gold. I got the chance to observe firsthand what she meant when, a few months later, my son started dating Jacqueline, and I watched Clark become "more Clark." When Clark asked for our blessing to marry her, Brent and I were able to give our wholehearted approval. Her positive godly influence had demonstrated to us that she was pure gold. She was the type of woman who would do her husband "good, and not harm, all the days of her life" (Proverbs 31:12).

This is often not the case. Many women have the opposite effect. They have a negative influence on men. They make him less and not more. Less responsible. Less considerate. Less reasonable. Less strong. Less good-humored. Less focused. Less committed to Christ. Less grown-up . . . less of the man God made him to be.

Influence is another point of contrast between the wise and the wild. Influence is the power to sway. It's the power that somebody has to affect another person's thinking or actions. A Girl-Gone-Wild exerts and is affected by negative influence. A Girl-Gone-Wise exerts and is affected by positive influence.

FATAL ATTRACTION

Back to our story . . . "With much seductive speech she persuades him; with her smooth talk she compels him." Her seductive words take hold. She succeeds in getting him to go home with her. "All at once he follows her, as an ox goes to the slaughter, or as a stag is caught fast till an arrow pierces its liver; as a bird rushes into a snare; he does not know that it will cost him his life" (Proverbs 7:21–23).

The woman succeeds in "persuading" and "compelling" the young man to sin. *Persuades* translates as a Hebrew verb meaning *to bend or turn*. It indicates that the woman turned the young man away from the direction he was headed. The other verb, *compels*, in Hebrew means to forcibly drive a flock of sheep away. It's used, for instance, for a lion or other predator that hunts and scatters them (Jeremiah 50:17; Isaiah 13:14). It's also used for inept shepherds who are guilty of doing the opposite of what they are supposed to do. Instead of compelling them to move in the right direction, the irresponsible shepherds scatter and/or lead the sheep astray (Ezekiel 34:4). The Old Testament uses both verbs repeatedly to refer to those who influence God's people to follow other gods (1 Kings 11:2; Deuteronomy 13:5).

That's exactly what the Wild Thing did. She seduced the young man to reject the true God for a false god of self-indulgence and sex. She was the negative influence that compelled him to sin. That's not to say the young man wasn't responsible for his behavior. He was just as guilty as she was. When he followed the seductress instead of God, he became a "traitor" (Proverbs 23:28). The Bible says that such a man will find himself "under the Lord's wrath" (Proverbs 22:14 NIV). Falling for a forbidden woman is a fatal attraction that will cost him his life.

The young man's illicit relationship leads to spiritual death. He falls into a deep dark pit. But the woman sets the trap. She "lies in wait like a robber and increases the traitors among mankind" (Proverbs 23:27–28). She robs the young man of his allegiance to God, his commitment to follow God's ways, his purity, his future, and ultimately his eternal destiny. It would be impossible to overstate how heinous her destructive influence is in God's eyes. Bad influence is a sin so wicked that God commanded the Israelites to put to death anyone who enticed a brother or sister to turn away from the ways of the Lord.

> If your brother, the son of your mother, or your son or your daughter or the wife you embrace or your friend who is as your own soul entices you secretly, saying, "Let us go and serve other gods" . . . you shall not yield to him or listen to him, nor shall your eye pity him, nor shall you spare him, nor shall you conceal him. But you shall kill him. . . . And all Israel shall hear and fear and never again do any such wickedness as this among you. (Deuteronomy 13:6–11)

Do you think God was being a bit harsh? Do you think He was overreacting? Is bad influence truly a sin deserving of death? Is it a threat so dangerous that it requires total annihilation? Or is the problem with us—that we're just too trendy to "get" how wrong it is to influence someone to sin? This passage is talking about leading someone to idolatry. A false god of sex is what the Wild Woman is ultimately calling her prey to. She is calling him to care more about illicit sexual pleasure than about God. Jesus also taught that bad influence was deserving of death. In Matthew 18:6 He said, "Whoever causes one of these little ones who believe in me to sin, it would be better for him to have a great millstone fastened around his neck and to be drowned in the depth of the sea." And let's not forget that in the Old Testament, the penalty for adultery was death (Leviticus 20:10).

Christ's death paid the penalty for our sin. He died so we might live. When the Pharisees caught a seductress in the act and asked Jesus if they should kill her as stipulated in the Law, Jesus directed that the person without sin should throw the first stone. Her accusers soon disappeared. Jesus asked, "Woman, where are they? Has no one condemned you?" She said, "No one, Lord." And Jesus said, "Neither do I condemn you; go, and from now on sin no more" (John 8:4–11).

God's grace is amazing. He didn't send His Son into the world to condemn us, but to save us from sin's condemnation (John 3:17). Jesus knew that the adulteress standing in front of Him deserved death. He knew that the man who succumbed to her charms also deserved to die. She sinned. He sinned. We all sin. We all deserve death. The fact that Jesus bore our punishment is the essence of the gospel and the great hope to which we cling. But the sad fact is, we often take His sacrifice for granted. We fail to appreciate the seriousness of sin. We fail to understand that a sin like negative influence is a "big deal." I hope that you're beginning to figure out how much God hates it when people entice others to sin. The sin of seduction is abhorrent to Him. I hope that you're starting to get it. He wants us to expropriate this wrong from our lives and from the Christian community. Does He extend grace? Yes, absolutely. However, He expects that those who receive it will "go, and from now on sin no more."

THE COMPANY YOU KEEP

I wonder if the young man thought he was immune to the Wild Thing's negative influence. I wonder if he rationalized that he'd just hang out for a short while and keep her company that evening. She was obviously lonely, unhappy with her marriage, and in desperate need of a friend. Maybe he thought he could help her—maybe he thought he could be a positive influence in her life. The fact that she had to persuade, compel, and sweet-talk him into the affair, and that he hesitated before giving in, indicates that his standards for sexual conduct were higher than hers were, and that he wasn't planning on having an affair.

Negative influence is very powerful. Not only does the Bible want us to stop being a negative influence on others, but it also wants us to avoid people who might exert a negative influence on us. The Sage says, "A righteous man is cautious in friendship, but the way of the wicked leads them astray" (Proverbs 12:26 NIV). A Girl-Gone-Wise chooses her friends carefully. She does not take on just anybody as a friend. Being "cautious" means that she searches out and investigates a person's character. She knows that if she constantly and exclusively hangs out with people who don't love the Lord, chances are they'll have a greater influence on her than she will have on them. They will affect her negatively.

Paul warned the Christians in Corinth that hanging out with the wrong people would have a bad effect on their behavior. Just because they'd become Christians didn't mean they were immune to negative influence. They were still susceptible. Paul cites a proverb that was in popular circulation in his day. His point is that *everybody*—even unbelievers—knows that the saying is true. It's common knowledge. The young believers shouldn't be deceived: "Bad company ruins good morals" (1 Corinthians 15:33).

Have you ever heard that saying? Or how about, "Tell me your friends, and I'll tell you who you are," or, "Birds of a feather flock together," or, "A man is known by the company he keeps"? That last one was in a *A Preparative to Marriage* book published in the year 1591: "If a man can be known by nothing els, then he maye bee known by his companions."[1] The saying has endured for centuries. In 1967, recording artist Dolly Parton used it as the basis for her breakout hit, "The Company You Keep."

You say you're doin' nothing wrong
I don't believe you are
I'm only trying to help you, sis
Before you go too far
'Cause I think you're an angel
But folks think that you're cheap
'Cause you're known by the company you keep

The company you keep keeps you out too long
Mom and Dad don't go to sleep until you get home
Sis, you're gettin' in too deep
You'd better look before you leap
'Cause you're known by the company you keep.[2]

The lyrics indicate that it's not just the little sister's reputation the big sister is worried about. She's worried that her little sister is "gettin' in too deep." She's afraid that the friends are going to influence her little sister negatively and make her stumble. *Everyone* knows that that's usually the case. Not only are you known by the company you keep, you're also shaped by the company you keep.

Paul was aware of the incredible power of negative influence. He told the Corinthians not to associate "with anyone who bears the name of brother if he is guilty of sexual immorality or greed, or is an idolater, reviler, drunkard, or swindler—not even to eat with such a one" (1 Corinthians 5:11).

That's pretty radical talk in our "I'm OK—you're OK" culture. But Paul knew that the people who have the most negative influence on believers are other people in the community of faith who profess to follow Christ, but who are hypocrites. There's less danger in associating with those who openly reject Jesus than those who claim to follow Him but who promote mediocrity and compromise.

IT WON'T HAPPEN TO ME

The Sage Father said, "Whoever walks with the wise becomes wise, but the companion of fools will suffer harm" (Proverbs 13:20). What's really sad is that later in life, he ended up going against his own advice. He started keeping the wrong kind of company. The women he associated with were a negative influence on him and turned his heart away from wholeheartedly following the Lord.

Now King Solomon loved many foreign women . . . from the nations concerning which the Lord had said to the people of Israel, "You shall not enter into marriage with them, neither shall they with you, for surely they will turn away your heart after their gods." Solomon clung to these in love. . . . When Solomon was old his wives turned away his heart after other gods,

226

and his heart was not wholly true to the Lord his God, as was the heart of David his father. . . . And the Lord was angry with Solomon, because his heart had turned away from the Lord, the God of Israel, who had appeared to him twice and had commanded him concerning this thing, that he should not go after other gods. But he did not keep what the Lord commanded. (1 Kings 11:1–4, 9–10)

Solomon was probably tripped up by the classic, foolish assumption that "it won't happen to me."

I'm amazed at the number of women who think they are immune to the power of negative influence. They think they're strong enough, and that they've walked with the Lord long enough, to be above the threat. So they start taking foolish risks in relationships. They let down their defenses, transgress boundaries, and crash and burn—and then wonder how it happened to them.

Scripture repeatedly warns against the assumption that we are beyond being affected by negative influence. "Therefore let anyone who thinks that he stands take heed lest he fall" (1 Corinthians 10:12). "Beware lest there be among you a root bearing poisonous and bitter fruit, one who . . . blesses himself in his heart, saying, 'I shall be safe, though I walk in the stubbornness of my heart'" (Deuteronomy 29:18–19).

If you are wise, you will walk in humble dependence on the Lord and avoid people who exert negative influence. You'll recognize that it could indeed happen to you, and that you are not beyond becoming a Girl-Gone-Wild . . . not at any stage in life.

POSITIVE INFLUENCE

The Lord created women with a unique relational bent. Therefore, women are powerful influencers—particularly in their relationships with men. How do we use this gift wisely? How can we make sure that we are influencing others in a positive way? The Bible gives some suggestions:

Choosing Positive and Not Negative Influence

Positive influencers seek out the company of those whose hearts are wholly inclined toward the Lord. Daniel 3 records the story of Shadrach, Meshach, and Abednego. It's an example of good friends who were a positive influence on each other. They stuck together as friends and positively encouraged one another to obey God, even in the face of difficulty and opposition. Queen Esther, one of the most prominent female influencers in the Bible, was careful to seek out godly input from her uncle and to surround herself with friends who supported and joined her in godly spiritual disciplines. Wise Women will make sure that their best friends are wise women.

Positive influencers not only surround themselves with positive influence; they are also careful to avoid negative influence. They are acutely aware of their own susceptibility to sin, so they do not form close associations with people who will influence them to compromise their obedience to God (Proverbs 13:20; 14:7).

Affecting Others through Strength of Character

Peter told female believers that the best way to be a positive influence was through their strength of character. He said, "Likewise, wives, be subject to your own husbands, so that even if some do not obey the word, they may be won without a word by the conduct of their wives, when they see your respectful and pure conduct" (1 Peter 3:1–2). The "respectful" and "pure" conduct of the women is what would have the greatest impact.

A wise woman knows that it's not her words, but her behavior that carries the biggest clout when it comes to compelling change. The more Christlike you are, the more positive your influence will be. If you truly want to influence someone else for good, you won't focus on changing *his* behavior. You'll focus on changing *your* behavior. You'll work at becoming more godly, and on interacting with him in a more godly way.

Judicious with Words

A positive influencer is very wise and careful with words. She wins others over "without a word." She's not a blabber, jabber, nagger, whiner, complainer, or yammerer. Nor does she use wiles, charms, smooth talk, or sweet talk to manipulate. She gives very little in the way of advice—so the little she says is extremely powerful and effective. "The heart of the wise makes his speech judicious and adds persuasiveness to his lips" (Proverbs 16:23).

Relying on God to Effect Change

A positive influencer knows that ultimately it is God, and not she, who effects positive change in a person's life. So she relies on Him and on her most potent, influential tool—prayer. Take Queen Esther, for example. When she wanted to influence King Ahasuerus, she didn't self-confidently burst in and start making demands. Nor did she try to influence him with crying, nagging, or pouting. What did she do? She called a fast. She asked her family and friends to fast and pray with her for three solid days. Only then did she approach the king. And she approached him with humility, few words, and much wisdom, knowing that in the end it was the Lord, and not she, who had the power to turn the king's heart.

How about you? Are you a positive influence? Are you surrounding yourself with positive influences and avoiding negative ones? Are you working on your strength of character and at controlling your mouth? Do you pray and rely on God to effect change? When it comes to the influence you accept and exert in your life, are you living wild or wise?

Now do the study questions in the *Girls Gone Wise Companion Guide*. They will help you apply the Word to your life and influence you to be increasingly wise.

Point of Contrast #19

SUSTAINABILITY
Her Ability to Nurture
and Sustain a Relationship

Girl-Gone-Wild: **Relationships Deteriorate**	Girl-Gone-Wise: **Relationships Grow**
"For many a victim has she laid low, and all her slain are a mighty throng." (Proverbs 7:26)	"The wisest of women builds her house, but folly with her own hands tears it down." (Proverbs 14:1)

W hat's your sexual history? How many sexual partners have you had?"

"Three. No, wait . . . make that four, including my fiancé." Emily's blue eyes blinked. "But I don't sleep around," she added, as though that somehow added an element of integrity to her pattern of behavior. Not sleeping around meant that she remained sexually faithful to her current love interest. That, and the fact that her number of partners hadn't yet reached the double digits, indicated to me that she considered her conduct to be respectable, and not promiscuous or whorish.

I sighed and silently asked the Holy Spirit how to start praying for this twenty-something Christian young woman. I felt as though I was looking at a massive, tangled ball of string with ends sticking out all over the place. Pulling on one would do little good, since it was attached to all the others. It would take years of prayer ministry and discipleship training to unravel the tangled knots. I only had a few short minutes.

As I prayed, the Lord met Emily in a significant way, but my heart was heavy and ached for her as I watched her walk across the room and out the door. I could tell she was carrying around a father-wound, a demonic stronghold, wrong patterns of thinking, bitterness, deception, and bondage to sin. I turned and asked a friend, "Is it just me? Or is the amount of sexual sin and bondage in the average woman's life piling up higher and higher?" Twenty years ago in women's ministry, it was extremely rare for me to encounter someone who had experienced so much relational dysfunction and sexual sin. Today, I am routinely seeing in women in their twenties more carnage than most women of the past accumulated in a lifetime. A woman who hasn't burned through a string of ugly, fractured relationships and had a succession of men in her bed, is now the exception rather than the rule.

Serial monogamy, the repeated leaping from one sexually monogamous relationship to another, has become a popular relationship trend of this generation. According to the Urban Dictionary, the most popularly accepted definition of a serial monogamist is this:

> One who spends as little time as possible being single, moving from the end of one relationship to the beginning of a new relationship as quickly as possible. Although the relationships in which many serial monogamists find themselves are also often short lived, the defining aspect of serial monogamy is the desire and ability to enter new relationships very quickly, thus abbreviating any period of single life during which the serial monogamist may begin to ask questions of an existential nature.[1]

Serial monogamy involves a succession of intense "committed" relationships, separated by tragic breakups. Take Karin, for example. This girl breaks up with Brad, whom she's been going out with for a year and a half, to go out with Scott. After a couple of months, she moves in with Scott, and they live together for two years. When her relationship with Scott seems irreparable, she starts dating Adam, who she then dumps after a few months because Harry has asked her out. She's sure Harry's the one. She convinces him that he is. They get engaged, move in together, and soon thereafter get married. But three years later, she's got a list of grievances. Her coworker, Bryan, lends a sympathetic shoulder and helps her through the divorce. Not long after, she moves in with Bryan. By the time she's twenty-five, she has cohabited with three men, married and divorced one of them, and slept with two others. She's had five serious, "committed" relationships.

I see it all the time. Older women aren't much better. They're into chain marriages. Perhaps they've been able to sustain a marriage for ten or twenty years before moving on to the next, but whether it's two or twenty-two sexual relationships a woman has in her lifetime, it's still serial monogamy. It goes against God's plan for one love between one man and one woman for life—an exclusive, permanent, "till death do us part" union.

The Proverbs 7 woman cheated on her husband. So she obviously wasn't monogamous. But that wasn't always the case. The Sage says that this type of woman "forsakes the companion of her youth and forgets the covenant of her God" (Proverbs 2:17). That indicates that she was committed to her husband and to monogamy at the start of her marriage. She didn't plan on being unfaithful. We don't know what her premarital sexual history was, but perhaps she had a number of "committed" relationships prior to getting married. Perhaps she was serially monogamous with one or more boyfriends prior to marriage. Perhaps her husband was one of them. Maybe she had remained faithful to him for a number of years and had only recently started having flings behind his back. We do know that by the time we encounter her, she had had several sexual partners, and the revolving door of men was a well-established pattern. "For many a victim has she laid low, and all her slain are a mighty throng."

Sleeping with one man at a time, in one "committed" relationship after another, is not substantially different from promiscuously sleeping with more than one at a time. The timing and the intent is different (the serial monogamist doesn't "intend" to sleep with anyone but her current partner), but the offense and the effect are the same. Both patterns involve sexual sin and leave multiple victims in their wake.

The ability to sustain and nurture a relationship is another point of contrast between a Girl-Gone-Wise and a Girl-Gone-Wild. Wise Things guard their hearts. They choose friends and a life companion very carefully and are usually able to make relationships work. Wild Things rush in and suffer through one tragic relational breakdown after another. Wise Things nurture and grow their relationships. Wild Things behave in such a way as to destroy them. They "shoot themselves in the foot," tragically crippling and sabotaging the very thing they hope to gain. As the Sage observes, "The wisest of women builds her house, but folly with her own hands tears it down" (Proverbs 14:1).

The reason a Wild Thing's relationships break down are many and varied, but I think they generally boil down to one thing, disrespect —disrespect for God and disrespect for others.

DISRESPECT FOR GOD

Many women think that God's plan for relationships and sexuality is prudish, repressive, and seriously outdated. Just yesterday, I received a comment on my blog from Christy. She said that encouraging girls to be pure and holy virgins promotes sexual repression. She argued that I was creating problems for women by bestowing a Madonna/whore complex on their sexuality. Christy wasn't against morals, she just thought God's standards were extreme. They're "damaging" to women. And by teaching what the Bible says about sexuality, I am "part of the problem."[2] Christy obviously doesn't have a very high regard for God or for His Word. She wants to come up with her own set of standards. She thinks she knows better than God does. While most Christians wouldn't come right out and say it, their behavior indicates that they have this same attitude of disrespect.

We disrespect God when we reject His pattern and purpose for our lives. God is our Creator. He knows what's best for us. God says, "You turn things upside down! Shall the potter be regarded as the clay, that the thing made should say of its maker, 'He did not make me'; or the thing formed say of him who formed it, 'He has no understanding'?" (Isaiah 29:16). God is not a mean ogre trying to rain on our parade. When He tells us how we ought to behave, it's because He knows and wants what is best for us. He has all wisdom and understanding. He is the Creator. He is God!

We respect God by respecting what He says we ought to respect. He tells us to respect the institution of marriage and not to sleep around outside of it. "Let marriage be held in honor among all, and let the marriage bed be undefiled, for God will judge the sexually immoral and adulterous" (Hebrews 13:4). He tells us to honor the fact that our bodies are the temple of the Holy Spirit, and to glorify Him with our bodies by keeping them sexually pure (1 Corinthians 6:15–20). He tells us to control our bodies in holiness and honor, not in the passion of lust (1 Thessalonians 4:4). He tells us not to marry unbelievers (2 Corinthians 6:14). He tells us that marriage is a permanent union, and in God's eyes, divorce and remarriage isn't an option (Mark 10:4–12). The woman who thumbs her nose at His plan and does things her own way is foolish. She will undoubtedly suffer negative consequences.

Sherie Adams Christensen, a student at Brigham Young University, did an extensive survey of research on premarital sex and marital satisfaction. The results are staggering. In study after study, premarital sex correlates negatively with marital stability. In other words, those who don't have premarital sex have more stable marriages. Women who were sexually active prior to marriage face a considerably higher risk of marriage breakdown than women who were virgin brides. Premarital sexual activity, even with one's future spouse, can decrease future marital satisfaction, and increase the chance of infidelity and divorce by up to almost 80 percent. The risk of divorce for women engaging in premarital sex with someone other than their future husband was 114 percent higher than those who did not!

Premarital cohabitation significantly lowers subsequent marital quality and happiness. Premarital cohabiters had significantly lower levels of problem solving and support behaviors than those who had not cohabited before marriage. On average, cohabiting relationships only last about a year. The statistics also show that sex is more satisfying in marriage than in any other context. Christensen concludes that "premarital sexual promiscuity must be considered among other documented 'risks' that negatively affect marital and sexual satisfaction."[3]

That's not to say that doing things God's way guarantees that you will never face serious problems or difficulties in your marriage. But the girl who commented on my blog is wrong when she maintains that following God's plan "damages" women. Women are far more "damaged" when they disrespect God and do things their own way. Following His plan for manhood, womanhood, relationships, marriage, sex, and family is not only good—it's also good for you. If you want a lasting, fulfilling relationship, you will go about it in God's way. You will respect Him.

DISRESPECT FOR OTHERS

The Proverbs 7 woman didn't respect men. She just wanted to have a good time. She didn't care if anyone got hurt in the process. She didn't care that her fling would wound her husband, or that her behavior would have negative consequences for her lover. She was too selfish to be concerned about hurting them.

"For many a victim she laid low, and all her slain are a mighty throng" is military language. Several commentators think the Sage used this description to bring to his son's mind the familiar image of the Phoenician goddess, Astarte. Astarte is queen of the Morning Star, goddess of war—a wild and furious warrior who sadistically "plunges knee-deep in knights' blood; hip deep in the gore of heroes."[4] She is also Queen of the Evening Star, goddess of sensuality and passion. She is beautiful, desirable, sexual, savage, and deadly. She's a ruthless conqueror who leaves the battlefield strewn with corpses. Solomon hoped the allusion would help his son grasp the danger of associating with such a woman.

The seductress causes the downfall and destruction of many men. From all outward appearances, she's just a beautiful woman looking for a friend. But in actuality, she's a "man-slayer." She uses men. She hurts them. She's not a builder, she's a destroyer. She tears her "victim" down and "lays him low." The fact that she uses him to meet her own selfish ends, disregards that it will affect him negatively, and discards him when he no longer serves her purposes demonstrates contempt and a severe lack of respect.

Have you noticed how prevalent disrespect toward men has become? In the sixties, women complained that men victimized and disrespected them. Now the tables have turned. Our sons, husbands, fathers, and men-friends are subjected to malicious jokes and attitudes that wouldn't be tolerated toward any other group. Women portray them as selfish, lazy, inconsiderate, hormone-crazed buffoons.

They gleefully slander and tear them down simply because they are male. Women today are like the Phoenician goddess. One moment, they entice men with their beauty and sexual prowess, and the next, they pull out their swords and slice them down.

Christians are not innocent of this sin. I am astonished when I see the haughtiness and contempt with which Christian women treat men. I feel grieved when I hear them tell jokes, mock, deride, put down, and criticize their male colleagues, friends, boyfriends, and husbands. I wonder how they can have the audacity to disrespect and hurt those whom God has created. Sadly, the church is filled with man-slayers. Instead of building men up, we attack, destroy, and bring them down. We use the sword of our tongues to lay them low. Disrespect is one of the main reasons relationships break down. Can you imagine how much longer they'd last if we treated our husbands and friends with respect and didn't lash out to wound them? If, instead of criticizing, complaining, whining, and demanding that they live up to their responsibilities, we took care to ensure that we lived up to ours?

The following list summarizes some of the Bible's directives on how we ought to regard and respect others. They represent the nuts and bolts on what God requires of us in our relationships with one another:

- "Do nothing from rivalry or conceit, but in humility count others more significant than yourselves. Let each of you look not only to his own interests, but also to the interests of others. Have this mind among yourselves, which is yours in Christ Jesus." (Philippians 2:3–5)
- "Love builds up." (1 Corinthians 8:1)
- "Let each of us please his neighbor for his good, to build him up." (Romans 15:2)
- "Encourage one another and build one another up." (1 Thessalonians 5:11)
- "Let no corrupting talk come out of your mouths, but only such as is good for building up, as fits the occasion, that it may give grace to those who hear." (Ephesians 4:29)

- "See that no one repays anyone evil for evil, but always seek to do good to one another." (1 Thessalonians 5:15)
- "Do not grumble against one another." (James 5:9)
- "Bear one another's burdens." (Galatians 6:2)
- "With all humility and gentleness, with patience, bearing with one another in love." (Ephesians 4:2)
- "Be kind to one another, tenderhearted, forgiving one another, as God in Christ forgave you." (Ephesians 4:32)
- "Bearing with one another and, if one has a complaint against another, forgiving each other; as the Lord has forgiven you, so you also must forgive." (Colossians 3:13)
- "A new commandment I give to you, that you love one another: just as I have loved you, you also are to love one another." (John 13:34)
- "Let all things be done for building up." (1 Corinthians 14:26)

The thing about these commands is that they have no qualifiers. They're not dependent on how our partner behaves. They don't say, "Let no corrupting talk come out of your mouth *if* no corrupting talk comes out of his." Or "Build him up *if* he builds you up." Or "Be kind and tenderhearted, forgiving him *if* he is kind and tenderhearted, forgiving you." God doesn't give us the option of respecting only those who are respectable. He commands, "Honor *everyone*!" (1 Peter 2:17). The reasons most relationships break down is that the parties spend more time pointing fingers at how the other person is failing to be honorable, rather than making sure that they themselves are.

It breaks my heart when I see wives "man-slaying" their husbands— cutting them down instead of building them up. Women, don't ever forget that when you hurt your husband, you hurt yourself. "The wisest of women builds her house, but folly with her own hands tears it down" (Proverbs 14:1). A Girl-Gone-Wise does not tear down. She is a builder and not a destroyer. She demonstrates respect.

DEMANDING RESPECT

You might ask, "What about me? Don't I deserve some respect?" Pop culture incessantly chants the "you-deserve-it-so-demand-and-take-it" mantra. It teaches women to demand that others respect them before they will give respect in return. But that's not the way of Christ.

Peter anticipated that believers would ask the "Don't-I-deserve-respect?" question, when he instructed them to honor everyone. He knew that some of his friends would face situations where people would respond to good with evil. He told them that they should be honorable and respectful nonetheless.

> If when you do good and suffer for it you endure, this is a gracious thing in the sight of God. For to this you have been called, because Christ also suffered for you, leaving you an example, so that you might follow in his steps. He committed no sin, neither was deceit found in his mouth. When he was reviled, he did not revile in return; when he suffered, he did not threaten, but continued entrusting himself to him who judges justly. (1 Peter 2:20–23)

What did Christ do when others disrespected Him? Did He "demand" respect? Did He scream, yell, and attack them with caustic remarks? No. He responded by "entrusting himself" to God. That's what we're to do too. That's not to say that we don't have protective boundaries, or shouldn't clearly express our opinions or work to change our circumstances, but that everything we say and do is honorable and respectful. Entrusting ourselves to God means that we don't try to control how the other person responds. We behave in the right way and leave the rest up to the Lord.

How are your relationships doing? Are you nurturing and sustaining them? Are they growing? Or are you stuck in a revolving door of broken ones? If you are married, is your love growing deeper? Are you more in love with your husband now than you first were? If you're not, you may need to take a serious look at whether you're behaving with the proper respect toward God and toward your husband. Evaluate your other relationships too. For them to grow, you need to behave in an honorable and respectful way. Remember: Girl-Gone-Wise builds her house—but a Wild One with her own hands tears it down.

Point of Contrast #20

TEACHABILITY
Her Willingness to Be Corrected and Instructed

Girl-Gone-Wild: Scornful	Girl-Gone-Wise: Teachable
"Woe to her who is rebellious and defiled. . . . She listens to no voice; she accepts no correction. She does not trust in the Lord; she does not draw near to her God." (Zephaniah 3:1–2)	"The ear that listens to life-giving reproof will dwell among the wise." (Proverbs 15:31)

Sadly, the man falls for the seduction. He follows the woman home and they spend the night together. The "stolen water is sweet, and bread eaten in secret is pleasant," but the story doesn't have a happy ending (Proverbs 9:17–18). The young man didn't realize that when he went to her house, he went to his grave. Maybe her husband finds out. Maybe she gets pregnant. Maybe he gets an STD. Maybe he loses his reputation. Maybe he's overcome with guilt and shame. Maybe she breaks his heart. Maybe he gets drawn deeper into sin. We don't know the details, but we do know that his decision disrupts his relationship to God. It leads to spiritual death. She promises him a slice of heaven, but he ends up in the pit of hell.

We've come to the end of the story, and to the last point of contrast between the wild and the wise. The simple young man who lacked sense and the wily seductress who caused his downfall are examples of two individuals who failed to walk in the way of wisdom. The Sage urged his son to pay close attention to their mistakes, so that he might learn from them. That's why he told the story. And that's why he wrote his book. The dad wanted his son to become wise. He wanted him to understand words of insight, to receive instruction, to be discerning and not naive, and to advance in knowledge and discretion. The Sage figured that everybody who was wise would pay attention to the meaning of the story and to all the proverbs that he wrote down. His wise words would help readers increase in learning and knowledge. They would make the wise increasingly wise (1:2–5).

SIMPLE, FOOLISH, OR SCOFFING

The final point of contrast between wise and wild is teachability, which is a woman's willingness to be corrected and instructed. A Girl-Gone-Wise is teachable. She's eager to grow. She welcomes correction and training. A Girl-Gone-Wild scorns instruction. She doesn't think she needs input. She resists change. In the book of Proverbs, the Sage profiles three types of individuals who turn their backs on God's invitation to become wise. They are the simple, the fools, and the scoffers. Proverbs 1:22 mentions all three. Wisdom asks, "How long, O *simple ones*, will you love being simple? How long will *scoffers* delight in their scoffing and *fools* hate knowledge?" (italics added).

The three categories aren't mutually exclusive. The characteristics of simple people, fools, and scoffers overlap. At times, the Sage uses the word *fool* in a general way to refer to anyone who resists wisdom. He sometimes calls a simple one a fool, and sometimes accuses a fool of scoffing. Nevertheless, he seems to make a distinction between these three types of foolish people—a distinction based on their likelihood to learn. The three represent a continuum of teachability. The simple person is somewhat open to instruction; the fool, less so; and the scoffer, completely closed to attaining wisdom. From the simple one to the fool to the scoffer, there is an increasing hostility and resistance to learning, and to doing things God's way. A Wild Thing will fall somewhere along this continuum. She will be like Simple Sally, Foolish Fran, or Scoffing Sue.

Simple Sally

Simple Sally is the female version of the young man in our story. The Sage described the victim as "young," "simple," and "lacking sense." "Young" refers to age, but also, and more importantly, to a lack of life experience. To be simple means that a woman doesn't have the necessary know-how. She doesn't clearly understand the implications or consequences of her actions (Proverbs 22:3). She doesn't see the danger, so she's easily taken in (27:12). She naively "believes everything" and fails to give thought to her steps (14:15). Unfortunately, this means that she's open to negative influence and that she'll likely get burned. Since she can't tell the difference between good and evil, folly and wisdom, she'll fall prey to the wicked.

The simplemindedness of the young man prevented him from seeing through the Wild Thing's wily scheme. He was naive. He didn't fully grasp that meeting up with the woman and having an affair would be bad for him. He hadn't bothered to think things through and to educate himself in the ways of wisdom.

Like him, Simple Sally is uninformed. She doesn't think that learning is all that important, so she doesn't make the effort to figure out what's wild and what's wise. She's blissfully ignorant. She "loves being simple." In short, she's childish. Children are open, trusting, and naive. This mind-set is to be expected in a child, but for a grown woman, it's a recipe for disaster. The danger is that Simple Sally will listen to the instruction of fools (Proverbs 16:22). She'll get mixed up with the wrong crowd and start taking the wrong advice. She'll believe the guy who tells her he loves her or who makes hollow promises so he can get her into bed, or she'll believe the girlfriend who tells her that going to the bar or strip club is a good idea, or she'll believe the ad that entices her to look at porn. If she fails to seek wisdom, she'll inevitably "inherit folly" (14:18). She'll be killed by inadvertently turning away (1:32).

The Sage says Sally needs to give some serious thought to her steps (Proverbs 14:15). She needs to learn how to think things through and behave with knowledge and discretion (1:4). In order to succeed in life, she needs to grow up and stop being so naive—to stop and look before she leaps. The Sage urges, "Leave your simple ways, and live, and walk in the way of insight" (9:6). To grow in wisdom, Simple Sally has to accept the challenge to learn. She must eagerly study the Word of God, pay attention to the pitfalls and dangers of sin, and learn from the mistakes and failures of others (19:7; 21:11). Sally has to stop being so simple. If she doesn't, she'll become like her sister, Foolish Fran.

Foolish Fran

Unlike Sally, Foolish Fran isn't uninformed. Fran has heard the message of wisdom. But she's unconcerned. She just doesn't care. She thinks she's got life figured out and under control. Fran is overconfident (Proverbs 14:16). She doesn't take God seriously (14:9). She takes no pleasure in understanding, but only in expressing her own opinion (18:2). Fran knows best. Her way is right in her own eyes (12:15). If a friend warns her about the consequences of sin, Foolish Fran tells her to "just lighten up." Doing wrong is like a joke to her (10:23). Nothing bad will happen! She'll be able to stop before going too far. She's got the situation under control. The thing that matters most to Fran is that she enjoys herself and has fun (Ecclesiastes 7:4).

Fran's problem is that she's reckless and careless (Proverbs 14:16). She despises wisdom and instruction, and especially the advice of her parents (1:7; 15:5). What do they know? Fran doesn't need another lecture. She knows what could happen; she just doesn't think it could happen to her. So she doesn't turn away from evil (13:19). If it looks like fun, she wades right in. She sins and makes mistakes. But she doesn't learn from them. Like a dog that returns to his vomit, she repeats her folly (26:11). She promises herself she won't, but she ends up making the same mistake over and over again.

Foolish Fran denies the danger of sin. She doesn't really believe that folly leads to more and greater folly (Proverbs 14:24). She thinks the consequences of sin are way overblown. She won't get sucked in. She can handle it—she's got things under control. Fran's lack of concern will lead to her ruin (10:14). She'll be destroyed by her complacency. The more she sins, the more she'll be enslaved to the bondage of sin.

Sin will lead to more sin. Much like Israel, who paid an awful price for depending more on other countries' military power than God's, the more she sins, the more the bonds will "be made strong" (Isaiah 28:22), until she becomes a scoffer. Her heart will get increasingly hard. Eventually, Foolish Fran will pass the point of no return. She'll get to the place where she is so enslaved to sin that she is unable and unwilling to change (Proverbs 27:22). In the process, she'll make a mess of her life.

What does Foolish Fran need to do to break out of this destructive pattern? The Sage says she needs to learn to love God's ways (Proverbs 1:22–23). She needs to stop feeding on folly (15:14) and start developing some self-control (18:7). Fran needs to have more respect for God (1:7). Usually a woman like Foolish Fran won't be motivated to change until she reaches a crisis point (3:35). She'll run headlong after the pleasures of sin until she hits a wall and the consequences beat her down (19:29).

If she's too far gone, even this won't bring change (Proverbs 27:22). But if she humbly repents and learns some sense, the Lord will help her get her life back on track (8:5). In either case, she'll have to live with the consequences of her sin. For example, she will never regain her virginity, her relationship will still break down, the STD will still flare up, the baby will still be born, the memories will still haunt, the dark temptation will still knock, bad thoughts will still nag, and new relationships will live under the shadow of it all. If she repents, the Lord will redeem what Satan intended for harm and bring good out of it, but the damage will rarely be completely undone.

Scoffing Sue

Scoffing Sue isn't interested in learning the way of wisdom. While Sally is uninformed, and Fran is unconcerned, Sue is unashamed. She unabashedly insists that God's way is wrong. Like the Babylonian army in Habakkuk, she makes believe she has the power to be her own god (Habakkuk 1:10–11).

She is proud, arrogant, and insolent (Proverbs 21:24). She doesn't hesitate to "stick her tongue out" and thumb her nose at the Lord (Isaiah 57:4). She doesn't care what He thinks, nor does she care what others have to say about it (Psalm 74:10; Proverbs 15:12). She hates people who think she's doing something wrong. If someone tries to correct her, she lashes out to injure and abuse (9:7–8).

Scoffing Sue is a slave to her own sinful desires (Jude 18). What's more, she's intent on seducing others to indulge in sin with her (Proverbs 7:21). She doesn't care if she hurts or exploits them in the process (7:26; 29:8). When Scoffing Sue is presented with wisdom, she doesn't "get" it. She can't grasp truth (14:6). She's convinced her way is right, so she refuses to change (13:1).

The danger of being a scoffer is profound. Sue is spiritually dead, condemned, cut off from God (Proverbs 19:29; Isaiah 29:20). Her life will be tough. She won't be able to sustain relationships, and the consequences of her sin will come back to haunt her, bringing pain and suffering down on her head (Proverbs 9:12; 22:10). Scoffing Sue won't escape God's punishment (Isaiah 29:20). Scripture says she'll come to nothing (Isaiah 29:20).

We don't know exactly where the seductress of Proverbs 7 was on the continuum of the three profiles, but I think it's safe to say that if she hadn't already crossed over from being a Foolish Fran to a Scoffing Sue, she was extremely close to doing so. What a woman like this needs is to encounter Christ. She has no desire to change and no inherent ability to do so. Apart from God's intervention and the regenerative work of the Holy Spirit, she's doomed. The Lord will let her "eat the fruit of her way, and have her fill of her own devices" (1:31).

A Girl-Gone-Wild, like the city of Jerusalem in the days of Zephaniah, "listens to no voice; she accepts no correction. She does not trust in the Lord; she does not draw near to her God" (Zephaniah 3:1–2). Simple Sally can't be bothered to listen, Foolish Fran doesn't see a reason to, and Scoffing Sue brashly refuses. The following chart summarizes their three profiles. As you read and compare them, think about whether you fit into any of the categories. (Note: Unless otherwise indicated, all references on this chart are from the book of Proverbs.)

Point of Contrast #20: Teachability

	Simple Sally	Foolish Fran	Scoffing Sue
Trait	She's uninformed—she doesn't make an effort to learn.	She's unconcerned—she thinks she's got it all figured out.	She's unashamed—she insists God's way is wrong.
Attitude	She doesn't think that learning is all that important (9:4–6). She likes not having to think about serious things (1:22).	She doesn't take God seriously (14:9). She's overconfident (14:16). She thinks she knows better (13:16; 18:2). Her way is right in her own eyes (12:15). Doing wrong is like a joke to her (10:23). She just wants to have fun (Ecclesiastes 7:4).	She is her own god (Habakkuk 1:10–11). She sticks out her tongue at God (Isaiah 57:4). She is proud, arrogant, and insolent (21:24). She doesn't care what God thinks (Psalm 74:10). She doesn't care what wise people say (15:12). She hates those who say she's wrong (9:8).
Problem	She lacks sense (7:7). She fails to see the danger (22:3). She doesn't understand the implications (27:12). She's gullible (14:15).	She's reckless and careless (14:16). She despises wisdom and instruction (1:7), especially of parents (15:5). She doesn't turn away from evil (13:19). She repeats and doesn't learn from her mistakes (26:11).	She's a slave to sin (Jude 18). She seduces others to sin (7:21). She doesn't care if she hurts and exploits (7:26; 29:8). She can't grasp truth (14:6). She refuses to change (13:1).
Danger	She'll listen to the instruction of fools (16:22).	Her folly will lead to more folly (14:24).	She's spiritually dead (9:18).

247

	Simple Sally	Foolish Fran	Scoffing Sue
Danger (cont'd)	She will inherit folly (14:18). She will be killed by inadvertently turning away (1:32).	She'll ruin her own life (10:14). She'll be destroyed by her complacency (1:32). Her bondage will be made strong (Isaiah 28:22). She'll pass the point of being able to change (27:22).	She is condemned (19:29). She will be cut off (Isaiah 29:20). She'll be unable to sustain relationships (22:10). She'll suffer (9:12). She'll be punished (21:11). She'll come to nothing (Isaiah 29:20).
Need	She needs to give thought to her steps (14:15). She needs to leave simple ways (9:6). She needs insight (9:6). She needs to be cautious (1:4).	She needs to appreciate knowledge (1:22). She needs to stop feeding on folly (15:14). She needs to develop self-discipline (18:7). She needs to start hearing God (1:7).	She needs to encounter Christ.
Corrective	She accepts the challenge to become wise (9:4). She eagerly studies the Word (Psalm 19:7). She learns from the failures of others (21:11).	She reaches a crisis point (1:31; 3:35). She experiences the consequences of her sin (19:29; 26:3). She humbly repents and works at change (8:5).	She has little or no desire to change. Change will only come through God's intervention (1:20–33).

THE BEGINNING OF WISDOM

One of the best-known verses in Proverbs is "The fear of the Lord is the beginning of knowledge; fools despise wisdom and instruction" (1:7). These words have been used as a motto and inscribed over the entrance of many schools and colleges. The Sage probably would have approved. This concept was so important to him that he mentioned it at the outset of his first collection of proverbs, and then repeated it, with a slightly different twist, at the end of it (9:10). This was his way of emphasizing that the fear of the Lord was the all-important idea behind all the sayings in the section and the all-important idea behind the lesson of the Wild Thing of Proverbs 7.

The "fear of the Lord" is an important theme throughout Scripture. The Lord is infinitely good and loving, but fear is the natural and appropriate response of all who catch a glimpse of His glory. When the Lord appeared to Moses, Moses trembled with fear and did not dare look at the spectacular sight. Isaiah came undone. Daniel fell trembling on hands and knees. Ezekiel fell on his face. John dropped down as though dead. Even the disciples, who were good friends with the incarnate Lord, were terrified of Jesus when He calmed the storm. Scripture reports that they felt more frightened of Him than they had of the raging wind and waves.

To know God is to know fear. The fear of God is a heart-pounding, knee-trembling, spine-tingling, shuddering recognition that God is infinitely more good, powerful, and important than I. It means that I live, think, act, and speak with a keen awareness that He is the Creator and I am the creature; He is holy and I am not; He is wise and I am a fool; He is powerful and I am weak; He is ruler and I am servant; He is self-sufficient and I am utterly dependent.

To fear God means to be ever aware of His all-pervasive presence, conscious of my absolute need for Him, mindful of my responsibility to follow His way, determined to obey Him, cautious of offending Him, and overwhelmed in amazement and gratitude at His incredible goodness and grace. As the early-twentieth-century philosopher Rudolf Otto said, "It is the emotion of the creature, submerged and overwhelmed by its own nothingness in contrast to that which is supreme above all creatures."[1]

So how is the fear of the Lord the beginning of wisdom? A woman won't figure out what's right if she starts at the wrong point. God is the starting point. We aren't. It's impossible for us to understand how we should live apart from our Creator. He knows the purpose and plan for our existence. If we follow His rules and His precepts, then we will live wisely. *Beginning* also means the capstone or essence. The fear of the Lord is wisdom's choicest feature, its foremost and most essential element.

Do you fear God? Do your knees knock when you think about His greatness? Do you tremble when you consider His holiness? Do you respect Him enough to listen and obey? Do you have any idea who He is? The fear of the Lord is twofold. First, it involves knowing who God is. Second, it involves obedience—loving righteousness, hating sin, and humbly following His way. The Sage says, "The fear of the Lord is the beginning of wisdom, and *the knowledge of the Holy One is insight*," and, "The fear of the Lord *is hatred of evil*" (Proverbs 9:10; 8:13, italics added). If you want to be wise, you'll start by getting to know God and doing what He says. You'll love the things He loves and hate the things He hates. You'll be humble and teachable, willing, eager, and determined to learn His ways.

He promises that those who do this will reap the rewards. He will pour out His Spirit on them, make His words known to them, guide them, and protect them. They will dwell securely, be at ease without dread of disaster, walk in the way of insight, and truly live.

LADY WISE CALLS

The Sage presents another idea at the beginning and end, and peppered throughout this section of his sayings—the concept of a personal invitation. A personification of the trait of wisdom, Lady Wise invites you to her feast. Above the din and bustle of daily life, she cries out and summons you to sit down at her table and listen to her correction and counsel.

Wisdom cries aloud in the street, in the markets she raises her voice; at the head of the noisy streets she cries out; at the entrance of the city gates she speaks: "How long, O simple ones, will you love being simple? How long will scoffers delight in their scoffing and fools hate knowledge? If you turn at my reproof, behold, I will pour out my spirit to you; I will make my words known to you. . . . For the simple are killed by their turning away, and the complacency of fools destroys them; but whoever listens to me will dwell secure and will be at ease, without dread of disaster." (Proverbs 1:20–33)

Does not wisdom call? Does not understanding raise her voice? . . . Take my instruction instead of silver, and knowledge rather than choice gold, for wisdom is better than jewels, and all that you may desire cannot compare with her. (Proverbs 8:1, 10–11)

[Wisdom] has slaughtered her beasts; she has mixed her wine; she has also set her table. She has sent out her young women to call from the highest places in the town, "Whoever is simple, let him turn in here!" To him who lacks sense she says, "Come, eat of my bread and drink of the wine I have mixed. Leave your simple ways, and live, and walk in the way of insight." (Proverbs 9:2–6)

Hers is not the only, nor the loudest, voice you'll hear. Lady Wild is also extending an invitation for you to go over to her place.

The woman Folly is loud; she is seductive and knows nothing. She sits at the door of her house; she takes a seat on the highest places of the town, calling to those who pass by, who are going straight on their way, "Whoever is simple, let him turn in here!" And to him who lacks sense she says, "Stolen water is sweet, and bread eaten in secret is pleasant." But . . . the dead are there . . . her guests are in the depths of Sheol. (Proverbs 9:13–18)

Lady Wise and Lady Wild both call for guests to come and dine at their tables. Lady Wise has slaughtered a beast and served up bread and wine. She serves up a rich and bountiful feast that will be sure to satisfy. Her only stipulation is that her guests be willing to forsake foolishness and walk in the way of wisdom. The "feast" of Lady Wild is a cheap imitation. She offers stolen water and bread—a veiled reference to illicit sex and everything else that God says is off limits. Lady Wild invites you to indulge in foolishness. She entices you with the idea that sin is sweet and pleasant, that you don't have to listen to God—that you can do whatever you want. But the simple young man who accepted her invitation discovered it was a ruse. Her seductive invitation leads to spiritual death.

The choice is up to you. Are you teachable? Are you willing to listen and accept God's wisdom for your life? Are you committed to learning and making the necessary adjustments? "The ear that listens to life-giving reproof will dwell among the wise" (Proverbs 15:31). The three Wild Things would refuse the invitation. Scoffing Sue would respond with, "How dare you suggest my way is wrong?" Foolish Fran would say, "No, thanks. I've got it all figured out." And Simple Sally would pipe in with, "Not right now. Maybe later." How about you? How will you respond? Lady Wise and Lady Wild are calling you to their tables. You will dine with one or the other. Whose invitation will you accept? Will you be a Girl-Gone-Wild or a Girl-Gone-Wise?

Conclusion:

WILD TO WISE

"The beginning of wisdom is this: Get wisdom,
and whatever you get, get insight.
Prize her highly, and she will exalt you;
she will honor you if you embrace her.
She will place on your head a graceful garland;
she will bestow on you a beautiful crown."
—Proverbs 4:7–9

D o you remember the seventy-year-old woman I told you about in the introduction? She came up to me after a workshop with tears streaming down her face saying, "I came to your workshop to get some ideas about how to help my granddaughter, but I see now that it's me who is a Girl-Gone-Wild."

I hope as you've worked your way through the twenty points of contrast, that you've noticed areas in your life where you need to learn and grow—and become less wild and more wise. I know I have. To refresh your memory about the ones you need to work on, you can go to GirlsGoneWise.com and do the "Wild or Wise?" twenty-question survey. The questions correspond to each point of contrast between a wild woman and a wise woman. Your answers to the survey will help you determine which wild parts of your character the Lord wants you to tame.

Being a Girl-Gone-Wise in a world gone wild isn't easy. In our culture, Lady Wild cries out more loudly and clamorously than ever before. Women are congregating at her table in droves. That's where the party is. That's where all the noise and commotion is. All the popular girls are members of her sorority. All the celebs are endorsing her club. All the guys are ogling her guests. I pray that you've grown wise to the ruse. I hope that you've seen through her deceptive scheme and you understand the danger of setting foot in her house. I hope that you've realized that the dead are there—that "her guests are in the depths of Sheol."

Throughout the pages of this book, a quieter voice has been calling. Lady Wise is asking you to come to her house instead. If you accept, you'll have to say no to the conflicting invitation. You'll have to leave Lady Wild's party. You'll have to choose to be different. You'll have to stand against popular opinion and also, perhaps, against the opinion of family and friends. Joining Lady Wise means thinking differently, speaking differently, dressing differently, and behaving differently than the throng of women around you. As you've seen in the Twenty Points of Contrast, being obedient to Christ affects every area of our lives. Like my son exclaimed, "Everything about a woman who loves God is different!"

In the past fifty years, we have witnessed a monumental shift in our culture's idea about what it means to be a woman. Feminism infused us with the idea that womanhood means deciding for ourselves what womanhood, manhood, marriage, sex, and sexuality are all about. The carnage of this way of thinking is almost beyond belief. Marriages and families are breaking down. STDs are rampant. Pornography has gone mainstream. Sexual identity is becoming a matter of choice. Gender confusion is on the rise. We live in a world of women who have had sex changes and make the headlines as pregnant "men," and men who manipulate their hormones to lose their beards and become "women," adolescents seeking to figure out their gender identity and "preference," and same-sex couples necking on TV.

Women and men are having a crisis of identity. Few people know, anymore, what it really means to be a woman or a man. What's worse is that even fewer care. They have no idea how important our God-given design is to our personal identity, our purpose, our wholeness, our well-being, and our capacity to enjoy healthy, fulfilling relationships. It matters how you live your life as a woman. It matters a great deal!

THE ALTERNATE ENDING

The Proverbs 7 woman messed up big time. Her story didn't have a happy ending. Scripture talks about another Wild Thing whose story was very similar, but had an alternate ending.

Have you ever read one of those kids' Choose Your Own Adventure books? They were quite popular in the eighties and nineties. Our kids constantly clamored for Brent to read them one. Each story was written from a second-person point of view, with the reader taking on the role of the main character and making choices that determined the main character's actions. Depending on the reader's choice, the plot and its outcome would change. At the end of each scene, the reader stood at a crossroad and had to determine the protagonist's next course of action. For instance, "If you decide to call the police, turn to page 24. If you decide to go after the intruder, turn to page 8." The plot branched out and unfolded, leading to more decisions and, eventually, to some alternate endings—some good and others bad.

There was a Wild Thing whose Choose Your Own Adventure story followed the same basic pattern as the Proverbs 7 woman. She was a party girl—incredibly beautiful and personable—but as her life unfolded, she just couldn't seem to make life work. Every relationship started out with a lot of promise, but then inevitably broke down. She could have been called "The Woman Who Had Five Husbands" or "The Woman Who Changed Husbands Like Vacuum Cleaner Bags." Nowadays, she'd have made an interesting guest on Jerry Springer's talk show, on a sleazy episode entitled something like "Break-up and Pick-up Techniques of Serial Seductresses." But we know her by less sensational titles: "The Samaritan Woman" or "The Woman at the Well."

Up to the point where we meet her, the plot in her Choose Your

Own Adventure story had been essentially the same as her Proverbs counterpart. In each scene, at each crossroad, she made the same sort of decision. But in this scene, her story takes an incredible twist. The choice she makes changes everything. Instead of the deadly ending for which she and the Wild Thing of Proverbs 7 were both destined, her choice leads to a happily-ever-after ending. You've probably heard her story. The Samaritan woman was looking for that which would satisfy her thirst. Her bucket was empty. And she had come to the well hoping to fill it up.

She came to the well alone. Women normally came to the well in groups. And they came either earlier or later in the day, when the heat wasn't so intense. But the Samaritan woman came alone in the blistering heat. She was lonely, isolated, and excluded from regular social contact with other women. Her public shame about her relationships with men likely contributed to this. She didn't belong to the group. She also had identity issues. When Jesus approached her, she immediately cited their differences: "Hey, why are you talking to me? You are a Jew, and I am a Samaritan *and* a woman." Right at the onset, she was anticipating conflict and rejection. It was what she was accustomed to. She thought Christ wouldn't accept her once He knew who she really was. She was suspicious of His friendliness. And she was even more suspicious when he implied that He could give her what she was really looking for. Yeah, right! She had heard *that* from men before!

The Samaritan woman thought that Jesus wasn't quite telling the truth when He offered her living water. But at the same time, underlying her caution, her interest was piqued. That's because she was acutely aware of her longing. Jesus' offer had touched a chord in her heart. She had come to the well feeling empty. Every day she felt dry and thirsty on the inside. She wanted to belong. She wanted to feel worthwhile, respected, and loved. She wanted purpose and meaning. She wanted to know truth. She wanted to find someone worthy of trust. She was so tired of the emptiness. She wanted to find fullness and satisfaction instead of constantly carting around an empty bucket.

No matter how she tried to fill it, her bucket remained empty. To satisfy her longings, she had engaged in a lifestyle of pursuit and indulgence. She went after everything that she thought would satisfy her desires. She had had five husbands and hadn't even bothered to marry the man she was living with now. When Jesus met her, she was on serial monogamy relationship number six. She was undoubtedly very alluring to have attracted all those men. She knew how to turn on the feminine wiles and charms. And the men provided her with what she thought she wanted—power, affirmation, marriage, sex, material provisions, a home, and a family. But it was all empty. It didn't satisfy.

Her story is all too familiar, isn't it? How often do we pursue and indulge in that which we think will satisfy? We try to fill our buckets with sex, romance, getting a husband, having kids, having a perfect husband and perfect kids, perfect looks, perfect friends, a perfect house, a perfect wardrobe, or car, or job, or education, or income, or holiday, or retirement, or a host of other things. We pour those things into our buckets, seeking to fill them up, but the water keeps running out. And on the inside, we begin to wither and die of thirst.

The Samaritan woman was tired of trying to fill her bucket. Jesus looks right into her heart, puts His finger on that tender place of all her shattered dreams and failures, and promises to quench her longing with living water. She pleads, "Sir, give me this water, so that I will not be thirsty or have to come here to draw water" (John 4:15). As the conversation unfolds, Jesus reveals that He is the living water—the Messiah, the deliverer. He is the object of all her longings and dreams. He is the only One who can fill her bucket. He reiterates the age-old invitation that the Lord extended in the pages of Proverbs through Lady Wisdom—the same invitation He extended through the prophet Isaiah:

> Come, everyone who thirsts, come to the waters; and he who has no money, come, buy and eat! Come, buy wine and milk without money and without price. Why do you spend your money for that which is not bread, and your labor for that which does not satisfy? Listen diligently to me, and eat what is good, and delight yourselves in rich food. Incline your ear, and come to me; hear, that your soul may live. . . . Seek the Lord while he may be found; call upon him while he is near; let the wicked forsake his way, and the unrighteous man his thoughts; let him return to the Lord, that he may have compassion on him, and to our God, for he will abundantly pardon. (Isaiah 55:1–3, 6–7)

The Samaritan woman made the decision to believe and follow Christ. He offered to fill her bucket brimful. In Him, she'd find forgiveness and life. Instead of the poisonous "stolen water and bread" of Lady Wild, she'd find good, rich, delightful, and satisfying food and drink. Jesus promised that she would find all this and more at His banquet table. So she left the house of Lady Wild and sat down under the correction and counsel of Lady Wise. Her choice at that crossroad made all the difference. It led to the alternate ending.

Now that you've read this book about the Wild Thing of Proverbs 7, who chose the house of Lady Wild over Lady Wise, and heard the story of the ex-Wild-Thing-at-the-Well, who met Christ and left the house of Lady Wild for Lady Wise, you are at a crossroad. You have a decision to make. It doesn't matter how wild you've been in the past, Christ is extending you an invitation. Today, you can make a choice that will lead to the alternate ending. God is giving you the opportunity to choose your adventure.

The message of the gospel is that Jesus Christ died to pay the penalty for our sins and restore us to a right relationship with God. All of us fall short of the glory of God. We all fall short of who He created us to be. As our study of the Proverbs 7 woman indicates, we all fall short of being the *women* He created us to be. All of us have messed up. Our guilt before God is undeniable. We are not worthy to be in a relationship with Him. Our sin and guilt condemn us. Yet Christ pours out His marvelous gift of grace on all who respond in faith to His offer of forgiveness and an eternal relationship with God. "For all have sinned and fall short of the glory of God, and are justified by his grace as a gift, through the redemption that is in Christ Jesus" (Romans 3:23–24).

The Wild-Thing-at-the-Well recognized her sin and her need for a Savior. Can you imagine how she felt when she met Jesus and He filled her bucket to the brim with living water? Can you imagine the emotions that flooded her heart when she realized that Christ would forgive her sin and quench her thirst? Can you imagine the joy? Can you imagine the overwhelming gratitude? Can you imagine the resolve to change and follow His ways? Can you imagine the transformation that took place in her life?

Maybe this book has been difficult for you to read. Maybe it has opened your eyes to the sin in your life. Maybe it's highlighted just how much you've messed things up. I hope you understand that God's grace is bigger than all your sin. I hope you understand that Jesus Christ was killed on a cross to cancel your debt to God, take away your sin and shame, and help you live the right way. I think of Christ's words to the adulterous Wild Thing who was thrown down at His feet by the self-righteous Pharisees who wanted to stone her to death.

The Pharisees were right—according to the law, she deserved death. But God did not send His Son into the world to condemn the world, but in order that the world might be saved through Him (John 3:17). When Christ saw the Wild Thing trembling in shame and fear, He did not condemn her, but extended undeserved grace. He said, "Neither do I condemn you; go, and from now on sin no more" (John 8:11). I suspect that that's what she did. Author Nancy Leigh DeMoss says, "Undeniable guilt, plus undeserved grace, should equal unbridled gratitude."[1] Wild Things who recognize their guilt and encounter the amazing love and grace of God, will respond to Him with gratitude and a resolve to become a Girl-Gone-Wise.

For all you Wild Things, I'd love to reach past these pages and embrace you as daughters, sisters, and mothers. I'd look you in the eyes and plead with you to respond to Wisdom's call. Listen, and live. Leave the way of wildness, and follow the way of Christ. Obey Him. Live your life the way He says you ought to live, and trust that *He* will fill your bucket. He will. Your thirst will be quenched at His table.

For those of you have already made the decision to ditch the Wild sorority and dine with Lady Wise, I urge you to stand strong. Follow the way of wisdom. Grow in wisdom. Do not flinch. Do not waver. Do not get careless as you get older. Be salt and light to a generation of women who are broken, floundering, and looking for answers.

For you older women, I challenge you to take up the mantle of sage motherhood and speak truth to the young. Mentor them in how to be a Girl-Gone-Wise. A sage mother "opens her mouth with wisdom, and the teaching of kindness is on her tongue" (Proverbs 31:26).

For you young women, it's never too early to start exerting some "motherly" influence. Remember Job? He said, "From my youth the fatherless grew up with me as with a father" (Job 31:18). He exerted a fatherly influence on his fatherless friends. The girls of this generation are "motherless." I challenge you young women to start spiritually mothering them. Your girlfriends desperately need input on how to live wise and not wild.

As I've said before, "I believe the time is ripe for a new movement—a seismic holy quake of countercultural women who dare to take God at His word, those who have the courage to stand against the popular tide, and believe and delight in God's plan for male and female."[2] Women are looking for something to fill their buckets. Christ is the only answer. Will you join the quiet counterrevolution of women who are committed to living according to God's design?

THE MOST BEAUTIFUL WOMAN IN THE WORLD

After hearing me on the radio, speaking about the points of contrast between Wild and Wise Women, a young man e-mailed me. He said he was so "wowed" that he shared the script of the radio show with all his buddies and posted it on his Facebook page. He said it was refreshing to hear something that wasn't "man-bashing" and would build, rather than destroy, male-female relationships. He wished every woman would encounter the material and learn the way of wisdom. He concluded with this statement: "My impression is the woman who has this [wisdom] would be the most beautiful woman in the world!"

I think the young man has the right impression. No woman is quite as beautiful as a Girl-Gone-Wise. So, look carefully how you walk, not as wild but as wise. Get wisdom! Prize her highly, and she will exalt you; she will honor you if you embrace her. She will place on your head a graceful garland; she will bestow on you a beautiful crown. Lady Wisdom will make you over, head to toe. Amazingly, she extends this opportunity to everyone. Any woman can become a Wise Thing. Any woman can become that most beautiful woman in the world. The choice is yours. Will it be you?

NOTES

Wild Thing

1. "Wild Thing," Words and Music by Chip Taylor ©1965 (Renewed 1993) EMI BLACKWOOD MUSICE INC. All Rights Reserved. International Copyright Secured. Used by Permission. Reprinted by permission of Hal Leonard Corporation.

20 Points of Contrast

Point of Contrast #1. Heart

1. Quotes from "A Faithful Narrative of the Surprising Work of God." By Jonathan Edwards. http://www.iclnet.org/pub/resources/text/ipb-e/epl-10/web/edwards-narrative.html.

Point of Contrast #2. Counsel

1. Data and calculations based on statistics by the U.S. Census Bureau. Table 1089. Media Usage and Consumer Spending: 2001 to 2011. http://www.census. gov/compendia/statab/tables/09s1089.pdf.
2. A. W. Tozer. http://christianquotes.org/search/quick/heart/30.
3. Nancy Leigh DeMoss has a great book and Bible study that expands on this concept of women being deceived: *Lies Women Believe: And the Truth That Sets Them Free* (Chicago: Moody, 2001).
4. Joshua Harris, "Like to Watch." http://www.boundless.org/2005/articles/a0001258.cfm.
5. C. S. Lewis, *The Silver Chair* (New York: HarperCollins, 1994), 181–82.

Point of Contrast #3. Approach

1. Hugh Kenner, *Chuck Jones: A Flurry of Drawings, Portraits of American Genius* (Berkeley: Univ. of California Press, 1994). http://ark.cdlib.org/ark:/13030/ft6q2nb3x1/, http://www.escholarship.org/editions/view?docId=ft6q2nb3x1&query=&brand=ucpress.
2. Ten-Year Magazine Readership Trend. 1997-2006 by the Magazine Publishers of America (MPA). http://www.magazine.org/content/Files/TenYrReader Trend97-06%2011-27-06.doc.

3. Eric and Leslie Ludy, *When God Writes Your Love Story: The Ultimate Approach to Guy/Girl Relationships* (Multnomah, 1999), 13.

Point of Contrast #5. Habits

1 . Eric Zorn. http://www.great-quotes.com/cgi-bin/viewquotes.cgi?action=search&orderby=&keyword=priorities&startlist=45.

Point of Contrast #7. Appearance

1 . Patrice A. Opplinger, *Girls Gone Skank: The Sexualization of Girls in American Culture* (Jefferson, N.C.: McFarland & Company, 2008), 1.

2. "What's the Problem with Nudity?" *Horizon*, aired Saturday, March 3, 2009, http://www.bbc.co.uk/programmes/b00j0hnm, and "Can People Unlearn Their Naked Shame?" by Paul King, http://news.bbc.co.uk/2/hi/uk_news/ maga-zine/7915369.stm.

3. John Piper, "Nudity in Drama and the Clothing of Christ." Sermon preached on November 20, 2006. http://www.desiringgod.org/ResourceLibrary/TasteAnd See/ByDate/2006/1884_Nudity_in_Drama_and_the_Clothing_of_Christ/.

4. John Piper, "The Rebellion of Nudity and the Meaning of Clothing." Sermon preached on April 24, 2008. http://www.desiringgod.org/ResourceLibrary/ TasteAndSee/ByDate/2008/2737_The_Rebellion_of_Nudity_and_the_ Meaning_of_Clothing/.

Point of Contrast #10. Sexual Conduct

1 . W. Barclay, *The Letters to the Philippians, Colossians, and Thessalonians*, The Daily study Bible series, rev. ed. (Philadelphia: Westminster Press, 2000), 198.

2. Ibid.

3. Ben Patterson, "The Goodness of Sex and the Glory of God." In *Sex and the Supremacy of Christ*, Eds. John Piper and Justin Taylor (Wheaton, Ill.: Crossway, 2005), 52.

Point of Contrast #11. Boundaries

1 . Miguel De Cervantes, cited in http://www.cybernation.com/victory/quotations/.

Point of Contrast #13. Neediness

1 . Martin Luther, http://www.brainyquote.com/quotes/authors/m/martin_luther_3.html.

2. C. S. Lewis, *The Pilgrim's Regress* (Grand Rapids: Eerdmans, 1981), 123.

Point of Contrast #14. Possessions

1 . "The vase that dreams are made of," by Giancarlo Rinaldi, South of Scotland reporter, BBC Scotland News website, http://news.bbc.co.uk/2/hi/uk_news/scotland/south_of_scotland/7789458.stm.

Point of Contrast #15. Entitlement

1 . 2009 News Releases from Voices of Martyrs, http://www.persecution.com.

2. *Foxe's Book of Martyrs* (Grand Rapids, Mich.: Revell, 2008).

3. Augustine, *Confessions*, 181 (IX.1).

Point of Contrast #17. Speech

1 . Bernard de Bovier de Fontenelle, http://www.giga-usa.com/quotes/topics/flattery_t002.htm.

2. William Penn, http://www.giga-usa.com/quotes/authors/william_penn_a001.htm.

Point of Contrast #18. Influence

1 . H. Smith, *A Preparative to Marriage*, 1591, p.42, cited on http://www.answers.com/topic/a-man-is-known-by-the-company-he-keeps.

2. Dolly Parton, "The Company You Keep." Lyrics copyright 1967, Monument Records. Used by permission.

Point of Contrast #19. Sustainability

1 . Urban Dictionary, Definition for Serial Monogamist, http://www.urbandictionary.com/define.php?term=serial%20monogamist, October 2009.

2. You can read Christy's comment at http://www.marykassian.com/archives/1136#comment-1417. You can also leave a comment on the GirlsGoneWise.com blog.

3. "The Effects of Premarital Sexual Promiscuity on Subsequent Marital Sexual Satisfaction" by Sherie Adams Christensen. A thesis submitted to the faculty of Brigham Young University, Marriage and Family Therapy Program, School of Family Life, Brigham Young University, June 2004. http://contentdm.lib.byu.edu/ETD/image/etd454.pdf.

4. Duane A. Garrett, *Proverbs, Ecclesiastes, Song of Songs*, electronic ed. (Nashville: Broadman & Holman, 2001), c1993 (Logos Library System; The New American Commentary 14), S. 104.

Point of Contrast #20. Teachability

1 . Quoted by Mary Kassian in *Knowing God by Name: A Personal Encounter* (Nashville: LifeWay, 2008), 1 14.

Conclusion: Wild to Wise

1 . Betsey Stevenson and Justin Wolfers, "The Paradox of Declining Female Happiness," *American Economic Journal:* Economic Policy 2009, 1:2, 190–225, http://www.aeaweb.org/articles.php?doi=10.1257/pol.1.2.190, http://bpp.wharton.upenn.edu/betseys/papers/Paradox%20of%20declining%20female%20happiness.pdf.

2. Mary A. Kassian, *The Feminist Mistake: The Radical Impact of Feminism on Church and Culture,* rev. ed. (Wheaton, Ill.: Crossway, 2005), 299.

MORE RESOURCES ...

**Girls Gone Wise
Companion Guide**

**Girls Gone Wise
DVD**

**Girls Gone Wise
Group Study Kit**